W9-CEU-123

At Home in the Land of Oz

of related interest

The Complete Guide to Asperger's Syndrome
Tony Attwood
ISBN 978 1 84310 495 7

Voices from the Spectrum
Parents, Grandparents, Siblings, People with Autism,
and Professionals Share Their Wisdom
Edited by Cindy N. Ariel and Robert A. Naseef
ISBN 978 1 84310 786 6

Laughter and Tears
A Family's Journey to Understanding the Autism Spectrum
Ann Hewetson
ISBN 978 1 84310 331 8

Elijah's Cup
A Family's Journey into the Community and Culture of
High-functioning Autism and Asperger's Syndrome (Revised edition)
Valerie Paradiž
ISBN 978 1 84310 802 3

Pretending to be Normal
Living with Asperger's Syndrome
Liane Holliday Willey
Foreword by Tony Attwood
ISBN 978 1 85302 749 9

Snapshots of Autism
A Family Album
Jennifer Overton
ISBN 978 1 84310 723 1

2 41 7 1 3 8

1/07

Butler Area Public Library
218 North McKean St.
Butler, PA 16001

At Home in the Land of Oz

Autism, My Sister, and Me

Anne Clinard Barnhill

362.196
BAR

***Funding for this book has been
provided through***
*PA Parents and Caregivers Resource
Network's*
***Mini Money Grant Program
(1-888-572-7368)***

Jessica Kingsley Publishers
London and Philadelphia

First published in the United States in 2007
by Jessica Kingsley Publishers
116 Pentonville Road
London N1 9JB, UK
and
400 Market Street, Suite 400
Philadelphia, PA 19106, USA

www.jkp.com

Copyright © Anne Clinard Barnhill 2007

All rights reserved. No part of this publication may be reproduced in any material form (including photocopying or storing it in any medium by electronic means and whether or not transiently or incidentally to some other use of this publication) without the written permission of the copyright owner except in accordance with the provisions of the Copyright, Designs and Patents Act 1988 or under the terms of a licence issued by the Copyright Licensing Agency Ltd, 90 Tottenham Court Road, London, England W1T 4LP. Applications for the copyright owner's written permission to reproduce any part of this publication should be addressed to the publisher.

Warning: The doing of an unauthorised act in relation to a copyright work may result in both a civil claim for damages and criminal prosecution.

Library of Congress Cataloging in Publication Data
Barnhill, Anne Clinard.
  At home in the land of Oz : autism, my sister, and me / Anne Clinard Barnhill.
    p. cm.
  ISBN 978-1-84310-859-7 (pb : alk. paper) 1. Clinard, Rebecca Jane—Mental health. 2. Autism—Patients—Biography. I. Title.
  RC553.A88B367 2007
  362.196'858820092—dc22
  [B]
                                                                    2007007806

British Library Cataloguing in Publication Data
A CIP catalogue record for this book is available from the British Library

ISBN 9781 84310 859 7

Printed and bound in the United States by Thomson-Shore, Inc.

For my parents, Jack and Virginia,
who taught me how to love

And for my sister, Becky, the bravest woman I know

Acknowledgements

Without Paul Wilkes, Visiting Professor at the University of North Carolina at Wilmington, this book would not have existed. Many thanks. Also, thanks to Jack and Virginia Clinard for access to their documents and their memories. My writing friends, Barbara Crooker, Becky Gibson, Mary Elizabeth Parker, Sandra Redding, and Isabel Zuber gave great encouragement and feedback throughout the process— thanks. A special thanks to Jessica Kingsley for her warm response to the book and to Jessica Stevens and Melanie Wilson for their invaluable help.

Emily and Kristi, thanks for your insight and conversation. My sons, Michael, Jason, and Adam, thanks for your love and excellent criticism. Special thanks to Jason for the beautiful song he wrote as a tribute to Becky. To hear "The Family House" go to www.myspace.com/nightsbrightcolors. No writing could have taken place without the support and encouragement of my husband of thirty years, Frank. Thanks to you all.

A Domino factum est istud et hoc mirabile in oculis nostris.

Contents

My head is quite empty but once I had brains, and a heart also; so, having tried them both, I should much rather have a heart.
—The Tin Woodman, *The Wonderful Wizard of Oz*

Introduction

On summery afternoons when I was a girl, I'd sprawl across my twin bed and study the scarlet tanager that nested outside my window in a nearby tulip tree. I'd found an old pair of opera glasses in my father's desk drawer and used them to spy on birds. The glasses magnified the bird so I could watch as he twitched his little head first one way, then another. He moved almost mechanically while on the limb and only achieved grace when he flew.

For hours I'd observe his habits, worry to see if his babies had hatched, stare as he worked alongside his plain, khaki-colored wife to build and repair and clean the nest. No one knew I spent so much time dreaming about the airy world of birds. No one knew how important birds would become to me later as I discovered them appearing over and over in my work, flashes of bright feathers that brushed across the pages of my writing, reminders of how each species of bird is distinct from the other, yet from a distance, a cardinal could be mistaken for a tanager, a crow for a falcon. Such errors are common among novice bird watchers; even experts can make mistakes.

I know about such confusion. And I know about the mistakes people can make when one thing looks like another.

I grew up with a sister who was confused, in a time when doctors couldn't tell the difference between one mental condition and another, when parents were blamed if a child was "not right," when mental illness was whispered about in the privacy of kitchens and in secret family meetings. I grew up in the years before talk shows broadcasted from every channel on TV, when people didn't divulge their heartache, their disappointment. I grew up in a time when private grief was the only kind around.

Being a child of that time, I learned my lessons well. I kept silent when I watched my sister, Becky, mash her food to a sloppy mush before eating it, something she does to this day. I kept silent when she ripped the heads off all her dolls, arms and legs, too. We'd find body parts strewn across the floor or tucked in some corner, the plastic flesh brittle and cold. I didn't speak the night my parents and I came home from grocery shopping to discover my sister had filed her front teeth into sharp points against the stone mantle over the fireplace.

She was fourteen and we'd only been gone a half-hour. And I kept silent when she went to an institution, her little girl body pressed against the window, watching my parents and me drive down the road.

Now, after forty years, I'm ready to tell my story.

It's not an earth-shattering tale, nor is it filled with easy answers about life. It's only the story of a mother, a father, and two daughters who must weave together a nest of broken twigs, bits of string, and an occasional feather, though one of them will never fly on her own. The nest must be strong enough to support the needs of each person inside. It must be long-lasting and trustworthy, so when the parents die, they can leave knowing their treasured daughter, the one without wings, will be lovingly cared for.

It's the story of how this family manages, with little money and no expertise (like most families, I suspect) to love when love seems hard, maybe even impossible. It's the story of two parents who are overwhelmed and confused about how to help their younger daughter—the one who talks to herself, the one who grinds her teeth and speaks in riddles—to find her place in the world, a safe place, a nest to call her own. And it's the story of how these same parents discover moments of joy, even flights of freedom and how they share this with their girls.

This is also my story—the story of how I learned to speak another language, the language of my sister Becky. And how I found my own meaning in our strange conversations—a meaning I am still discovering.

There are no happy endings here, but this is not a tragedy either. It's a chronicle of one family's struggle against despair, four people who chose to stay and fight the demons when it might have been easier to run away. It's about how much we depend on each other, how we truly are our brother's (or in my case, sister's) keeper.

Like life, these memories are a crazy mix of humor and grief, success and failure, good intentions and serious neglect. I don't claim to have all the facts straight. These are, after all, my own moments of reflection. It's a weighty thing to try to reconstruct a life. I hope my words will fly into the wind with the courage of my sister, a strange bird if ever there was one, yet one who soars when she gets the chance. Just soars.

Recently, while driving Becky back to her home in Winston-Salem, North Carolina, she and I had a theological discussion, one of many we've shared. The sky was darkening, though the light lingered longer than I'd anticipated so late in September. Shafts of orange-gold filtered through low-hanging clouds, which were puffy and as solid-looking as cotton bolls pulled from the stems, their long filaments trailing across the pinkish sky. I was tired. I'd read two collections of ghost stories aloud to Becky, watched *Little Shop of Horrors* for at least the tenth time, cooked several grilled cheese sandwiches and plates of spaghetti, made pots of coffee, and answered a zillion questions. Keeping my sister happy could be exhausting.

We'd been reminiscing about our maternal grandparents, Gwennie and Ernie, both of whom have been dead for about fifteen years. Maybe it was the sky, the way the heavens seemed to open up above us, or maybe it was the fact that we were returning to Becky's house, or maybe Becky had heard something on television—whatever the stimulus, our conversation turned from dental problems to questions about life after death.

"Do you think Ernie has his teeth in heaven?" Becky asked. Our grandfather had had cancer of the jaw and all of his teeth had been removed, along with part of his tongue. Because of this, it was impossible for him to wear false teeth. This worried Becky, who'd had a "dental fascination" for many years.

"Yep. Yep, I do, Beck. I believe in heaven, everything will be restored," I said. I didn't really believe in heaven, but I fostered such belief in Becky. I thought it might comfort her.

"Do you think Gwennie's back won't hurt in heaven? Will she be young again?" Becky stared at the tattered pictures she held in her lap, pictures of The Monkees, a musical group popular in the 60s.

"I don't think her back'll hurt but I'm not sure about her getting younger. But, hey, it's heaven, right? Maybe anything is possible," I said, again trying to appease her. I didn't like the direction the conversation was going. I didn't want Becky to start crying or getting upset because our grandparents were dead.

Several minutes passed. The sky turned gray and a few stars appeared. My mind was occupied with thoughts of chores I planned to accomplish the next day. I had only a few weeks before school began and I wanted to make good use of my vacation. Once I returned to my teaching job at Guilford College in nearby Greensboro, my life would be crammed full and I'd have no time for gardening, baking, and puttering around the house. As I made my "to-do" list in my head, I almost forgot Becky was in the car with me—she'd grown so quiet.

"Jet, are there group homes in heaven?" Becky said.

Her question startled me. I knew what she was really saying—if heaven had group homes, she'd rather spend eternity somewhere else. I didn't blame her.

"Nope. Won't need any group homes in heaven. I'm sure of that," I said.

Again, she grew quiet. I felt the familiar knot begin to form at the back of my throat. I tried to steer my mind in another direction.

"When I die, will my autism be cured? Will Jesus come and put his finger right in the middle of my forehead and cure my brain?" Becky said, her voice tense and nervous.

Oh, hell. I hated taking Becky back to the group home. I hated her pain and my pain and all of it mixed up together. I wanted, just once, not to feel that lump grating against my esophagus. Just one time. But no, she had to ask questions like this, questions that broke my heart.

"Yes, Becky. I believe that. I really do believe that," I said, my own voice strained so that tears seemed to wring out of it. Mercifully, she returned to her thoughts and I hoped there'd be no more interrogations along this line. I focused on my chore list.

Several more minutes passed. I could hear Becky ruminating over our conversation, emitting a low humming sound, the kind she said sounded like the bass pipes on the church organ. I dreaded to hear what she might ask next.

"If my toenails need to be trimmed when I die, will Jesus be my heavenly podiatrist?" Becky blurted out, then laughed that bubbly, sort of guttural laugh of hers.

"Heavenly podiatrist? Well, sure, why not?" I said, laughing with her.

The mood was broken, the sorrow drying up and blowing out the window like chaff. Becky had brought me back from the edge of despair with her quirky questions. The thing is, she knew she'd done it. She knew she was being funny and just a little sacrilegious.

I loved her for it. Because no matter how much I might grieve for Becky, there were moments when we connected and light broke through into our very spirits. I knew enough to hold on to those moments. And treasure them.

This is the story of such moments, both light and dark. I want to go back to the late 1950s and 60s when Becky and I were children, to explain and discover what those early years meant to me, having a sister like Becky. I want to explore events that happened to both of us, events we've never talked about, events that have molded us in ways we never could have dreamed.

My life has followed a fairly normal route. I went to college, married, gave birth to two sons, divorced, remarried and had another boy, taught high school for fourteen years, began a career as a writer. None of this was as easy as one sentence makes it sound. I did not have an orderly early life by any means. After ten years of struggling to write, I returned to graduate school at the University of North Carolina-Wilmington for an M.F.A. in Creative Writing, graduating in 2001 at the age of forty-nine. Since then, I have taught writing and continue to write articles, short stories (several of which have been published), novels, and now a memoir.

While I dealt with "normal" life problems, Becky struggled with her own set of difficulties. She spent about twenty years at home with our parents, from the age of thirteen to thirty-three. While living in West Virginia, she earned a high school attendance degree for going to special education classes until she was twenty-one and no longer eligible. After that, she worked at a sheltered workshop for the next eight years until my parents and she relocated to Kernersville, North Carolina to be nearer to my family. In Kernersville, Becky again worked at a sheltered workshop. In 1990, at thirty-three, Becky moved into a group home.

We've both had our difficulties, our sorrows to bear, just like everyone else. In this, Becky is completely normal. But our childhoods were anything but ordinary, and it is this extraordinary period I want to explore.

❧

In 1943, Dr. Leo Kanner used the term *autism* to describe a condition in which children are socially withdrawn and preoccupied with routine. These children struggle to acquire spoken language but often possess intellectual gifts that rule out a diagnosis of mental retardation. Most of the children affected, according to Dr. Kanner, were male. One year later, Dr. Hans Asperger added his definition to Kanner's original and expanded the term to include children who were socially maladroit, developed bizarre obsessions, yet were highly verbal and sometimes, quite bright. Asperger also noted that there was a striking tendency for the disorder to run in families.

By the time my sister was born in 1958, much of the research of these two doctors had been discarded in the aftermath of World War II. No one is quite sure how such a loss occurred, but it was as if the scientific world had simply misplaced this information. By 1958, experts insisted that children weren't born autistic. Instead, autism was caused by cold and un-nurturing parents, mothers especially. Not only were parents blamed for this unusual condition, the condition itself wasn't widely known. At that time, an estimated one in 10,000 children suffered with autism and it was considered a rare disability. Now, experts estimate one in 150 children may be affected. There is definitely a rise in the occurrence worldwide. But no one knows why.

Autism is a mysterious condition, more so than most psychological disorders. No one knows the cause or the cure. The most current theories blame pollutants in our environment, mercury in particular. Some scientists are convinced the condition is completely genetic. Many parents and some researchers believe the vaccinations routinely given to babies spark a response in certain children who may be predisposed for autism. While one study suggests this might be true, several others have found no connection between the MMR (measles, mumps, rubella) vaccine and developing autism. But there are many parents who say their children were perfectly normal until they received the MMR at about fifteen months of age. The latest research suggests that autism may be a systemic disorder rather than a neurological one, and may even affect the digestive system. Some parents and physicians are exploring dietary restrictions as a way of modifying behavior.

The truth is, scientists are baffled, and even the condition itself has so many variables that there are several different labels to identify which strain of autism a person has. What psychiatrists now recognize is that autism runs an entire spectrum of symptoms and behaviors and can occur in varying degrees.

In 1981, Dr. Lorna Wing published a paper which compared the disorder identified by Asperger to the list of Dr. Kanner's descriptions of autism. Dr. Wing pointed out that the similarities were much more noticeable than the differences. As a result, doctors now believe the two are closely related disorders, and the definition of autism has been expanded to include a large array of symptoms and behaviors, including Asperger's syndrome.

Though interesting, these developments in the study of autism did my family little good. My sister was born before most doctors recognized the multifaceted condition, and since Becky could talk and communicate well, autism was ruled out in her case. Back then, autism was viewed strictly as a nonverbal condition. The varying degrees of autism that we now know are part of the disease weren't identified when Becky was a child. As a result, Becky didn't get the appropriate treatment.

But what is the appropriate treatment for a condition that's incurable? Currently, two methods of intervention vie for status as the most effective way to help children with autism. In one method, a regulated life where each moment is rigidly scheduled is seen as the way to help autistic kids make sense of their world. The TEACCH (Treatment and Education of Autistic and related Communication handicapped Children) program, headquartered in Greensboro, NC, favors this approach.

In the other method, teachers use the principles of ABA (applied behavioral analysis) to work with the children every hour of every day to break simple tasks into smaller parts so that learning these skills becomes easier. Each time a child successfully completes a step, the child is rewarded by being allowed to do something he likes, or by a special treat of food or beverage. The tremendous cost of this method can rise to $60,000 per year and isn't covered by most insurance policies. Practitioners of this method claim that if the child is diagnosed early enough and has very early intervention, the child may be able to attend public school on schedule. However, the autism doesn't go away completely and there are no guarantees that a child who can graduate from high school can function in the real world.

More attention is placed on autism now than when my sister was born. One reason is the marked and frightening increase in cases of autism. Some believe one reason there is such a big jump in the number of cases is simply that the definition of the disease has broadened and more doctors are aware of the condition, leading to more diagnoses. However, this doesn't account for the ever-increasing numbers of children who exhibit various aspects of the condition. For example, in North Carolina, the number of children receiving special-education services for autism increased from 1,464 in 1996–97 to 1,708 in 1997–98. For example, the number of students on the autism spectrum enrolled in public schools in the state of North Carolina has more than doubled over the past five years (from *The Spectrum*: the quarterly newsletter of the Autism Society of North Carolina, winter 2007, vol.23, no.1). Similar increases are occurring all over the country.

When I was growing up, few people had heard of autism. Though my parents were told my sister had some behaviors that resembled autism, the flipping of her hands and the echolalia (repeating what had been said to her or just repeating words and sentences), her verbal abilities ruled out autism as far as the experts were concerned.

I believe if Becky had received the appropriate treatment (whatever that might have been) at the right time, she might have been able to move into society with much more ease. Who can tell how things might have been? I must deal with things as they are. And as they are, my sister isn't and never will be "normal."

Because I was a child myself when my sister was struggling to learn how our world worked and fighting feelings of rejection from being sent away from home at the age of eight, I asked my mother to write down the major events that occurred in the correct order. Here is what my mother wrote:

Born January 31, 1958.

First, we thought Becky might be hard of hearing because she did not respond. She was checked for this and she could hear well. Before that, she never chewed on anything. Even when she was teething. Never put anything in her mouth. She was a little slow learning to walk. She had no trouble learning to talk. She kept to herself a lot. We allowed her to do this. We were remiss in doing this.

She started seeing Dr. M——, a child psychologist, on a regular basis either weekly or monthly (at age four). He explained her problem as having a brick wall between her and learning. We had to try to tear down that wall. It could have been Dr. M—— and his associate who diagnosed her as emotionally disturbed with secondary retardation. She saw Dr. M—— about two years. He told us to take her for walks.

When Becky was six, we moved to Nutter Fort, West Virginia, where she attended a small school for mentally retarded children for one year. It did not seem to be what she needed. In 1965, we moved to Philippi, WV where we consulted with Dr. L——, a teacher of psychology at Alderson-Broaddus College. Becky went to a school with Mrs. Coontz for a short while (Becky was expelled for extremely active and uncontrollable behavior); then she was tested at West Virginia University in Morgantown.

She then went to Amos Cottage in Winston-Salem, NC. Dr. Hinman (sp?) worked with her and helped her be able to go to Pressley House (later called Pressley Ridge School, no longer in existence). She was at Amos Cottage about nine months. She was at Pressley House for about four years. She worked with Dr. Eigenbrode while there and she attended the school they had there on campus. From age thirteen to twenty-one, Becky attended Mr. Smiley's special education classes at Philip-Barbour High School. She got a diploma (for attendance only) and then went to special ed classes in Belington, about ten miles from Philippi.

After she finished school, she went to the Barbour County Sheltered Workshop for two or three years. In 1987, we moved to Kernersville, NC, where she attended the Kernersville Sheltered Workshop. In 1990, she went to live at Rouses' group home near Mayodan, NC.

My mother is now eighty-three years old. In this account, she doesn't mention how all of this affected her. She has never expressed those feelings, at least not to me. I suspect she keeps them deep in her heart where only God has the key. What my mother and father have been through, rearing an autistic child in the 1950s and 60s, would be enough to crush the spirits of all but the very strongest people. My parents would not have survived the experience intact without their belief in God's infinite love. And, thanks to their courage and kindness, we—my parents, Becky, and I—have all survived. We may be a little shaky and we may carry our own nugget of sorrow, but we have made it this far. And that's all anyone can ask.

Chapter One

Birds fly over the rainbow...
— *Dorothy*

Sitting in the back seat of my parents' car made me feel like a kid again. My sister, Becky, was perched behind Mother, and I took my usual spot behind Dad. My parents, though smaller and grayer, still reigned over the front seat, dispensing Cokes from Dad's six-pack cooler, conversing in the rising and falling tones so familiar from childhood. Becky and I still teased and laughed in patterns established thirty years ago. I kidded her about stealing what was in her pocketbook and she responded with feigned alarm. I called her favorite Monkee, Davy Jones, a little chimpanzee and Becky yelled, "He is NOT!" I told her she was a heartless woman, fickle to boot, for changing her favorite Monkee from Micky Dolenz to Davy. She groaned and gritted her teeth, saying "I couldn't help it!" under her breath.

Playing those old games again reminded me of long trips with Becky, the two of us sequestered in a universe of our own, separated from the grown-ups by what then seemed an enormous distance. We'd count the cows; I'd tell her stories; and I'd try to teach her the alphabet game, the one where you picked out the letters from road signs. Unlike most siblings, my sister and I never fought. She was six years younger, so we didn't have the same interests, nothing over which to disagree. Besides, she preferred talking in that singsong voice of hers, asking questions over and over, giggling at things I couldn't share. She never minded when I stopped trying to entertain her, the way most little kids did. *I* was the one who desired games, conversation, intimacy. She was content to return to her own special realm, a world no one else could enter.

Now we found ourselves in the same spot, together again in the back of the car, driving with the folks, the four of us linked by my sister's problems, her unruly life. That part hadn't changed over the years, though Becky and I had each grown in different ways. In my own life, I was navigating the way toward middle-age and trying to find my place in a house empty of children. My three sons were grown, on their own. I even had two new granddaughters I intended to cuddle and spoil to my heart's content. I was trying to carve out a writing career from the stuff of my life, having quit my job as a high school teacher ten years earlier. I hoped to discover new activities to share with my husband. And yes, even rekindle romance.

While I struggled with the poignant emotions that mark mid-life, Becky tangled with her own problems. On the surface, her life looked almost perfect. She took horseback riding, ballet, aerobics twice a week. Each Wednesday, she went to the beauty shop for a haircut and manicure. She worked one day a week at Burger King and never had to worry about money. She owned more clothes than I could ever imagine possessing and she took a vacation twice a year to some fun-sounding place like Disney World or the Outer Banks.

But I had the one thing Becky lacked, the one thing she wanted more than anything else. I was in charge of my own life. I made my own decisions and steered my course as much as any normal adult could. Becky desperately desired that power.

My father put the car in reverse and drove from the driveway of the brick ranch where Becky lived. She gritted her teeth and made a low hum, sure signs that she was nervous. Her hands shook a little as she held them, one on top of the other, like hands folded in prayer, but turned sideways.

"Tiny," she said under her breath. "So tiny." Her voice scrunched up so that when she spoke, she sounded like a young child. Her voice was a low monotone when she conversed with people, but when she talked to herself, her conversation became melodic. She hit a certain rhythm, a slow iambic pen-tameter with the last syllable toned lower than the previous ones had been. I think she interrogated herself to comfort whatever was troubling her at the moment. After all, the iamb mimics the human heartbeat. Perhaps in some way, she was returning to the comfort of the womb while she worked things out in her mind.

When she babbled, she looked the way a small bird might look if it could speak. Her head bobbed from side to side in that same, quick way. This other-worldly motion often drew stares from strangers, looks of confusion that Becky never noticed, but I did. I was used to people checking her out, curiosity on their faces, amazement. I'd long ago recovered from the uncomfortable feelings such gaping caused. The judgments of people who didn't know me, or didn't know my sister, simply ceased to bother me.

Of course, that had not always been the case. Sometimes, being with Becky had been embarrassing. When I was a child, other kids would ask me what my crazy sister was doing when we were out playing in the yard. Becky would be flipping her hands against some plastic toy, a ball most likely, keeping it in the air for up to a half-hour at a time. Her flipping, referred to as "flapping" in professional terminology, was typical of autistic children, though we didn't know that then. She'd fling her fingers against whatever she was attracted to, brushing the object gently at first while listening to the sound her fingers made against the material. All the while she'd croon to herself, her voice going up and down, her legs moving in a skip-like fashion keeping time with her hand movements. I'd say casually, as if her behavior were the most normal thing in the world, "Oh, she's just flipping." That would be the end of it. I learned early on that if my attitude toward Becky was one of acceptance, other people would be more likely to accept her, too. Loving Becky became a kind of litmus test for my friends and boyfriends: if they couldn't find the beauty in her spirit, then I couldn't see much loveliness in theirs. Being Becky's sister taught me to select only the best kind of people for friends.

I've been married twice, the first marriage lasting four years, the second still going strong after almost thirty years. While the men differed in every other aspect, both husbands have been generous and warm to Becky, as have my women friends. Becky has bestowed nicknames on her favorites—Emmie is the "Coffeemate" because they both enjoy that beverage and I don't. Kathryn is "Dental Kathryn" because she's had twenty-three root canals, something we all regard as a record. My husband, Frank, is "The Dentist" because, as a great and courageous gift to Becky, he sang the lead in a shortened production of *Little Shop of Horrors*, Becky's favorite musical. The Dentist, played by Steve Martin in the movie version, is Becky's all-time favorite character, and to see her brother-in-law sing the familiar songs dressed in a dental coat, then leather jacket, was a moment of pure joy. And though Frank had never sung a solo in his life, he made it through the performance, something he would never have tried if not for his desire to please my sister.

Pleased as she was though, to this day she reminds him that he mixed up a few of the lines. Then she corrects him, giving him the exact lyrics, adding, "That's all right. I forgive you." And though he loves her, is kind during her brief visits to our home, he has confided to me that living with Becky on a permanent basis would drive him insane. "Those constant questions and the way she talks to herself all the time—it gets on my nerves after a while," he confessed once after a three-day visit. The fact that I utterly devote myself to Becky and her needs while she's at our house contributes to his unease. I suspect he prefers to have that spot for himself. Yet, he remains willing to let me handle Becky in my own way. He has accepted us both for better or worse.

My first husband, too, was invariably kind to Becky. One Halloween, he created a huge black mustache out of cardboard so Becky could dress the way she wanted for the occasion. He never once questioned her desire to be a mustache; instead, he set about making her dream come true. Becky has that rare capacity to experience the moment, as completely and as joyfully as humanly possible. Friends and family go to extreme lengths just to bring her to that point of ecstasy.

Becky never stopped caring for my first husband, though he and I had a bitter parting. Unfortunately, he cut off all contact with her after the divorce and never bothered to explain his actions to her. She still refers to him as "the original Tall One," and she likes to recall his "giant hands" which, in her frequent comparisons, made hers look even smaller than usual.

She's always loved her petite hands and enjoyed holding them up to mine (or anyone else's) to compare, pleased that hers were smaller. She'd been an abnormally little child and grew into a short woman, not reaching five feet. We've had numerous conversations about her stature, discussing the differences between dwarves and midgets, where she might fit in on the scale of the "height-challenged." She is proud of her size, considers herself "almost a dwarf" and seems to take comfort in the thought.

Interestingly, while browsing the Internet recently, I discovered a website created by a woman who considers herself "an elf." This woman suffers from the same disorder as my sister. She says that being "an elf" is like being an alien—constantly having to learn customs and language, manners and communication. Learning these things in our culture does not feel natural or particularly comfortable to this woman, much the same way Becky has trouble figuring out the rules of polite society. From childhood, people told the woman that her tall thin frame and her sculpted ears make her look like an elf. She writes that she doesn't feel she belongs with humans, so she proclaims her "elf-hood" with pride, much the way Becky claims a kinship with dwarves.

Sitting beside Becky in the car, I watched as she studied her hands, pressed them together hard until they shook a little.

"Nervous, Beck?" I reached for her, rubbed my thumb over her palms.

"A little." She allowed me to massage her hands for a brief moment, then pulled them away.

"Do you think they'll choose me?" Her voice was low and I could hear the fear in it.

"I don't know. They're choosing six out of ten people. You have a good chance, but I can't promise." I knew she would never understand if she weren't selected. She'd be hurt, feel rejected no matter how many times it was explained to her. My head began to ache.

As always, being with Becky brought to the surface feelings I'd rather remain buried deep inside. She wasn't happy in her current situation, and I couldn't stand to think of that. We shared so much pain from our past—the frequent separations, her inability to "fit" into the usual nooks and crannies of childhood, certain moments branded in my memory—I shook the gloomy thoughts from my head and tried to focus on the moment. Today was a red letter day for Becky, one she'd awaited for a long time. I didn't want to upset myself with memories gone by. Now was the important time. Today, my sister was going to interview for a new life.

I could tell she'd taken special care with her appearance. She'd chosen a royal blue pantsuit that matched her eyes and set off the blush in her cheeks. Her hair, cut as short as she could convince the beautician to chop it, was still damp from shampooing and had a slightly medicinal odor. But then, she always smelled like that, as if she'd been sprayed all over with a very light disinfectant. The scent was strong when you entered her house and it clung to Becky when she ventured out into the world.

Her face, small with delicate features, not at all like the slightly distorted faces of people with Down's syndrome, would have been pretty if not for the blankness usually found in her eyes. But today, her eyes were bright. Today, there was life, even excitement in them.

But you'd never mistake my sister for someone "normal" because of the way she held herself: head down, never looking directly at anyone, body a little hunched as if it couldn't quite find its place in the world. I glanced at her again because she was emitting a loud noise, much like the sound of a lawnmower that's running out of gas.

She was grinding her teeth, another indication of her anxiety.

"Quit that, Becky," my father said sternly. "Have a lifesaver." He handed one back and Becky plopped it into her mouth.

"Thanks," she muttered, her voice flat.

She began talking to herself, repeating questions over and over. She asked about herself and whether or not the interviewers would approve of her. She didn't expect an answer just yet. She would address a person directly if she really wanted a response. Now she was mulling something over, working it out in her own mind by a constant stream of inquiries that twisted through the air like a strange, surreal song. Asking questions, whether to herself or to someone else, was Becky's way of conversing. She's done it forever and I was used to the peculiar rhythm of her speech.

"Is she a nice person? Will they like her? Will they pick her?" She'd switched to the third person, an old habit from childhood. While this may seem odd, it wasn't to me. I could remember when she always talked about herself using "she" rather than "I". This distancing is common among people with autism. Becky only reverted back to third person when she was feeling especially vulnerable. I knew how badly she wanted this new beginning, and I ached for her. She continued her litany until my mother turned around and tried to explain everything.

"Honey, it's like this. If they pick five people who like rock-and-roll music and they are looking for a sixth person, would they choose someone who liked rock-and-roll music or would they select someone who enjoyed Beethoven? They're looking for people who have similar temperaments and interests." Mother's soft voice had a calming effect. She smiled at Becky and I wondered how she still managed to have patience with an adult daughter who would never really grow up. But then, she'd always tried to manage my sister with kindness, even when my sister drove her to distraction with her incessant questions.

"This is the place, I think," Dad said as he pulled the car into a driveway. The asphalt led up to a nice brick home with sliding glass doors. Dad found an empty slot next to a van with METHODIST GROUP HOMES printed on the side. My parents got out of the car. I leaned over to Becky and whispered, "Remember, be friendly. Talk. Look 'em in the eye." I gave her arm a little squeeze.

"I will, Jet." "Jet" is the pet name for me Becky coined in childhood. She explained it to me in those days, saying the shape of my face reminded her of a jet airplane. I couldn't see the connection because jets were angular and sleek and to my mind, my own face was chubby and round. But I was happy she saw me that way and laughed when she sometimes sang her first original composition, "Jet-shaped Face," composed in my honor. I've been nothing but Jet ever since.

I watched as she opened the car door and walked toward her future. I sat for a moment, alone in the back seat, remembering our past.

Chapter Two

There's a cyclone coming...
—*Uncle Henry*

In the 1950s, being an only child was a rare thing. It was, after all, the Baby Boom years. Young married couples must have felt confident in the post-war economy and the idea that the world had been made safe for democracy once again. By the time I was five years old, I already sensed the oddity of my "only" status. All of my playmates had siblings in varying combinations. The next-door neighbors had a bustling brood, which included my best friend, Betty. Each day, after Betty walked home from her first grade class, we'd play together with our dolls while her younger siblings constantly interrupted us. If one of the little ones cried, Betty would have to stop her play, try to comfort the child, then run inside to get her mother. Yet, though they were trouble-some, I desperately wanted a baby sister or brother. Already, I wanted to fit in, be like all the other kids.

So in December 1957, when my parents told me I'd be having a brother or sister soon, I bubbled with excitement. My mother let me put my ear to her stomach to hear the new baby. I'd gingerly touch her belly and feel the bumps and kicks from within. I didn't put my mother's suddenly fat appearance together with the idea of the baby inside. For years afterward, I thought my mother had grown bewilderingly large. In my mind, her body never returned to normal after my sister's birth.

Not only was I going to have a brother or sister, our family was moving from North Carolina to West Virginia. I still remember packing boxes of my toys and taking the long trip over the mountains to our new home in Hunting-ton, where my father had taken a job as Minister of Music at Fifth Avenue Baptist Church. Mother flew in an airplane because she was almost ready to give birth and the doctor didn't think a long, twisting car ride would be good for her. I still recall going with my father to pick her up at the airport, the night foggy and cold, so cold my fingers felt stiff and hard to bend. I'd never been to an airport before and can still remember seeing my mother climb down from the plane, the fog making her seem vague, ghostlike. Now, I wonder if that late-pregnancy plane ride had a damaging effect on my sister.

I loved our new house on South Queens Court. Two new constructions, exactly alike, sat side by side: one was yellow (ours) and the other green with a large oak tree in the front yard. Our house perched halfway up a steep hill, and the new backyard was nothing more than a long incline of grass that led to a stand of woods at the top. An enormous stone wall held the mountain at bay and provided us with what little flat yard we had. The hills and curved roads of West Virginia were very different from the flat, sandy region in North Carolina where I'd lived. I quickly grew to love the mountains and the rangy woods near the new house. Here, I had an upstairs room with two windows. One window overlooked the street, and I could watch all the kids at play; the other window was shaded by an enormous tulip tree. Having a room up so high made me feel as though I lived with the birds and squirrels. Early on, I caught sight of a Baltimore oriole outside my window. Later, I would see a scarlet tanager and lots of cardinals. I tried to imagine flying, swooping in for a landing on one of the gnarled branches outside my window. I'd discovered another universe, one that seemed ordered and beautiful. I spent a lot of time in my room, staring at the bare limbs of the nearby tree, wondering what my new brother or sister would be like. I tried to imagine us sharing this room, and I hoped having a new baby would start a whole chain of events that would lead to our family growing even larger.

Though I was more than ready for a new sibling, I recall my maternal grandmother's caution to me before the baby was born. Affectionately called Gwennie by the family, my mother's mother was a humorless woman with a surprisingly kind heart, the sort of woman who would have liked to order the world her way. As long as things moved along in a seemly fashion, she would have been quite content. In this perfect place, no one would be naughty, no one would be rude and no one would ever do anything that might cause the family reputation to be tarnished. Respectability and restraint were as necessary for my grandmother as bread and water. No negative emotions were allowed—no envy, no hatred, and especially no anger.

Gwennie had iron-gray hair she wore in a chic French twist. I used to watch her brush her hair and then put it up in one swift motion. She wore cat's eye glasses with silver rims, dabbed her lips with a dark pink lipstick, and powdered her nose lightly. Bustling around like a bumble-bee, she flitted from one chore to the next when I visited her house in Lincolnton, North Carolina and never lit on a chair for more than two or three minutes. Like a bee, she had a thick middle with long, spindly legs and arms. Gwennie never had a hair out of place and never wore anything other than dresses and skirts. She preferred shirtwaist dresses in pastel shades of green, lavender, and yellow.

Gwennie informed me that I was not to be "jealous of the new baby." I'd had my parents' attention for almost six years and to my grandmother's mind, that was enough to spoil me. She wanted to make sure I understood that the new addition was to be loved, nothing else.

And I, being the good little girl that I was, took her message to heart. I would never be jealous of the baby. I would take care of it and love it and be "very gentle," just as instructed.

In 1958, the January night my sister was born, I went to bed as usual, but was awakened in the wee hours before dawn. My father shook me from sleep, helped me into my clothes, explained that I would be spending the night with Martha Jane, our preacher's daughter who was a year younger than me. Martha Jane and I were in primary choir together, so staying a few nights with her seemed natural.

Mother didn't say much on our way to Martha Jane's home. She must have told me to be a good girl and kissed me goodbye, but I don't have an exact memory of it. Now I realize she was in labor and had entered that quiet state some women retreat to in order to focus on the hard work of giving birth. Though my memories of Mother are vague, I can see clearly in my mind's eye Martha Jane's mother welcoming me into their big white house and telling me that Martha Jane had crawled in bed with her daddy and I could join them. I was a little uneasy getting in bed with Martha Jane *and* her father, but I would never have questioned a grown-up. Years later, we all joked that I'd been in bed with the preacher.

That morning after breakfast, Martha Jane and I were playing in the living room. The telephone rang and Martha Jane's mother announced that I had a baby sister.

"A GIRL! It's a GIRL!!" I screamed and so did Martha Jane. We ran around the room and rolled somersaults on the carpet. My happiness was like a cold—everyone caught it and Martha Jane's house became festive.

Unfortunately, that night someone wet Martha Jane's bed. Martha Jane told her mother I did it and I was humiliated, though I was certain I was not at fault. I'd never wet the bed that I could recall. Looking back, I see the event as an omen. Already my sister was having a mixed effect on my life—even at this early stage. Joy and shame began to thread through the tapestry of who I was, and both feelings were stitched, somehow, to Becky, though back then I was only aware of the excitement of having a new baby sister. I would discover soon enough the embarrassment that often accompanied our relationship.

ॐ

Rebecca Jane Clinard, born January 31, 1958, weighed 6 lb. 10¼ oz, an average-sized baby, though smaller than I'd been. My mother doesn't remember much about the delivery; she'd been knocked out with some sort of drug, the same medication she'd been given when she birthed to me. She told me later she slept through both deliveries and was groggy for quite some time afterward. This was the way babies were born in the 1950s. The doctor told her later that he'd had to use forceps to help Becky emerge. I wonder now if the drugs or the forceps caused damage—now, we know the infant cooperates in the birthing process if allowed to be born the natural way. Both Becky and I got off to the same sluggish start.

Becky's head was covered with light blond fuzz, which grew into golden curls that first year. Her eyes, big and bright blue, shone above a button nose. She had my father's smile, wide and thin.

I remember Gwennie staying with us that first month after Mother and Becky came home from the hospital. Mother mostly rested and couldn't be disturbed, but Gwennie let me hold my sister a few times. She made me sit on the couch and taught me how to cradle my arms just so. Then, she'd lay Becky in the little nest I'd made and tell me to be very still. Becky reminded me of a tiny sparrow, her almost bald head wobbling against my arm. I immediately felt protective of her. Mostly Becky slept, but sometimes she'd open her eyes and look at me. I couldn't wait for her to grow up so we could talk and I could teach her how to collect just the right cards to win at animal rummy.

After the novelty of having a sister had worn off, I didn't find Becky all that interesting. She slept and was quiet most of the time. I don't remember her crying much. Mostly, she just lay in her crib. But by the time she was six months old, she and I could play games: peek-a-boo and tickle feet. I used to hurry home from school to fool around with her. She'd be lying on Mom's big bed and I'd tickle her, make her giggle and laugh. She'd coo and do all the cute baby things. Sometimes, I'd pull her across the bed by her feet and she'd laugh even more. The more aggressively I swung her around on the bed, the better she liked it. Sometimes, Mother would tell me to settle down, to be more gentle. I don't remember Becky ever crying during this activity; she always wanted more.

Eventually, Becky started talking, though sometimes her words were hard to understand. But that was true of all babies, at least in my limited experience.

According to my mother, during those first two years of life, Becky developed much as I had.

But there were a few differences.

Becky was a very good baby. She rarely cried or demanded much attention. She seemed content to play with the toys in her playpen. She was a loner, even then. She didn't cuddle in Mother's lap the way I had, but she loved to rock. She'd crawl up into a rocking chair or a swing and stay there until someone moved her on to another activity.

Her first year was normal as far as my mother and Becky's pediatrician could tell. Though Becky and I had different baby personalities, my mother saw no cause for alarm. Becky did everything on schedule. Mother does mention one incident that happened during Becky's first year. I remember it too, and I've often wondered if this event had any impact on Becky's condition.

When Becky was about a year old, she had an accident. I recall walking up the hill to our house, tired and hot from school when my mother screamed at me to hurry. I'd never heard my mother's voice sound that way before—terrified, desperate. I ran, dropped my lunchbox on the way to the front door. Mother held Becky in her arms, a towel wrapped around Becky's head, making her seem smaller, more vulnerable. Becky's eyes were wet-looking, though she wasn't actually crying.

"She's gashed her head open. Monie's taking us to the hospital." Monie was our next-door neighbor. She could drive and my mother couldn't. We hurried into Monie's car and drove to the emergency room. I looked at the place on my sister's head, a two-inch cut that went all the way to her skull, it seemed to me. I waited with Monie while the doctor stitched Becky's head back together. He covered the stitches with a hard, waxy material and told us Becky would be okay.

"She was in the crib and I was vacuuming the rug. She leaned over toward the vacuum and fell. She hit her head on the side of the vacuum and screamed. I grabbed her and ran over to Monie's. Then I called your daddy." Mother kept explaining it, holding Becky and calming her. She was deeply upset, and when Daddy met us at the hospital, she went over the story again.

That was the only injury to Becky that I can recall. I wondered later if this fall had been the cause of Becky's problems. Mother and I discussed it after I'd become an adult. Once I'd grown up, Mother sometimes mused about the causes of my sister's condition. Now a mother myself, I know how the maternal mind grills itself on every possible mistake made, every opportunity lost, looking for flaws and searching for faults in the care and raising of a woman's most treasured responsibility—her children.

My parents didn't realize anything was amiss with Becky until she was between three and four years old. I suspected something was wrong before then. But I was a child and had no way to articulate my feelings. I just knew that Becky wasn't like the other children in the neighborhood, the ones her age. First of all, she didn't like candy or ice cream. She didn't care for anything sweet. What little kid has to be forced to take a bite of ice cream? She didn't eat regular food either. She ate Gerber baby food or else she gobbled soft stuff that Mother mashed for her. Other little kids chewed on pretzels or crackers. Becky never would, and I knew this was strange, even early on. But the biggest give-away was the time she entered Mr. Green's perfectly manicured yard when she was around two.

Mr. Green and his wife lived three houses down from us on our dead-end street that grew more children than flowers. His yard was the only one with a well-tended garden, a plot that was never disturbed. All the children in the neighborhood had better sense than to go anywhere near the Greens' house. Mr. Green's temper was legendary and even the atmosphere around the place was prohibitive. The house was always quiet and the Greens never smiled or waved at anyone. I rarely ventured to that part of the street, partly out of fear, but also because in the afternoons after school it was my job to keep an eye on Becky while my mother prepared supper. Usually, Becky stayed in our front yard and I anchored myself close by. Sometimes, one of my friends would join me in a game of cowboys and Indians or freeze tag. Any game was allowed as long as I could watch over Becky. But one day, Becky slipped away from me, and before I could stop her she did what every other kid in the neighborhood knew *not* to do—she marched onto the Greens' lawn.

The Greens had no children and no patience. Mr. Green, especially, was scary. He'd chase any living thing out of his yard with a baseball bat he kept on the front porch for such purposes. If one of the boys threw a ball into his shrubs, it stayed there until it rotted. No one, not even the brattiest boy on the street, crossed into Green territory.

Imagine how I felt when I saw my little sister charging behind enemy lines with the zeal of a bull elephant. I ran after her, pumping my legs and panting hard, but I was clumsy and slow and before I knew it, she'd plodded right into Mr. Green's tulips, trampling the red blossoms as she went. By the time I reached her, Mr. Green had his bat in hand.

"If she's too goddam dumb to stay out of my yard, then you'd better keep her out, you hear?" His spittle fell on my upturned face and I watched his cheeks grow red. No grown-up had ever cursed at me before. My own parents never went beyond a 'darn.'

"Let's get out of here, Becky. He's mean," I said in the strongest voice I could muster. I didn't care if he chased me with that bat of his. He'd called

Becky dumb and he'd acted like there was something wrong with me, too. He'd lumped us together and I didn't like it. Anger propelled me out of his yard faster than I thought I could go. And I dragged Becky behind me by her skinny arm.

"Don't ever go in there again. He's a bad man. A bad man. Understand?" I shook her shoulders just a little for emphasis. She wouldn't look at me but she gritted her teeth. "Stop gritting." I worried that she'd wear her baby teeth away before the big ones had a chance to come in. She seemed oblivious to the danger we'd both been in, and at that moment I knew something wasn't quite right with her.

That wasn't the only time Becky strayed far from home. Once she became mobile, my parents had a hard time keeping up with her. She would take off any time she got the chance. Her forays into the neighborhood got her into trouble. If my father was home and Becky wandered out of the yard and I didn't catch her, he would go after her, carry her home wrapped tight in his arms. Then he would cut a hickory switch from outside and switch her little legs, carefully explaining that she was not allowed to travel from our yard without one of us with her. I remember thin, red stripes across her legs. The strange thing was, Becky rarely cried when she got a whipping. And the spankings never seemed to "sink in;" they never deterred Becky from future roving.

Because of Becky's propensity for wandering out of our small yard, my parents fenced in the back portion, using the stone wall behind the house as the rear of the enclosure, the house itself as the front, then closing in the two sides with strong metal fencing. The back porch opened into this space and my parents put a swing set on one side of the yard, and there was a small patch of grass on the other side where Becky and I could play "Mother May I?" or "Red Light/Green Light." When my mother needed to iron clothes or cook a meal, she would let Becky go outside to play for a little while. Becky loved the swing and usually rocked back and forth without complaint, at least for a few minutes. But one day, while I was in school, Becky escaped.

Mother recalls the incident like this:

> I was working in the house and had just left Becky swinging. I checked on her every so often, peering out the door to make sure she was okay. When I finished ironing one of your daddy's shirts, I went to gather Becky back in the house. But she was gone! I ran outside and called her. No answer. I ran back into the house, down the steps, and out the front door to see if she'd gone into the street. I wasn't too worried about traffic because we lived on a dead-end road. I was more worried about Becky getting into something dangerous.
>
> She was nowhere in sight. I ran all over the neighborhood, screaming her name. Monie, our neighbor, joined me in the search. Finally, I had to

call your daddy at work for him to come and look for her in the car. He found her about a mile away, just marching along. She wasn't crying or scared. But I was. I still don't know how she got out of the fence. But I realized then I could never leave her unsupervised, not even for a minute.

Becky's adventurous spirit didn't seem quite normal to me. None of the other little kids in the neighborhood left home the way Becky would if she got the opportunity. It was as if Becky didn't realize she belonged with us, like she didn't understand that the four of us were family. Instead, Becky was a soul unto herself, a force of nature almost. And I knew, before anyone else recognized it, that Becky wasn't like other children.

I imagine my parents didn't want to think anything was wrong with their beautiful little daughter. Like most of us, they probably thought that given time, she'd come around, develop the way she should. Besides, she didn't look abnormal in any way. She'd been a pretty baby with golden curls and fine features. By the time she'd turned three, she was a real beauty. I can remember being jealous of her looks. I'd already decided that I was more of a plain Jane with stringy brown locks and the infamous "Clinard" nose, a large, hooked proboscis passed down on my paternal side. There was nothing that could be mistaken for beauty about me. But Becky looked like a cherub. No one knew she was anything beyond an armful of sweetness until the visit to my paternal grandparents in North Carolina when Becky was around four.

Mrs. Phelps, Mamaw and Papaw's neighbor, first suggested Becky might have a problem. While chatting with our family, Mrs. Phelps called Becky but got no response. She mentioned it to my folks, saying, "I believe that baby can't hear." The more my parents thought about the possibility, the more sense it made. Deafness would explain why Becky didn't always obey, why she didn't come when called. It's a mistake commonly made by parents of children who share Becky's disability. When a child doesn't respond when spoken to, the first assumption is that the child can't hear. My parents took Becky to a hearing specialist once we had returned to our West Virginia home.

At the specialist's office, my father ran into the first hint that trouble was ahead for Becky. And for all of us. Becky had no interest in being examined by a doctor, so she began to fight him off with all of the vigor her four-year-old body possessed. My father was amazed at her strength, how she fought. But what impressed him most was that she wouldn't listen to reason. She refused to allow the doctor near her, even when my father tried to bribe her with a visit to the park. My father couldn't succeed; the doctor got nowhere fast. He instructed his nurse to wrap Becky in a sheet so he could perform the exam, creating a sort of straitjacket for toddlers. Though my father didn't like it, he didn't know what else to do. He stood beside Becky and tried to comfort her while she turned red with screaming. It wouldn't be the last time he had to do something unpleasant, thinking it would be in Becky's best interest. He couldn't know it then, but seeing her restrained would be one of his easier trials.

After the exam, the doctor, tired and irritated by Becky's behavior, declared there was nothing wrong with Becky's ears. This news was both good and bad. Good that her hearing was normal, but bad because the tone of the doctor's voice suggested something much, much worse was the matter with my sister.

My parents can't retrace the exact steps that took them to the office of Dr. M——, a local psychologist, after Becky's hearing tested normal. Becky was around four years old. My father vaguely recalls that his boss recommended Dr. M——, who was also a member of our church. Dr. M—— was a child psychologist in practice with a psychiatrist and he worked with Becky for two years while we still lived in Huntington.

He diagnosed Becky as being "emotionally disturbed and mildly retarded due to her emotional problems," though he admitted that an accurate diagnosis was impossible since Becky refused to cooperate with any testing. She wouldn't pay attention to the tasks he set before her and an accurate measure of her intelligence was impossible. He gave my parents his "best guess."

As my mother recalls, he explained to her that Becky had built a sort of "wall" between herself and learning. In order to help her learn, we had to destroy the wall. Because Becky's behavior wasn't conducive to testing, Dr. M—— could never measure her IQ. She didn't want to participate in his "games," so he guessed that she was somewhat retarded. He was never able to unlock the secret of her intellect because she simply avoided his tests.

Unfortunately, neither Dr. M—— nor the doctors who came after him could ever find the key to my sister's condition, although each believed such a key existed. As a result of this belief, my parents began to search for the "right" treatment, a search that would last far beyond Becky's childhood. At first, no doctors could give a clear diagnosis beyond the vague phrase "emotional disturbance."

Becky's behavior grew more bizarre as she grew older. My parents remember her as hyperactive, constantly in motion, flipping and skipping around the house the way a hummingbird flits around a garden, buzzing here and there, pausing only long enough to get a sip of nectar. Becky was like that—never stopping, always in flight. She was a loner and didn't seem to require contact with others. Since she loved to rock, one Christmas my parents gave her a large hobbyhorse. She rode the daylights out of the toy, scooting Trigger (my name for the honey-colored horse, not hers) all over her room. Finally, in desperation, my father bolted Trigger to the floor in her room so she would be able to ride as hard as she wanted with no danger to life or limb. Or furniture, for that matter.

While under Dr. M——'s care, Becky went to a special preschool one day a week. Dr. M—— also gave my father an assignment: to spend an hour every day playing with Becky. My mother was to teach her the basics—shapes, colors, sizes—while Dad would concentrate on her emotional needs. In those days, problems were often blamed on parents and though Dr. M—— probably didn't come out and say so, I suspect he was ready to find any flaws he could with the way my parents did things. I don't know if my parents felt this or not. But I do know that outsiders who don't know all the facts can often judge harshly and find fault where no fault exists.

I can still remember how, after supper, Dad and Becky would go to the living room where the stereo system was set up. Being a musician, Dad wanted a nice record player and had built one for himself from a mail-order electronics course he'd taken. We didn't have a lot of money or furniture in those days and the living room was spacious enough to run, or gallop, as the case turned out, in big circles round and round. Dad would put on Becky's favorite record, "Who Wants a Ride," and let her clamber up on his back. Then he would become the "trotting pony" mentioned in the song. He'd circle the living room over and over until he was huffing and puffing. When he could trot no longer, he'd sling Becky off his back in one quick movement. She'd giggle and laugh, begging for more. After he'd caught his breath, he'd pick her up again and off they'd go—"Giddy up pony lift that knee"—once more. Finally, out of breath, he'd quiz her on her shapes—circle, triangle, square—then hand her over to Mom, who'd give her a bath and tuck her into bed.

I have to say I was jealous of Becky for the time my father spent with her. I adored him and he wasn't home that much. Like most fathers in the 50s, he was our sole support and he worked long hours. The fact that Becky got some of his time each day, assigned time he was determined to fulfill, brought out feelings of envy. I wanted him to do something fun with me—not carry me around or anything—but maybe play cards or Monopoly. But I knew, even at ten, that Becky needed his extra attention. I knew something was wrong with her. The minute I felt jealousy coming on, I'd begin to chastise myself for it. After all, I was okay. I didn't have problems. If this was what Becky needed, then so be it. I knew my father loved me; I knew my sister needed him, needed everything. I began to learn how to put another person's needs ahead of my own. I figured out how to say nothing when I wanted something for myself. In some ways, these skills have served me well over the years; in other ways, they have been a stumbling block to honest relationships. But I began to learn them in our small living room while my father and Becky trotted in even circles, listening to "Who Wants a Ride" over and over.

During those early years, Becky and I had separate bedrooms. I'd tell her a story or we'd sing a couple of songs, then I'd head for my own room where I could read or finish my homework. I was in the fourth grade when Becky began seeing Dr. M——, and my folks explained as well as they could about her condition. It was then I began to pray for Becky. Being the daughter of a minister of music meant I was at church for every Sunday school lesson, every Bible school session in the summer, church camp and children's choir. I walked in an atmosphere of faith and grew up in what I know now to be an innocent, safe environment. This innocence and optimism was very much a part of my family's attitude toward the world. Even my grandparents on both sides were strong church-goers. But it went further than mere attendance. I can still remember Mamaw listening to sermons on the radio. It was she who told me about her grandfather, a preacher who established a church in Winston-Salem, North Carolina. She also taught me the Lord's Prayer when I was about six. On the other side of the family, my grandfather, Ernie, read his Bible every day, and I'd often find him in the parlor of a morning with the book open across his knees.

I came from a long line of believers and, at ten, I'd already felt the presence of God in my walks through the woods; I'd already been struck with a deep desire to be "good." And so, in complete faith, I began to pray for my sister, for her instant and miraculous recovery. Later, as I realized there would be no quick fix to this problem, I started praying for Dr. M—— to be the best doctor in the world and find a cure for Becky. I prayed each night, sometimes growing hot with the effort, often ending my prayer in tears that ran all the way into my ears and dampened my pillow. I prayed for Becky to be normal, just like all the other little kids. And I cried, I think, for me. Because I would never have a normal sister, something I wanted very much. I wanted to know what it was like to have a real conversation, not a question-and-answer game. I wanted to be able to tell Becky all my secrets and listen to hers. I was tired of feeling embarrassed about her oddities and I was tired of feeling guilty about my embarrassment. I wanted her to be normal, normal, normal. But she wasn't.

Though Dr. M——'s treatment wasn't successful with my sister, he gave my parents something to work toward. After all, he'd implied if my parents could just fix the emotional problems, Becky might learn to be "normal."

After Becky was diagnosed as emotionally disturbed, her unusual behavior placed a stigma on our family, at least in the eyes of the extended family members. Gwennie didn't believe there was anything wrong with her "Rebecca" and once, when she was taking care of Becky and me while our parents were at a church choir retreat, Gwennie took Becky to Dr. Fitzgerald, a general practitioner who lived in Lincolnton.

I'd been to Dr. Fitzgerald many times myself as a small child and still remember him as a kind man. Unfortunately, mental disturbances weren't his specialty and he told my grandmother there was nothing wrong with Becky that a little discipline and attention couldn't cure, as if my parents were remiss in these areas. Being told that Becky was all right must have been music to Gwennie's ears. I imagine she couldn't wait for my parents' return to share this wonderful news with them.

My parents were not happy with Gwennie's diagnosis, particularly my father. In fact, Dad was livid. He resented the fact that Gwennie had taken it upon herself to seek consultation from a doctor who was not even a specialist in psychology. He resented the implication that neither he nor my mother gave Becky enough attention, and as for discipline, Dr. M—— had suggested "time-out" for Becky when she misbehaved where she sat in a chair for a certain number of minutes. This they did, though it was hard to enforce. Dad spanked Becky sometimes, though not often. But Becky was almost impossible in certain situations and no one knew exactly how to handle her. In Dad's mind, he and Mother were coping with a difficult situation to the best of their abilities, doing exactly what Dr. M—— told them to do. To hear that Becky's problems were simple and relatively easy to solve infuriated my father. I still remember their argument upon my parents' return from the retreat.

Though I didn't know at the time what all the shouting was about, I do recall Gwennie trying to give my parents a little pink potty that Becky loved. Gwennie had toilet trained Becky while my parents had been gone and Becky was very proud of her achievement. After all, she was four years old, way past the time most children learned to use the potty. Though she used it, Becky still had to be cleaned up afterwards, a job that fell to me. I wasn't particularly happy about having such a duty, but I wiped her little bottom almost as often as I wiped my own. And, since Becky had learned her new trick with the pink potty, that was the one she wanted and my grandmother wanted her to have it. But my father disagreed.

"I'll buy her a potty! We are not taking that with us! I'll get her one on my own!" my father shouted.

"But she loves this one! She might as well take it!" Gwennie shouted right back, though her voice shook and I knew she was going to cry in a minute. And cry she did. But my father stood firm, even through her tears. We packed up in record time and left my grandmother sobbing in the back room. The ride home was very quiet and I remember not knowing what was going on, but being upset that such yelling would happen at my grandmother's house.

After that, my grandmother spent lots of time with her "Rebecca" whenever we visited. Gwennie took Becky for long walks; she told Becky stories about what life had been like when Gwennie had been a little girl; she constantly encouraged my mother to spend more time with Becky, though my mother was already spending a great deal of time teaching Becky her letters, colors, shapes. Gwennie became Becky's advocate and didn't seem to fear my father's anger when she interceded for Becky. Unlike me, Gwennie didn't quake in her shoes when my father's voice rose.

I remember another time when Gwennie took Becky's part. It was Thanksgiving. Gwennie and Ernie had come to our house in West Virginia to visit. I was playing a game with my father and some kids from the neighborhood. Becky was crying and my mother had gone upstairs to get her and bring her down with the family. Once Becky was downstairs, she toddled over to where we were playing and upset the game. She did this several times before my father told my mother to "take that young'un back upstairs."

"That child is a part of this family and she needs to be with the family," Gwennie said firmly. "She shouldn't be shunted to the upstairs."

"Take her back," my father said again, his voice tight with impatience.

My mother must have felt at odds because her mother was telling her one thing and her husband was telling her the opposite. She turned with a sigh, picked Becky up, and returned to the upstairs part of the house where she stayed and played with Becky.

When my father told me this story recently, he said, "Your grandmother was right. We should have kept Becky downstairs with us for that game. She was absolutely right." This must have been a hard admission for him to make; Gwennie, with her bossy ways, wasn't one of his favorite people. But Gwennie loved her "Rebecca;" even my father knew that, though they expressed their love in different ways

One evening during that same visit, Mother called us to dinner. Becky was rocking on Trigger in her room and I could hear the rhythmic sound of the horse hitting against the floor, ka-thump, ka-thump, ka-thump.

"Go get that child and bring her down to supper," my grandmother told my father.

"She'd rather rock than eat. Let's just go ahead and eat in peace. She'll come down when she's hungry," he said, a tight smile forming on his lips.

"That child needs to be with her family. If you won't go get her, I will," my grandmother said. And she did.

My father was about thirty-seven years old at the time; he hadn't the experience to see things as clearly as my grandmother saw them. And, he resented her telling him what to do. She was, after all, a bossy woman, something my father couldn't abide. I never thought I'd hear him say she was right about anything, but now, at eighty-two, my father sees that some of Gwennie's impulses regarding Becky were correct.

Because Becky loved being by herself even as a baby, it was easy to leave her alone, especially if there was work to be done around the house. My mother explained it like this:

> Becky didn't cry much. She would amuse herself in her playpen for a long time. She liked to be alone and sometimes we let her. We were remiss in this. We should have made her interact with the family.

Perhaps Mother's assessment is true. Perhaps Becky should have had more time interacting with the family in those early years. But as I remember things, Becky did get lots of time. She got her "pony" time with Dad, her school time with Mother and her playtime with me. In my memory, we were all invested in helping Becky become normal and we took that very seriously. And we were optimistic, believing that Becky would someday become a normal child and, through our love and attention, we could somehow cure her. In October 1962, just after Becky had been diagnosed by Dr. M——, my father wrote this to his mother:

> Dearest Mother,
>
> Becky is continuing to improve, doing new things almost daily now. Not all of them are desirable, but all of them show progress, so we try to be grateful even for the changes that create problems. She hasn't had a diaper on since vacation. She still has accidents from time to time, maybe an average of one a day, but gradually that, too, is improving. She says many words and phrases now, and is able to tell us what she wants some of the time. I believe more than ever that she is going to come out of it all one of these days! Praise God from Whom all blessings flow!

Such was the optimism with which all three of us considered Becky's condition. I knew my prayers would be answered; my father and mother believed the same about their own pleas to God. How could a God of love do anything but cure my sister? It was merely a matter of time.

But two years passed and, though Becky did improve under Dr. M——'s care, she still wasn't a normal child. She still referred to herself as "the Becky" in most of her questions. "Can the Becky have some peaches? Does the Becky need to use the potty?" Even though she was six years old by this time, she still needed help wiping her bottom after using the bathroom; she couldn't be trusted to stay in our yard; she still flipped everything in sight and she held her hands in front of her face for long periods of time. However, some progress was evident. Becky was learning her shapes and colors; she could talk, though her speech was rapid and hard to understand. Sometimes, I understood what she was saying when no one else could. I don't know why this was so. But over the years, I began to understand Becky in a way my parents did not. Maybe because we were in the same generation, maybe because we spent more time together, or maybe because I taught myself to pick up on her cues—whatever the reason, I was becoming Becky's interpreter for other people in the world. In turn, I began to interpret the world for her. I even explained about God and helped Becky learn to say "Now I lay me down to sleep" each night before bed. I believed in prayers and I knew our prayers for Becky had been working slowly. God was taking His own sweet time about answering them the way I wanted them answered. Presto!—A normal sister.

I remember a few times when Becky and I seemed to be normal sisters, especially during my early years. After school, I'd cuddle up with Becky. I was usually tired and ready for a nap but Becky was raring to go. I invented a game for us to play called "Sleep Ghost." Becky and I would pretend to fall asleep with our eyes closed and our bodies still. If she moved, I'd tell her the Sleep Ghost was coming down out of the sky to snatch her up. At three, she believed me! Eventually, we'd both fall asleep for real. I was pleased with my cleverness, tricking Becky into napping with me.

Later, when she was around four and I was ten, we'd play "Mother May I" in the back yard. I'd allow her to take fifteen baby steps, then three giant steps and finally, one ballerina step until she finally could tag me. Then she'd become the mother and I'd have to work my way to her, step by step. Looking at us from a distance, we must have seemed as normal as any kids. I always loved those quicksilver moments of real sisterhood.

Often, these memories centered around the Christmas holidays. Once, Becky and I received matching stuffed elephants with long trunks and red, velvet saddles with gold tassels. I wanted her to name her elephant but she refused. I ended up not naming mine, either. We didn't play much with the elephants; mine sat on my bed with some other stuffed animals. Becky didn't do anything with hers. It ended up in her room but I don't think she even flipped it.

Another Christmas morning when I was around eleven, I recall getting a globe. I was disappointed because I'd wanted a transistor radio. Most of the cool kids in my sixth-grade class walked around with a transistor radio held up to their ear and I wanted one, too. I'd not mentioned a globe to Santa, not even once.

That year, Becky got a baby doll and lots of coloring books with crayons, the fat waxy kind I used back in the first grade. Becky never seemed disappointed with anything she received from Santa. Instead, she liked to rip open her packages, flip the paper for a while, then hold whatever was in the box up for a good flipping. Even when I thought her presents were dull, Becky never complained. I felt guilty for not loving my globe, especially when Becky seemed to like all her stuff. While I hid my disappointment from my parents, or so I thought, I was truly devastated about the radio. At my first opportunity, I ran into the bathroom to cry.

I wasn't in the toilet long before I heard a soft tapping against the door.

"What?" I said, sniffling back the tears.

"Are you okay in there?" my father asked.

"Yeah. I'm fine," I said, my voice wobbly.

"Are you sure you looked real good for all your gifts? I'm not sure you found everything," my father said.

My heart beat faster. He was giving me a hint. Whether or not I got my transistor wasn't important at that moment. What was important was the fact that I'd gotten more than a stupid old globe! I hurried out of the bathroom and ran to the Christmas tree, searching through the discarded wrapping paper and throwing wads of it this way and that. Suddenly, there it was—my transistor radio in its own black leather case. I couldn't have been happier. Now, I could walk with a jive step; snap my fingers like Kookie on *77 Sunset Strip*. I'd joined the cool gang just by having a transistor radio, leather cover, made in Japan and small enough to fit in my pocket. Becky flipped her new doll while I turned the white dial on my radio to find some tunes, Elvis hopefully.

"Will your radio play music, Jet?" Becky asked.

"Soon as I find a station," I said.

"Can we dance to the music?" Becky replied while slinging her new doll around by its hair.

"Sure," I said.

Finally, I found the local rock-and-roll station. "I Want to Hold Your Hand" reverberated around the walls of our living room. I grabbed Becky's hand and swung her while we jitterbugged across the room. Just like the kids I watched on *American Bandstand*. We were dancing just like the kids on TV.

Chapter Three

I will use all the magic arts I know of to keep you from harm.
                                                    —*Glinda, the Good Witch*

My mother is seventeen in the old black-and-white photo snapped ten years before she married my father. She's standing at the foot of my grandparents' porch steps in what looks like a white chiffon dress that skirts her ankles. Next to her, Margaret, her younger sister, poses for the camera and wrinkles up her nose and lips. Mother is watching Margaret and giggling, her small arms flung open, her smile wide and wanton, as if she has nothing in the world to do but laugh.

Her black hair curves around her shoulders and is pinned into a sort of roll on top—what they called a "bop" back in the 1940s—and her lips are dark with what I know is very red lipstick. It's the only shade she's ever worn.

Mother is glamorous, just like a movie star, just like Rita Hayworth. Chestnut highlights flicker in her hair when she's in the sunlight, warming the color to prove she's human after all, not somebody's romantic vision.

In the snapshot, her shoulders are bare and white, smooth-looking and delicate. She is a small woman, 5'2" at most, with a well-proportioned figure that's mostly hidden by her dress. She and her sister are going somewhere special, maybe to a prom, perhaps to the May Day celebration they had every year at Lincolnton High School. Wherever she's going, my mother looks happy.

In the picture, my mother's face is tilted down just a little. That exact moment catches her shyness, even when she's at home surrounded by family. I can almost see her blushing as my grandfather, Ernie, takes the shot. She's still quiet, shy. She doesn't like crowds, hates to speak out in public, and is most comfortable at home, a place she doesn't leave often. Her beauty never granted her confidence, the way it does with some women. Instead, she's wrapped her shyness around her like a shawl, a soft comfortable fabric she can use to hide herself from the world.

My mother was a natural beauty and she must have known it, though she never acted the way you might think such a woman would. I don't believe having a child like Becky changed that about her, but I do believe it crystalized her strong belief that "pretty is as pretty does," a maxim she drilled into me.

She was the middle daughter, the dark-haired one, the quiet one. A definite follower, she had no desire to be the boss or run things. While she was clearly the beauty of the family, she didn't fit in the way her sisters did. Gwennie and the other two girls chattered nonstop most of the time. Often, they all three talked at once. My mother must have had a hard time getting in a word. And because she was not assertive, she never learned the art of butting in. Instead, she listened and spoke only when there was a lull in the family chitchat. After Becky's diagnosis, Mother seemed even farther outside her family circle. I felt outside the circle, too. I sensed at an early age that Mother, Becky, and I were the oddballs in that old Southern family. At first, my feelings were hurt, but later, as I grew into my teens, I felt vaguely superior to what I considered an everyday sort of person, the sort of persons my aunts and cousins were. I don't believe my mother ever felt superior to anyone. She seemed content to retire from the world and let somebody else lead the way. She was perfect for my father.

❧

In the early 60s, after we'd moved from Huntington to Philippi and my father had become a professor of music, he left our house every January for two full weeks as part of his job. He toured up and down the eastern seaboard with the Alderson-Broaddus Tour Choir while Mother stayed home with me and, when she wasn't institutionalized, Becky. The minute he hurried out the front door, a hearty "See you in two weeks" on the air, Mother would turn to me and say, "We're on vacation now!" Then she'd plop down in front of the TV and pat the couch beside her. I'd sit and together we'd find something to watch.

Once I heard those magic words, it seemed to me the house itself breathed a sigh of relief. Everything relaxed. Mother would go about for days in her gown and bathrobe. I'd come home to find her curled in a chair, reading novel after novel. We'd scurry something up for supper—peanut butter crackers, soda pop, tossed salads, sliced apples—and eat in front of the television rather than around our kitchen table. We'd watch *Concentration* or *The Andy Griffith*

Show. Sometimes, she'd let me stay up until ten or even eleven o'clock, a treat that was unthinkable with my dad home.

"Let's have a backwards dinner tonight. We'll start with a bowl of chocolate ice cream and end up with scrambled eggs," Mother would say in a girlish voice.

"I love backwards dinners! How come we don't ever have them when Daddy's here?" I said. I watched as she got out two big plastic bowls and filled them with scoops of rich-looking ice cream.

"Oh, he wouldn't like them. And don't you tell on us. It's between us girls," she'd whisper in a papery voice.

"Give me a little more," I urged. She dug deeper into the carton and plopped a big chunk into my bowl.

After she'd filled our bowls, we'd head to the couch and click the channel to *The Price is Right.* Mother would set up TV trays, white with gold leaves swirled over the top. The bluish light from the TV set would cast strange shadows on the walls and Mother would turn out all the lights. We'd guess how much the dish detergent cost and keep score. She'd argue with the results.

We'd watch *Queen for a Day,* that sappy show where women would tell the audience how rotten their lives were and the audience would clap for the one they felt most sorry for. Mother would disagree with the choice almost every time. She rarely picked women who cried and carried on about their misery. She preferred the stoic "gray" women. I thought of them as gray because usually they were plain and spoke their stories in quiet, calm tones. I think back now about Mother's admiration for those women who refused to dramatize their circumstances. How she must have thought of them as examples. When she was faced with difficult, heart-breaking decisions, she must have remembered those women on TV because she, too, became stoic. I never saw her cry or show any emotion about Becky's diagnosis.

I still had to follow my routine—doing homework, bathing, selecting my clothes for the next day—those parts of my life went on as usual, even though Daddy was gone. But the atmosphere of the house was easier. Mother and I did what she called "girl things." They weren't what you might expect. We never experimented with makeup or put on costumes. But sometimes she'd play dolls with me and pretend to cook supper on the toy stove that Becky and I shared. If Becky was home, she'd spend a lot of time reading to us until I could hear her throat go dry. But you could count on her to finish the book, even if it was a long one like *Black Beauty.* The first time she read it to me, I was sick with scarlet fever. Mother kept my room dark and sat next to me each day, reading about the brave black horse that trotted out to good pastures in the end. She didn't mind repeating a book and often reread her own favorites. Her voice was precise and soft, and I can imagine her tiptoeing out of my room, thinking I was asleep.

As I grew older, my mother began to get on my nerves. By the time I was around twelve years old, I couldn't stand the idea of becoming like her, becoming someone who gave herself away the way my mom surrendered to my father, Becky and me. I had my own ideas about everything and saw no reason why I should ever put a man or a family above myself. Where my mother was acquiescent, I was headstrong. Where she was quiet, I spoke my piece even when it got me in trouble. Where she was patient and long-suffering, I ranted and raved about any slight I imagined.

The worst years were between eleven and thirteen, the years I began puberty. She made her first mistake on my eleventh birthday. She gave me bras. Nothing but bras.

For a tomboy, the idea of turning into a woman wasn't a pleasant one. From what I could see, women didn't lead very interesting lives. They folded laundry, cooked, did ironing, vacuumed the rugs, scrubbed the toilets, dusted, mopped, and generally kept everything going at home. I watched as my mother worried over, what to me, were silly things. Did I remember to wear my sweater? Had I done my homework?

Her focus was always on me, my dad (were his shirts ironed?), and Becky. We were her life and she was very much a woman of her time. Born in 1924, she lived the June Cleaver life I watched on *Leave It to Beaver*. I didn't understand then exactly what the role of mother required. But I knew I didn't want to have anything to do with becoming a woman.

So the bras infuriated me. After opening them, three pairs of cotton triangles that formed what was then called a "training bra"—training what, I wondered—I ran to my room and threw the bras to the floor, stomping on them over and over. No girl in the fifth grade wore a bra and I'd be damned if I'd be the first. The little thin undershirts that I'd worn up until that moment would continue to work just fine. I stared at my chest. I hadn't noticed any breasts. There wasn't anything there except a little bit of fat. I could work that off easily. Nobody would notice my rising nipples. Mother was just plain ridiculous to think I was ready for a bra. I sobbed into my pillow, then hid the bras deep down in my underwear drawer. I decided to quit speaking to my mother altogether. And I did.

When she walked into a room, I'd leave. When she asked me a question, I'd refuse to answer until I forced her to scream at me. Then, I'd mumble a word with as much disgust as I could pack into it. When I saw her, I'd snarl my lip and release a sigh that spoke volumes about how much I hated her. Which is exactly what I remember yelling at her when she asked if I wanted ice cream on my cake.

I don't know how long I would have acted that way. She didn't get angry except when I refused to answer a direct question. She never scolded me about my behavior, and I think this made me despise her even more. At this time, Becky would have been around five; she would have been seeing Dr. M——, and my mother would have been following his orders about trying to teach Becky the rudiments of self-care.

The war with my mother would never have stopped if not for my father's intervention.

He picked me up from school one day, something very unusual.

"Where are we going?" I plopped in the front seat, my lunchbox and books tossed carelessly in the back.

"Oh, I thought we'd drive over to the park. Take a walk."

The park? He'd never taken me to the park that I could remember, not just me by myself. That was weird and it tipped me off that I might be in some kind of trouble. But he didn't act mad.

"How was school today?"

"Okay. I made an A on my spelling test."

"Good for you." He turned into the park and pulled our station wagon under a big tree. We both got out of the car.

"Let's walk up this trail for a ways, okay?" He still didn't seem angry. Instead, he was deadly calm. My stomach tensed up a little.

"Okay."

We walked along the path in silence, him leading. Up the hill, then back down, then across a little bridge we traveled. Finally, we came to a small bench.

"Let's sit down here for a while. I want to talk to you." He sat on one end, I on the other.

"What about?" The moment I was dreading. I must have done something really bad to warrant a trip to the park.

"About the way you're acting towards your mother."

The words hung in the air between us, heavy as bricks. I knew exactly what he was talking about.

"What do you mean?"

"I mean the ugly way you're treating her. She's told me how you leave the room when she comes in, the mean way you speak to her, when you even bother to say something. You've hurt her feelings." His voice stayed soft and calm. He didn't sound angry. He sounded sad. I couldn't get much air in my lungs.

"Your mother loves you, Anne. I want you to think for a minute of all the things she does for you." He paused for a moment, then continued. "You never go hungry because your mother cooks your food and packs your lunch every day. You wear clean clothes because your mother washes them for you. She hems your dresses and even fixes you an after-school snack. She doesn't deserve to be treated the way you've been treating her."

My face burned and I felt tears bunching up at the back of my throat. Suddenly, I considered the idea that maybe my mother didn't really want to take care of us; maybe, when she'd dreamed gauzy teen-age dreams, she hadn't thought of ironing and cooking. The way my dad explained things, I began to see that what my mother did, she did for love. And I had missed it—I'd failed to understand. I'd taken all her work and care for granted. I saw very clearly that my father admired her and was grateful for all she did and he was very disappointed to find I wasn't. My chest started to ache.

"What can I do?" The words sputtered out.

For a long time, he didn't respond. Then, finally, "I think you ought to write her a letter and apologize."

I could only nod my head in agreement.

I wrote the letter with a truly contrite heart. My mother never mentioned it, only hugged me after I'd given it to her. I ran across it a couple of years ago in her jewelry box, yellowed and creased, with M-O-M scrawled across the outside in my grade-school hand. Here is what it said:

Dear Mom,

I'm so sorry for being ugly to you. I appreciate you cooking my dinner and washing my clothes. I'm very sorry.

Love,
Anne

Though my letter wasn't very long, it must have done the trick. Mother didn't hold my bad behavior against me. She still loved me.

Chapter Four

I've a feeling we're not in Kansas anymore.
                                              —*Dorothy*

When I turned twelve, we moved because my father accepted a position as Chairman of the Music Department at Alderson-Broaddus College, located in Philippi, West Virginia, nestled in the primitive mountains in the north-central part of the state, an area of sparse population and rugged, but beautiful terrain. I was excited about the move, but hated leaving my friends. I hated having to say goodbye to our dog, Fluffy, a black-and-white cocker spaniel with long, droopy ears. We weren't allowed to take him because, rather than move directly to Philippi, my father had rented a duplex in nearby Nutter Fort, so Becky could attend a special school there. Once again, Becky had cost me something, though I didn't know it at the time. Oddly, Becky didn't object to leaving Fluffy at all. She paid him little mind, unlike most kids her age who seemed to love animals. I don't recall how Becky might have felt about the move; at six, she was too young to understand such things.

I was disappointed we didn't settle immediately in the picturesque village of Philippi but I tried to make the best of things. In Nutter Fort, I entered Roosevelt Junior High School.

It was 1964, the year I went Beatle crazy.

The seventh grade brought many changes. I was the new kid in school, scared at first, as I imagined Becky might be. But I made a best friend, Judy, two years older and a true Beatle-maniac. Our mutual devotion to the Beatles was our strongest bond, and we spent hours in her room, talking about, listening to and dreaming over the Fab Four. Paul was her favorite, John mine. We knew the words to every song, and to this day I do a mean rendition of "I Wanna Hold Your Hand." The Beatles were the perfect vehicle for adolescent fantasy—totally unattainable and therefore, safe. At that time, real boys seemed gross and scary. But the Beatles—they were across the ocean and they seemed full of nothing but fun.

I can still see Judy leaning over the ironing board in her mother's bedroom, ironing her long curly hair until it hung almost straight, with a small flip at the very end. She was trying to mimic the style of the day (think Cher and Jean Shrimpton) but with her curls, it was difficult. I, on the other hand, had stick-straight hair without the use of appliances. For so long, I'd envied Becky's golden curls, but finally I had something that was "in." Though I'd wanted hair like Becky's, she didn't like her curls; she put up a huge fuss every time Mother tried to rake a comb through her long locks. She'd scream and try to pull away; sometimes, she'd hide when it was time to get ready to go somewhere and Mother would yell for her to show herself.

Entering seventh grade brought with it a sudden interest in hair, lipstick, eyeliner and having the "right" clothes. Prior to our move, I'd been a tomboy. I liked dolls well enough (at least *I* didn't dismember them, something Becky was prone to do), but what I really enjoyed was riding my bike, following trails through the woods behind our house, and climbing trees. Back in Huntington, I'd had plenty of friends and we kept ourselves busy with imaginary games. One of our favorites was to pretend one of us was crippled. The "crippled" one would hobble around on a croquet mallet, limping here and there. The other girl would be the evil queen and make the "crippled" girl do all the work, sort of like Cinderella. And then, through the magic of a kiss from the handsome prince, there would be a reversal, and the "crippled" girl would become queen.

I invented the game and looking back, I can't imagine why anyone would want to play, but surprisingly, my whole gang loved it; everyone vied to be the "crippled" girl. Now I can see a lot of projection in the game; perhaps I was hoping that Becky would experience the same sort of reversal in real life as the "crippled" girl in my fantasy. Or maybe my sympathies for Becky manifested in this "disabling" game.

My favorite activity was reading, a love I'd caught from my mother. By the end of the sixth grade, I'd discovered Sir Arthur Conan Doyle's Sherlock Holmes books. That summer, I became a sleuth and formed a detective club with the other girls in the neighborhood.

I was convinced someone was living in the nearby woods. The idea wasn't as far-fetched as you might imagine. Our neighborhood was within walking distance of the mental hospital, and a couple of times, mental patients had wandered onto our street. One man, dressed in his institutional pajamas, was found hopping around on Mr. Green's immaculate yard. Rumor was the man thought he actually *was* a frog. I seemed to be surrounded by insanity.

Thinking of an asylum escapee was scarier than thinking about Becky's problems—after all, grownups were supposed to be okay. The whole neighborhood had been spooked by the appearance of the Frog Man. Someone hiding out in the woods seemed possible. After all, I'd found clues—a cigarette box with several cigarettes still intact. From this, I deduced a person must have been in a hurry and dropped his cigarettes while running. Running from what? I would ask myself. That one clue was enough to encourage our detective club to search the woods for more. We found footprints; a candy wrapper; a shoestring. At night, I'd lie in bed and sometimes, a spotlight would shine into my window from the woods behind the house. Terrified, I'd run into my parents' bedroom to tell them about it. Many nights, my father would rise to check the window and point out the full moon to me. I was convinced the light came from another source, but my father insisted it was the moon. On those nights, I envied Becky who slept peacefully in her own room, the same room that contained her bolted-to-the-floor rocking horse.

I had time for meetings with the detective club and bike riding, though I still was required to keep an eye on Becky. But she was in special school a couple of times a week and saw Dr. M——, too. Those activities gave me some time of my own. Though Becky wasn't in the detective club, she and I would get together in the late evenings after my adventures, and I'd tell Becky about my clues, the little treasures I'd found in the woods, and stories about strange creatures lurking about; those were her favorites.

That summer, everything seemed plausible; I liked the idea of someone hiding in my backyard; the line between what was real and what was imaginary stretched thin as a fairy's wing. I wonder if that's how Becky saw the world all the time.

That was the last summer of my true girlhood. The previous year, along with birthday bras, I had also gotten my period. No one was more surprised than I, with the possible exception of my mother. She hadn't expected me to be such an early bloomer, so she hadn't told me anything about women and their cycles. The entire event caught me unprepared.

I suspect my mother had much more on her mind than explaining the facts of life to an eleven-year-old. Becky was in school but her behavior was still uncontrollable at times. She was struggling to learn how to act in her special class, trying to grasp the basics of elementary education—rule one: Do Not Flip Everything. Mother had her hands full, but I was completely unaware of what she must have been going through. At any rate, I was furious about growing up into a woman—especially when Mother explained that during my period, which would come *every* month forever, I couldn't go swimming. I thought this was the most unfair situation in the world—boys didn't have to curtail their swim schedules; boys didn't have to worry about leaking through their clothes and being embarrassed to death; boys didn't have to tug on bra straps to keep them in place. I hated the idea that girls had all these problems and boys didn't have anything to worry about. Life seemed unfair. I went through a long spell of hating boys—the entire sixth grade. But by seventh grade, I was primed to go from hating boys to becoming boy crazy.

The Beatles came at the moment between those two extremes.

While I was in the throes of Beatlemania, Becky was trying to get up to speed with her education in a white clapboard school house with other kids who were "different." We had moved to Nutter Fort in the hopes that this special school might help Becky, even though it meant a 45-minute drive for my father each day to and from work in Philippi. Most of the students in the school suffered from Down's syndrome and shared an oriental look my sister didn't have. Many, including Becky, were shorter than normal and some were chubby. Becky was small but delicate, skinny. I guess she flipped and bounced away any extra calories. She still didn't like sweets and her appetite wasn't huge, so she never had to worry about being fat. I, of course, obsessed about my weight and my looks. What seventh-grader doesn't?

Becky didn't seem to fit with the other children. She spoke clearly, though rapidly. She didn't drool. She knew her colors and shapes. Sometimes, I thought she knew more than anybody, if only we knew how to "get the information out of her head." Each day, she brought home coloring book pictures where she wavered crazily out of the lines with a thick, black crayon, her favorite color. Every drawing was black, even little bunnies, squirrels flowers—all black scribble-scrabble. Even I had to admit her pictures looked weird and slightly demonic.

Her school building was a couple of blocks away from mine, so I didn't have much contact with her during the day. A special bus drove her home while I walked to the house with my friends.

That suited me fine. I wasn't eager for everyone to know my sister went to the "retarded" school. In the seventh grade, a person wants to fit in, be like everyone else. Inside, I knew I'd never really be a part of the popular gang. I was already different because my sister was different. The concept of "guilt by association" wasn't one with which I was familiar at that age, but I understood the underlying assumption: in my child's viewpoint, I figured there must be something strange hiding inside of me because there was something wrong with Becky. After all, we shared the same blood. I came to see us as twin spirits bonded by family and love; it became very important to me not to let her down, not to "deny" her, the way Peter had denied Jesus as I'd learned in Sunday School. It was here, in the seventh grade, when I felt a strong urge to disassociate myself from Becky, that I decided never to do so. I don't know what prompted my choice. Maybe it was the example of my parents, the way they kept trying with Becky, the way they so obviously loved her; maybe it had something to do with all the things I'd learned in church about the way we are supposed to treat each other on this planet; whatever it was, I was determined that no matter how bad things got, I'd never leave Becky and I'd never try to pretend she didn't belong to me.

I became the storyteller; I often told ghost tales to Becky and my younger cousins. But Becky was the poet—she inhabited ethereal realms that I couldn't imagine. And though I loved her and refused to show any shame over her unusual actions, inside I wished she were normal and I didn't have to worry about her.

Even though I didn't call attention to the fact that Becky was my sister at school, somehow the kids found out. Having a "crazy" sister wasn't exactly the claim to fame I'd wanted at twelve and thirteen. But, I'd made myself the promise not to be embarrassed by Becky, so I learned to ignore taunts by boys my age.

"Retard! Loony!" they'd shout across the schoolyard. I wanted to hit them, shoot them even. But they were older boys, eighth and ninth graders; all I could do was turn my head away. And I taught Becky to ignore them, too. Of course, that part was easy—Becky didn't pay them any attention anyway; she remained in her own little world, bouncing and flipping without a care.

My girlfriends never said much about Becky one way or the other—they had to treat her well when they came over, or they wouldn't have stayed my friends for long. I didn't broadcast any information about Becky to the kids at school. I kept my secret.

Once home, though, Becky and I spent a lot of time together. We shared a room for the first time, me on the top bunk, her on the lower. I'd crawl down or she'd crawl up after we'd been told to hit the sack and we'd talk together in the dark. I'd ask her what she did at school that day and she'd explain about coloring and playing games. She'd tell me about each person in her class, their name and what they liked to do. She rarely asked me a question about my own life. She didn't initiate conversation but was happy to listen to my fractured fairy tales, skewed inventions geared to elicit a laugh from her. I teased her about her hands, saying that mine were smaller and hers had grown gigantic overnight.

We both loved the old duplex where we lived, even though it was smaller than our house in Huntington had been. Shiny oak crown molding and a curved banister by the stairs made the place look elegant. The kitchen was bright white with lots of windows, and the atmosphere of the house made me think it must have been similar to the modest circumstances of John Lennon's adolescence. I'd spend hours telling Becky all about the Beatles and together we'd listen to their albums. She watched as I cut out photographs from magazines and taped them to the walls of our bedroom. She helped me catalogue my Beatle card collection and enjoyed listening to their music on my transistor radio with the lights turned off and our parents believing us asleep. Those nights, snuggled together, Becky and I both learned about being sisters. She learned to keep my secrets and I learned how to include her in the things that meant the most to me. I guess in our own way, we were becoming as close as "normal" sisters.

Though I didn't know it at the time, our year in Nutter Fort, 1964–65, would be idyllic for Becky and me. Though I was concerned about her, I was also at an age where I believed everything was possible. Maybe someday I *would* meet the Beatles. And if I wanted to, I could become a great actress—the next Katharine Hepburn, a woman I admired for her feisty spirit. Perhaps I'd be a famous writer and smoke cigarettes from a thin silver holder. Or I could start a special home for people like Becky. I'd buy a big old house and take care of Becky and a handful of others like her. I'd teach them and work with them until they were as normal as birdsong in the morning.

I was certain great romance lay in my future, some dark-haired man who would whisk me away to roam the world with him. We'd raise a family together—at least six kids—and loud, raucous fun would jangle the steady air in our home. We'd be happy and he would always think me beautiful, even in old age when my hair had turned white and my eyes sallow. My heart beat fast just thinking about the adventures waiting for me.

I was equally certain Becky would somehow be cured, and soon, too. Then we'd commiserate about our parents the way I imagined normal sisters did. We'd fuss about the rules they gave us—bedtime 9 PM, all veggies cleared from the plate before dessert, no lipstick until age thirteen—those decrees were for me. For Becky, the rules were a little different—she was to attempt to eat solid food, especially meat cut into infinitesimal bites; she should try to learn the ABCs; she would be in bed by 8 PM; and she would learn to wipe herself. Though our laws were a little different, I figured we both had objections we could make.

My rules were pretty typical, and I realize now such boundaries help a child feel cared for, cocooned in the warmth of family. But back then, I railed against such constraints, especially the one about not using lipstick. My friends had already started coloring their mouths with gooey lip-glosses with names like Cherry Kiss, April Frost, or my favorite—French Champagne. My emotions were swinging from one end of the spectrum to the other (much like now as I approach menopause), and I was convinced life was out there waiting for me, and the world was mine.

Around this time, I started reading poetry and found Wordsworth to my liking, especially the poem "I Wandered Lonely As a Cloud." John Lennon, my idol, wrote poetry, two books' worth. He was noted for being the 'intellectual' Beatle and if he could be a poet, so could I. I considered it very cool to be writing poems. I began to compose syrupy sagas, tales of tragic love mostly. I didn't know that my father was composing some lines of his own, only his weren't private. Instead, they were directed to other people, doctors mostly. His words, too, were about tragic love.

During the year Becky spent in the school for the educable retarded in Nutter Fort, my father, new to his position as college professor with the added responsibilities of being department chair, was making contacts across the eastern seaboard trying to find help for Becky. After we moved to Nutter Fort, away from Dr. M——, Becky came under the care of Dr. L——, a psychiatrist who also taught at the college. Becky would have sessions with Dr. L—— once a week. She must have liked Dr. L—— because she always talked about how she wanted to *be* Johnny L——, Dr. L——'s four-year-old son. I'd just learned about reverse psychology from my dad and so one day, after hearing Becky prattle on and on about Johnny L——, I thought I'd try my newly acquired technique on Becky.

"Why can't she be Johnny L——? She wants to be Johnny L——," Becky chanted, jumping that half-skip, half-jump of hers, flipping a plastic milk jug. I was struggling with math, the dreaded word problems. Mother was busy in the kitchen and I could smell onions and bread cooking. Outside, big snowflakes fell as they had on and off all day, covering the ground with about three inches, more to come. But inside, the house was warm and yeasty-smelling. I watched Becky as she circled around me again, flipping harder and faster against the milk jug.

"Why can't the Becky be Johnny L——, Jet? Why?" she echoed.

I saw my opportunity to test Dad's theory of reverse psychology.

"Well, go ahead, if that's what you want. Go ahead and *be* Johnny L——," I told her, certain that the little trick my dad had explained would work and we'd all be freed from her relentless questions about the L—— family. I felt very clever, pleased with the idea of manipulating someone's behavior. It gave me a sense of control.

"You walk all the way to Philippi and march right up to Dr. L——'s house and tell her you want to be Johnny." The distance between the two towns was about thirty miles. I knew Becky had no idea how long a walk it would be since she rode to her appointments and riding changes one's perspective of both distance and time, not that Becky had any sense of either. She'd sit forever on her potty, regardless of how often Mother yelled at her to get off. Time had little meaning in her life.

Becky went directly to the closet and put on her winter coat. She didn't say another word, just walked out the front door. I didn't go after her. Instead, I peeked out from the window to see how long it would take her to change her mind and come back home. It was still snowing, and the icy wind chilled to the bone.

I watched and waited until her figure became very small, a spot of quick motion on the horizon.

"Go get her right now. She isn't coming back," my mom told me as she peeked in the den drying her hands on her apron.

"Yes, she will. It's reverse psychology, Mother." I'd taken to explaining things to my mom, as if she were the most ignorant person in the world. She sighed.

"Go right this minute. You'd feel mighty bad if something happened to her." Mother's voice meant business.

"Oh, okay," I said in my huffy way, anger seeping out.

I put on my coat and ran to catch up with Becky. I thought I'd never get there and I was panting with the effort. She could really move when she wanted to. I called out to her, told her to stop, but she didn't even turn around. She must have been three blocks away, so I had to hustle. The dark clouds hung low in the sky and the sun was going down fast. The wind continued to howl around the corner, pushing itself into my lungs. My chest ached with cold.

Finally, I reached her.

"Becky, what are you doing? You can't walk all the way to Philippi!" I grabbed her arm and turned her around.

"Come on home, Beck."

She didn't give me any trouble about returning home, but the whole way back she discussed the matter with herself—"Why can't she be Johnny L——? Why can't she?" Her cheeks were ruddy and she hadn't bothered pulling up her hood, so I stopped and tied it tight under her chin. Her eyes had gone blank and I could tell she was someplace far away. I felt guilty for giving her false hope, suggesting that she could, somehow, be Johnny.

I didn't get into trouble for what I'd done. Instead, my dad had fun at my expense—he called me Doctor and we laughed at how my little experiment had backfired.

I didn't try any more reverse psychology with Becky. I was learning, along with the adults involved, that Becky was a law unto herself, a mystery, sometimes frustrating, sometimes irritating, and always just beyond my comprehension.

In March of 1965, my father wrote this letter to the Western Psychiatric Institute and Clinic Children's Residential Treatment Service:

> I have a seven-year-old daughter who is presumably mentally retarded, or perhaps emotionally retarded. For over two years, from ages four through six, she was treated and observed by Dr. M——, clinical psychologist in Huntington, WV. Last summer, we moved to Nutter Fort so that I could be near my new work, which is now at Alderson-Broaddus College in Philippi, WV. We settled at Nutter Fort in order that this daughter, Becky, might be a part of the 'trainable' class there, since there were no special classes in Philippi.

He went on to say he and Mother were interested in getting a complete evaluation of Becky which he had been told this clinic could provide. He then added:

> Becky was seven years old January 31. She is forty-four inches tall and weighs approximately forty-four pounds. Physically, she is perfect, and if I may be forgiven for saying so, a very pretty child with no apparent indication of anything wrong. She has a very good vocabulary and can express most any desire she wishes. However, she does refer to herself in third person, such as "Becky wants to have some ice cream." She is beginning to write just a little at her school. She can sing the ABC song, she can say the pledge of allegiance to the flag, she can count higher than twenty and she has very good musical aptitude. She goes to the toilet by herself, but has not yet learned to take care of herself when she is finished. She has never chewed any hard food. She is still eating junior baby food and soft foods such as ice cream, mashed potatoes and the like. We are interested particularly in discovering if there is any physical reason why she will not chew.

This stiff, rather formal letter doesn't match the way my father acted around the house. Playful, tender-hearted, a man who loved to start each day vocalizing his big tenor voice, this was my dad. At the dinner table he used to pun and wait anxiously for my girlish groan, "Oh, Daddy." He even punned with Becky and I remember one occasion when she got the joke.

When she was small, Becky used to put her palms together and then say, "Cheep, cheep." She called her hands "little chicks" and one evening, she was cheeping all over the place. We were trying to have a conversation but it was hard because of the cheeping—it sounded like a hen house. My dad looked straight at Becky and deadpanned, "Really, Becky, talk is cheap."

Becky looked at him for a brief moment, her clear blue eyes sizing him up. Then she chuckled wildly, an uncontrollable sort of laughter that lit her face in a strange way. Her mouth was stretched in a wide, zany grin and her eyes seemed suddenly to have a frenzied look. I would learn soon enough that once she got a joke, she had a hard time stopping her response, and one of the most disconcerting aspects of her behavior was the eruption of giggles out of the blue. But when she understood Dad's joke, the whole family joined in her delight—we were happy to know she could comprehend such things.

Although my dad loved to laugh, he also prided himself on being logical rather than emotional. Many a time he told me not to wear my heart on my sleeve, as I'm prone to do—"It's likely to get bruised on your arm like that," he'd tell me. He would try to reason with me whenever he gave me a talking to, usually after a report card had come home. He liked to build his argument one brick at a time until he had constructed a wall that seemed obvious and right. He rarely lost his temper, though there was no doubt who was the boss around the house. When he told you to do something, he meant business. I rarely challenged him directly, not so much because I was afraid of him but more because I didn't want to displease him.

My mother, Becky, and I must have driven him nuts, though. We frequently ganged up on him. He was governed by his reason, and Mother was anything but logical. She ran on pure emotion and she was a "screamer." She didn't do it often, but when she let loose, her voice could make the back of your neck tingle. I still recall Mother hunched inside our tent when we were camping for vacation, the light from the lantern flickering across her face.

"Don't you just want to scream? Let's all just scream as loud as we can," she'd conspire with Becky and me. Becky and I would join in "Ahhh!" at the top of our voices while Daddy just rolled his eyes.

The summer following the seventh grade, Mother, Becky, and I split the three-month holiday between Mamaw's house in Winston-Salem, and Gwennie's in Lincolnton. The reason was simple; my father was in graduate school that summer and in the fall, we'd be moving to Philippi for good. Rather than pay rent and leave Mother stranded with two kids and no car, my father asked the grandparents if we could stay with them. Since we only saw them briefly a couple of times a year, I suspect they were happy to oblige.

My father must have noticed the way Becky and I connected. Just before we packed up our station wagon for the long stay, he took me aside.

"Snookie, I want you to work with Becky this summer. Teach her to read a few words if you can and a little about numbers. Whatever you can get her to do. Maybe you could help her learn to print her letters a little better," he said, his voice serious.

"Okay," I said. I knew I could help Becky. I'd already suspected that I understood her better than my parents did. Again, I can't explain the way I seemed to "get" Becky when others couldn't—maybe my intuition helped me or my own powers of imagination. Whatever it was, I understood Becky in a way no one else could.

"She really needs to catch up with the other children her age. Remember, I'm counting on you," he said, patting my shoulder.

I didn't want to let my father down, so the first thing I did when we arrived at Mamaw's was to set up a miniature school in the living room. A card table, two chairs, a long hickory switch to use as a pointer (unless Becky's attention wandered; in that case, I intended to slam the hickory against the tabletop to bring her back to reality), paper, fat pencils like the ones I'd used in first grade, coloring books, and the flash cards my father had given me. I also established a schedule: in the morning after breakfast, we'd have school; if Becky did her lessons well, we'd walk to the nearby park for an afternoon of swinging, splashing around in the kiddie pool and spinning on the merry-go-round.

I was the teacher from hell. I don't know why Becky didn't run screaming out of the living room because I made her repeat, repeat, repeat letters and words until she knew them; I forced her to write her name over and over until it was almost legible; I cracked the hickory against the table more often than I'd ever dreamed and sometimes, I cracked it against her legs. Though I wasn't exactly the model teacher, I did keep my word and every afternoon, Becky and I walked down to the park for some fun.

My father wrote a couple of letters to me that summer:

Dear Snookie,

I miss you and Mommy and Becky very much. Wish we could all be together. You be good and don't forget to help Mamaw around the house. Listen to your mother and remember to work with Becky so she can learn what she needs to learn. I'm counting on you.

Love,

Daddy

I took my responsibility toward Becky seriously. Maybe I could be the one to save her. Maybe it all rested in my hands. I wasn't the only one in the family who took duties to Becky to heart. Both my parents did their best by her, but my father left a paper trail to document his efforts to help Becky.

The file of letters my father saved over the years regarding Becky and her progress shows a man sobered by the reality of his love and obligation to his daughter. Though the language is formal and distant, it was, perhaps the only way he could communicate about Becky and her problems. In his mind, helping Becky was serious business that called for his best logic, not runaway emotions. But I can hear the pain underneath the words and the letters leave a trail of desperation and heartbreak as my father tried to lead Becky into the world of the normal.

Looking back, I realize my parents must have been desperate to give Becky whatever she needed to fit into the world. For most children, that means an education, and for my parents, bringing Becky to the highest level of which she was capable was a major goal. The trouble was, no one could say with any certainty what that level was. Becky was still baffling to doctors. And, because of the label "emotionally disturbed," my parents must have thought that if someone could locate the reason for her problems, she might become a normal, healthy child. They continued to hope.

I, too, felt hopeful, and as I see it now, I would have approached the problem in much the same way. I know what it's like to be concerned about one's children, their education, their preparation for life. My three sons took up all my worry just in the normal course of growing up. When my eldest son, Michael, made Bs and Cs in high school, I worried and nagged at him about trying harder so he could get into a good college, maybe even be awarded financial aid. And when my youngest son, Adam, got not one but four tattoos, I took deep breaths to keep from screaming. I hated the fact that he'd ruined his beautiful skin, and he'd never regain that baby-purity I held dear. My middle boy, Jason, dropped out of college for a year to find himself. He was drinking too much and he didn't come home very often—on Christmas Day he spent one hour with us—but the worst part was he was miserable and there wasn't anything I could do about it. There were nights I cried myself to sleep, nights when sleep wouldn't come and all I could do was toss with worry. Raising my sons was the hardest job I've ever had.

I couldn't imagine raising a child like Becky, nor could I picture maintaining a fairly normal home life, as my parents had done. Because I'm never one to keep my feelings hidden, my heart would have broken, had I been Becky's mother. My unquenchable sorrow would have hung in the air like an unhealthy fog. As odd as it may seem, I didn't worry too much that I would have a child like Becky, though the thought crossed my mind once in a while, especially as I grew nearer to childbearing age. Though I thought about the possibility, I knew, somehow, God understood I could not have handled it. I believed God gave such children to very special people, the kind of people who didn't break apart easily. I still believe it, and I know deep down I simply don't have what it takes to mother a special kid like Becky. My spirit isn't buoyant enough to withstand the despair.

But despairing isn't the word I'd choose to describe the atmosphere in my childhood home. Oddly, the word normal comes to mind. As a child, I have no memories of seeing either of my parents cry over Becky. Instead, there was much laughter, teasing and playing. Now, I recognize the valiant effort my folks made to keep their hurt and disappointment private, something they dealt with together. Their sadness didn't really touch me or Becky. That kind of self-control springs only from one source—love. It was their love for Becky and me that kept laughter in our house, a forced light-heartedness that allowed us all to breathe.

Evidently, some time during that summer of 1965, an evaluation of Becky did take place. My father wrote in a letter to Mamaw:

> We finally heard from Becky's examination. In a nutshell, they could find nothing wrong physically, nothing wrong neurologically; they felt she was emotionally disturbed with a possibility of mental retardation, which couldn't be determined because of the emotional disturbance. Their only recommendation was that we consider the possibility of placing her in a residential school for treatment and education. We have not yet had time to look into these; we only know that all of them are terribly expensive. Within the next few weeks we will be investigating some places, visiting those we feel we could consider financially. We hate the thought of taking her out of our home, but are willing to if it is the best thing for her. We would hope of course that in a year or two she would be ready to come back home and get into a regular routine of school, etc. Of course, there are visiting privileges. We have made no decision but are trying to see what is best. Incidentally, just this morning she took several bites of toast (bit it off herself) and chewed it up and swallowed it. She is eating more and more things right along. She still doesn't chew well enough to want meat, but that's okay with you, isn't it, Mother?
>
> Dearest love,
>
> Jack

On August 30, my father wrote to the West Virginia University College of Human Resources and Education regarding Becky. Here, he mentioned an evaluation done in order for Becky to be admitted to the public school in Philippi for the educable retarded for the fall of the next year. He asked for a second evaluation since he and my mother agreed that Becky hadn't done her best on the first, and the superintendent of schools was "on the fence" about whether or not to admit Becky to the new class.

Becky received a second evaluation from the College of Human Resources, though no acceptance into the new class in Philippi was immediately forthcoming. Late that summer, we moved the few miles from Nutter Fort to Philippi to a bigger house on faculty row, about one mile from the college campus.

The campus was atop a mountain with a spectacular view of the little village below. The Tygart River meandered through the town separating the mountain on which the college was located from the main part of Philippi, on the other side. A covered bridge, built before the Civil War, connected the two banks. Philippi was the site of the first land battle of that war and its residents were very proud of their bridge and their history.

I fell in love with Philippi, the rolling hills very different from the crowded, dingy city of Nutter Fort. Philippi had grace and beauty; the quiet of the mountains became a special song for me. I knew the verses of each day—the birdsong at morning, the long, low whistle of the coal train as it chugged through the length of the town in the late afternoons, the quiet hoot of an owl at night. There was a wildness in the mountains, a solitude that reminded me of the woods behind our house back in Huntington, but this was better. Instead of one little section of tangled forest, there was a whole range surrounded by stark hills.

I started eighth grade that fall while Becky tried the new class for slow learners, as they were called then. She lasted one month before they kicked her out. According to a letter written by my father to a facility for disturbed children in Pittsburgh, Becky's "hyperactivity led them to ask for her removal." In a later letter to a different residential program geared toward helping emotionally disturbed children, he wrote:

> Recently we took Becky to Children's Hospital in Pittsburgh for a thorough examination. In short, the results of this evaluation seem to indicate that Becky is emotionally disturbed with possible mental retardation. It was the recommendation of the hospital staff that we consider placing Becky in a residential school with a focus toward rehabilitation. We've found such a school, Pressley House in Pittsburgh... Usually a child is there from one to three years, at which time he is 'graduated' to return to his family and public

school... We have tried enrolling Becky in a public school in a special class for the retarded but she is too active for them and they are running a new program with unprepared teachers. She has already lost two years of school. We are anxious to see her begin receiving some education, since she has been classified as educable. If this can be considered in the province of your foundation, we desperately need your help. We are enclosing a recent picture of Becky, hoping that it will help you in some little way to see her potential.

I learned only recently that my parents had tried to find local schooling for Becky. I'd always thought they sent her away because that was the only option. I didn't realize my sister had been expelled from the Philippi school; I just knew she was home all day. My folks didn't tell me Becky had been judged too rowdy for public school, or that her teacher was Mrs. Coontz, the mother of one of my friends. I would have died if I'd known Mrs. Coontz thought Becky was too unruly, and died yet again to think Mrs. Coontz might have told her daughter about my sister.

That fall, my mother worked with Becky on her writing and reading skills, but I didn't understand Becky had been tried and found wanting. After all, I was in another new school, busy with the problems of fitting in.

The Philippi Junior High School that I attended no longer exists. Now, there's a new brick building on the corner where my old school used to be, containing all the modern educational equipment. It wasn't like that in 1965.

In Huntington, I'd been a student at Gallaher Elementary, which had a reputation as the best elementary school in the area. One of the reasons my parents chose their home was so I could go to Gallaher. I got a solid base on which to build during my six years there, but was unprepared for the poor teachers I found in the tiny town of Philippi, not to mention the run-down building and the grinding poverty of many of my classmates.

Not that my family was wealthy, far from it. But we always had food in the house, electricity, and indoor plumbing. We didn't eat out until I was around fourteen, when Burger King brought 15-cent hamburgers to the nearby town of Clarksburg. I didn't have lots of store-bought clothes because my grandmother (Gwennie) made most of my things even in high school. But I didn't smell bad, as did some of my fellow students. In fact, the entire school building stank with the odor of coal, chewing tobacco (which most of the boys "rubbed," a big bulge in their cheeks, their teeth stained brown with bits of tobacco wedging into any crannies) and plain old human sweat, the kind that had been on the body for a while.

Many of the students were children of coal miners with strange-sounding names like Prutsok, Chevcko, and Charnoplosky. They seemed grimy to me, like the school itself. The schoolhouse was covered in gray dust from the mines, as were all the downtown buildings, and was at least fifty years old. Two-storied, the school sat next to the railroad tracks. Tall smokestacks spewed thick, dark smoke into the cloudy sky in winter. The school boasted no playground, no trees or greenery in the yard. Yellow buses crowded into the parking lot, dropped their load of children, then zoomed away, leaving a trail of exhaust that could choke even the healthiest child.

Inside, the halls were gloomy and crowded. Unruly children pushed and shoved their way around, very different from the quiet lines I was used to from elementary school.

Sprinkled among the children of coal miners and farmers were a few kids "from the college." To the townies, the "faculty brats" were rich, likely to be stuck-up and lumped together in the college-prep classes. I fit into this category. That made it hard to become friends with anyone because the "townies" were the more popular kids. They were all related—you had to be careful about gossiping.

Slowly, I made friends with the other kids "from the college" and began my job of "fitting in." My best friend was Sarah or "Dusty," as she was called, a girl who giggled as much as I did. By the end of the year, I'd been elected into the Kiwanettes, a group of smart, popular girls. I was firmly nestled in my little clique where Dusty, another friend, Libby, and I played guitars and sang folk songs, certain we would become the next great folk group, just like Peter, Paul, and Mary.

That year, I snagged my first boyfriend, John, a tall, dark-haired boy who was shy and very sweet. John used to hitchhike all the way from Century, a coal town about ten miles away, so we could meet at the movies in town. His father had been killed in the mines when he was just a boy. He never had much money. The last time I saw him was at a party right before we graduated from high school. He asked me to slow-dance and I can still remember how he smelled—clean with the sweet scent of English leather aftershave mixed with the tangy odor of chewing tobacco. He trembled when he put his hands on my waist. I wanted to stand there with him, barely moving, forever.

He was killed in Viet Nam the year after graduation.

∾

I have few memories of that year with Becky. She was at home, so there are no recollections of taunting by other kids, not many moments of embarrassment I recall, except at church when Becky could be heard cheeping and wooing in the sanctuary, even though she was downstairs in the nursery. Most of the nursery kids were toddlers and Becky towered over them. After church, she'd hop up the steps, singing, and talking to herself. I'd learned by then the bottom line with my sister was that she remained herself no matter where she was. On the playground, in a school room, in church, Becky flipped, skipped, ran all over, and talked to herself regardless of the circumstances. Sometimes this was funny. Sometimes it was not.

Still, I helped her with her learning, going over the ABCs and trying to teach her small words, though Mother did some of that as well. I created stories, custom-made, which Becky still loves to hear. She's still fond of ghost stories and horror stuff. And, of course, she loves a good dental yarn, one in which false teeth play a major part.

Becky's "dental fascination," as she calls it, started at an early age. She enjoys telling how she became interested in teeth to anyone who will listen.

"Was it because I saw Mamaw's false teeth in a jar when I was two years old? Is that what started it? How could she take her teeth out? Was it hard for a little child to understand? Yep, that's what got me started," Becky explained to my friend Emmy, her "coffee mate," over lunch one day. "Do I sing to my dentist whenever I go for a visit?" Then she burst into song: "I am your dentist/I get off on the pain I inflict…," she belted out in the restaurant. Heads turned to watch the performance. Emmy laughed and joined in.

"Is it from *Little Shop of Horrors*, my favorite movie?" she explained to Emmy in her unique method of communication. Talking about her dental fascination is one of her favorite topics. She even made up an original song—"Mamaw's False Teeth" to go with her other composition, the ever-popular "Jet-Shaped Face."

My eighth-grade year, the year Becky stayed at home, we had a lot of fun.

We played a game called the Bagoonda-Swoopa where I'd rear back like a horse, extend my arm as if it were the trunk of an elephant and do a sort of slide-step towards her. She'd run and scream until I caught her. Then we'd collapse in a fit of laughter, catch our breath and start again.

Sometime during the school year, my parents had an in-ground trampoline installed in our backyard. The tramp, as we called it, was for Becky. During the previous year at Nutter Fort, we discovered Becky loved to jump on trampolines. This wasn't a big surprise since she bounced everywhere she went. She hopped up and down on Mom and Dad's bed every chance she got. When Dad saw an actual trampoline arcade not far from our house in Nutter Fort, he figured Becky should give it a try. And she did.

She wanted to go to the "tramp place" every day, and my parents learned quickly they could bribe Becky into semi-good behavior by promising to take her to the trampoline arcade with its ten rectangular trampolines at ground level. For so much money, you got so much jumping time. Becky climbed onto the tramp with a couple of toys or plastic bottles and bounced surrounded by her treasures. The look on her face was ecstatic.

Once we had settled into our lives in Philippi, my parents proposed the idea of buying a community trampoline for the neighborhood. Each family could kick in their fair share and the trampoline would be installed in our backyard. As always, my father was concerned with money, the best way to conserve it. He and my mother were children of the Depression and even though he was a college professor, his salary was small, just enough for the basics and few extras.

My father made the purchase and soon our backyard was the center of action for all the kids on faculty row. Big kids, little kids, even the grownups tried out the new toy. Some of my best memories are of jumping on the tramp with Dusty and other friends.

You might have thought there'd have been fussing and fighting over whose turn it was on the tramp, but the kids got along amazingly well. I don't recall any fights. Becky would have her turn during the day when the other kids were in school. Then, in late afternoons, the bus would let us out and we'd all head for homework, then the tramp.

Becky learned to sit down, then bounce back up. She went to her knees and on her back, too. I learned the backward bounce, the face-down bounce, plus the same ones she learned. Soon, all the kids discovered that if you got more than one person on the tramp, you could really zing into the air. It must have been dangerous, but I can remember as many as four jumping at one time and the surprise take-off when all that energy would come up from the tramp and you'd bounce over twice your height. It was exhilarating.

I can also recall watching Becky out there alone, her toys bouncing gently beside her. None of the other kids would come around when she was having her turn on the weekends—it was as if she were some sort of "untouchable." However, they didn't hesitate to ring our doorbell and demand a turn after Becky had been on by herself for a while. Usually, we acquiesced because Becky tended to hog the tramp once she got on. Sometimes my dad and I would jump with her; but usually, it was just Becky, the tramp and her plastic toys. She didn't seem to mind being alone with her plastic milk jugs and her beach balls. She looked small out there in the backyard, a little person in the middle of the trampoline, a wild child misunderstood by everybody.

Finally, after two years of searching, my parents found a place they felt might help Becky. Pressley House, located in Pittsburgh, a two-hour drive from our house, had been recommended by the people at Children's Hospital who did Becky's total evaluation. My parents checked out the place both by visitation and letters. Out of the dozens my father had contacted, Pressley House seemed the best bet.

Pressley House took children from six to thirteen and gave them counseling, training and therapy with the hope of helping these emotionally disturbed kids move back into their families as quickly as possible. My parents must have been thrilled to have found a place that seemed to fit Becky's needs. In the mid-60s, facilities for emotionally disturbed children were scarce, as were homes for retarded kids. Many of the institutions my parents contacted were residential care facilities that didn't offer therapy or education. These were more like dumping grounds for difficult kids. My folks had no interest in that.

Unfortunately, Becky couldn't be accepted at Pressley House until she reached the level of competency they required. Proper potty procedure was one of their musts.

After having finally found a place that promised real hope for Becky, my parents must have been very disappointed when Pressley House rejected her first application. They immediately set out to find another facility where Becky might go in order to prepare her to attend Pressley House at a later time when she was better able. I was unaware of any of these struggles at the time. For me, life was chugging along just fine. I was making good grades, had a boyfriend as well as a couple of really close girlfriends. Life was good.

It was never my parents' intention to institutionalize Becky for any kind of indefinite stay. From the letters in her file, from my own memories of childhood conversations with them, it's evident my folks were looking for ways to help Becky be as normal as she could be. They were not looking for a way to rid the family of a difficult child. The myriad of doctors, psychologists, psychiatrists they consulted gave them the same advice—let professionals help Becky so she could take her place in the world someday. They insisted that she *could* learn, that she *was* capable of making progress. For years, our whole family believed an emotional disturbance was the block to Becky's mind and it was up to us to find a way to remove that block—through special treatment, through psychiatric help, and through prayer.

Eventually, my parents found another facility that would accept Becky—Amos Cottage in Winston-Salem, North Carolina, my father's hometown. Amos Cottage was a small brick building in the grounds of Graylyn, a large imposing mansion built in the 1920s. The thought of leaving Becky at such a grand place must have comforted my parents a little. She would not gain so many material advantages at home.

On October 1, 1966, my parents drove the long miles, an eight-hour trip, to take Becky to Amos Cottage at Graylyn. In the fall, the mountains of West Virginia are beautiful, and I imagine their trip was one filled with reds and yellows, bright orange, and rich brown. The two-lane roads would have curved pleasantly and the variegated color on the mountain views would have been breath-taking. And the poignancy that autumn brings must have stung them as they made their way to North Carolina—the sadness that comes at the peak of such loveliness.

That weekend, I stayed home with a babysitter. I knew they were taking Becky away, but I have no memory of the actual moment she left. Yet, even as I write, sadness comes over me, some vestige of memory, like the ghost of a lost limb—a missing arm that still aches. The remembrance of that day must be hidden from me in all but that sense of loss, as if I were bereft of a part of myself.

I do get a flash, just an image really, of myself lying across my bed, quietly crying, softly, ever so softly so the babysitter wouldn't hear me.

The cost of residential care was more than emotional and my father wrote to eighteen foundations explaining Becky's situation and his limited funds. In other words, he asked for help:

> … My annual salary is $7,700 and the cost for residential care is $6,205. As you can see, I could not possibly afford this cost, since I have a wife and older daughter to support…

Help didn't come from any of the foundations he contacted. Instead, his insurance paid for the first month of Becky's care; then the state of West Virginia paid for the remaining months that Becky spent at Amos Cottage, but only after many more letters requesting help, a tangle of red tape, and frequent delays.

It never occurred to me that my parents might be under financial strain. I begged for the things I wanted, like new shoes or money for the movies, as if they had all the money I needed but were too tight-fisted to give it to me. In reality, looking back, they were very generous—each school year, I got some new clothes; I received spending money once in a while. I never worried over money because I had no idea that lack of it might be a problem. I did know that sometimes my usually jovial father would be in a bad mood.

"What's wrong with Daddy?" I'd whisper to Mom in the kitchen.

"He's just blue, honey. Sometimes paying the bills makes him blue." She'd dry the dishes, then wipe the counters.

"Don't bother him right now. Why don't you go outside and take a walk? It's a pretty evening. You know he doesn't stay blue for very long," she reminded me as I hurried out the back door seeking the solace of the mountains.

My parents and I never discussed our feelings about sending Becky to Amos Cottage. I have those vague memories and I recall thinking about her being all alone in a strange place. But then, there were so many times I sobbed over Becky I can't isolate the very first time she went away. My parents didn't divulge their plans to me; they never brought up Becky's situation. They seemed to operate on a "need to know" basis as far as I was concerned. Only recently have I had the courage to ask them what it was like to leave behind a child, all those years ago.

When my own son was having some trouble, my husband and I made the hard decision to evict him. He was eighteen at the time, and I thought my bones would crack open with the pain of telling my boy he had to find someplace else to live. We gave him a deadline and he could either move out or have a full-time job by that date. Frank and I had sought counseling and were following a policy of "tough love," which, I discovered, meant it's tough on the parents, not, as you might think, the child. The day after I had delivered this ultimatum to my son, my mother and I were driving to town to shop for a birthday present for a mutual friend. I was steering around a curve, thoughts of my boy swirling through my brain when without warning, I started to cry. I pulled onto the shoulder of the road and my worries erupted from some deep place, hot as lava.

"This is the hardest thing I've ever done, Mom. I don't know if I'm doing the right thing or not. But what else can I do? We can't go on like we have been. It's not good for us and it's not good for him," I sobbed.

My mother was very quiet. I continued to cry while she dug into her purse and handed me a Kleenex. We sat for several moments in the quiet car and then she said in a soft voice, so soft I could barely hear her:

"The hardest thing I ever had to do was leave Becky at Amos Cottage."

Tension made the air in the car go stiff. The weight of that earlier hurt, the ache of my sister in my soul, slammed at me. I could barely breathe.

My mother had never spoken of that time, not once mentioned it in over thirty years. I didn't dare say a word.

"When we left her, I cried for three days. I begged your daddy to go back and get her. It was awful." Her voice caught in her throat.

I still didn't speak. I couldn't. Nothing I'd experienced could come close to the hole she must have had torn in her spirit that day so long ago. And, though my troubles seemed enormous, they didn't compare with what she'd endured. After a minute or two, she continued, "Mamaw gave me that pitcher that had belonged to Papaw's mother. It was her one treasure, the one thing she loved. But she gave it to me that weekend."

Mother grew silent again and I knew she was remembering everything. Finally, she continued, "That pitcher is real old, made before the Civil War. It was the hardest thing in the world to leave that baby. Maybe it was a mistake, I don't know. But it was all we knew to do."

Finally, I found my voice. I wanted to comfort her, thank her for sharing a little of her pain with me. It was a gift, I knew, more precious than the antique pitcher my grandmother had given her.

"It must have been just awful, Mom," I said as gently as I could. We sat for a few more minutes, then headed for the highway, the air between us lighter now.

My mother opened up to me that day. She finally shared her suffering with me so I'd know I wasn't alone with my own. I'll never forget it.

Recently, I asked my father what that weekend had been like for him, telling him what my mother had said about the experience. We were on the phone, so I couldn't see his face, but his voice became very subdued.

"I felt the same way she did. We both cried. And if I'd thought she really meant it, I would have gone back for Becky. But I knew it was just the emotional response to saying good-bye. We'd worked a long time to try to find help for Becky and we believed we'd found it. We wanted to do everything we could for Becky's good—no matter how it felt or the pain we were in. I guess reason won out over emotion," he said in a tight voice. We hadn't examined these feelings before; we hadn't brought them out of the darkness of sorrow into the light of discussion. Finally, our emotions had exposure to the healing element of air. This was sacred family history we were exploring, and the power of these shared events filled me with awe. Though I lack a firm memory of that fateful weekend in October when Becky went away, I'll never forget my first visit to her new home.

Chapter Five

Who are the Munchkins?
—*Dorothy to Glinda*

Becky left for Amos Cottage in October of my ninth-grade year when she was eight and I, fourteen. I saw her again that November. My parents and I traveled eight hours from Philippi to Winston-Salem to celebrate Thanksgiving at Mamaw and Papaw's house. We didn't usually go south for the holiday. Instead, my parents would spend the day in the kitchen preparing turkey, sweet potatoes, gravy, and all the rest, while Becky and I watched the Rose Bowl parade on our black and white television. Sometimes, Dad would build a fire and I'd keep it going while he helped Mom cook. But this year was different—this year we wanted to visit Becky.

One of the reasons my parents chose Amos Cottage for Becky was because our grandparents lived in the same town and we knew they would keep an eye out for her. My father's sister, Nearl, also lived in Winston and picked Becky up for weekend visits once such visits were allowed. Nearl was five years older than my father with three children of her own. She had red hair and that same love of life that Papaw and my father shared. She often told my mother that she'd like to take Becky and work with her. Like so many, Nearl thought she might be the one to "fix" my sister. But Nearl never did take Becky. She did, however, visit her on occasion. Sometimes, she'd bring Becky to Mamaw's for the day.

At first, the doctors were very careful about when and how often family could see Becky. They thought she would adjust better and make more progress if the family wasn't constantly around. I didn't understand why we couldn't visit her whenever we wanted and resented the doctors for limiting our time with her. Even now, I question that approach, though I can understand contact with family might prove distracting. Though I was fourteen at the time, I wasn't ready to leave home, so I could easily imagine how difficult it must have been for Becky. Becky didn't understand my parents were doing this for her own good. When you're eight years old, you don't understand things like that, even if you're normal.

We arrived at Mamaw's at dusk and found Papaw on the front porch smoking his evening cigar. I'll never forget how Papaw looked while pacing that porch—sort of like the profile of Alfred Hitchcock. Papaw had the famous "Clinard" nose, the one I feared I'd inherited. He loved to tell jokes and make sweet Scuppernong wine kept in vats in the basement.

As usual, Mamaw hugged us like she didn't want to let go and herded us into her warm old house to the kitchen where she'd prepared food. She never forgot my favorites—congealed cherry salad with slivered almonds and pineapple trifle. Mamaw had cottony hair, white and soft, that seemed to fly about in all directions. Her arms were strong and veiny-looking, her face mild; indeed, she was a loving woman who always saw the best in people.

After supper, I joined Papaw on the front porch swing. We didn't say much. I loved hearing the bells chime from the nearby Baptist church. Each evening, the bells played through several familiar hymns. I enjoyed their rich, honeyed tone and the way they marked time, ringing in the morning and the night. Hundreds of birds swarmed in the trees next to Papaw's house. I couldn't tell what kind they were in the dusk but they moved in concert as if by magic. I watched them, iron filings streaming one way, then another. I wondered if Becky paid any attention to the birds flying south for the approaching winter; I wondered if she looked at the birds and wished she could sprout wings and fly home to us.

When bedtime came, I didn't give my usual fuss but climbed the stairs to Mamaw's bedroom and crawled into the old poster bed. I slept with Mamaw in her bed and Becky slept on a small cot in Papaw's room when she was with us. My grandparents no longer slept together because Papaw snored so loudly; at least that's what Mamaw told me when I asked her about what was, to me, a strange arrangement.

I snuggled under the covers and traced the patterns of the mauve flowers on the wallpaper in Mamaw's room—round and round my eyes would follow the petals, one after another after the other—until I fell asleep to the sounds of the adults laughing and talking downstairs. This night, I tried to go to sleep faster than ever, because I knew my father would be picking Becky up in the morning and I wanted to see her, find out how she was doing at Amos Cottage. I wanted to hold her, curl myself around her like a protective shell, the way I did when we napped together. I wanted to smell the little-kid sweat in her hair, make her laugh and erase all the loneliness she must have felt since she went away. I drifted off to sleep with her face in my mind: her blues eyes that could hold mischief or nothing, her grin, her small nose and long, golden curls.

When Becky finally arrived at Mamaw's that next morning, I noticed right away they'd cut her hair. Her beautiful, soft curls had been chopped into what I'd call a "Little Dutchboy" style. The shorter hair gave Becky an impish quality she hadn't had before. Her blue eyes seemed more noticeable and they looked full of mischief. Maybe she was just so happy, her eyes took on extra light. I hated the fact she'd lost her beautiful hair; it seemed a shame for someone else to have made a decision like that for Becky, someone other than my mother. From the look on Mother's face, she wasn't too thrilled with Becky's new look, either. But she didn't say a word about it.

Becky didn't bounce around quite as much as she had before she'd gone to Amos. While she wasn't exactly subdued, she wasn't quite as hyper as I remembered. She still flipped everything in sight, especially plastic objects, but there was a subtle change in her I wasn't sure I liked. What had they done to her to make her calmer? Switches? Medicines? Threats?

I couldn't wait to get her alone. We worked our way upstairs to Mamaw's big bed where I could make sure for myself that she was all right.

"Tell me about Amos Cottage, Becky. What's it like?" I asked while she played with a red duck Mamaw had given her. Becky loved anything plastic, especially something hollow that would make a sound as she flipped it with her fingers.

"Is there Mama Clark who lets me drink coffee?" To many people, including my parents sometimes, Becky's questions were nothing more than rhythmic gibberish. But I knew that when she was nervous or happy, the questions would come in streams, one after the other, fast and furious as a mountain creek. That's the way they were churning up now. The longer we talked, the more like her old self Becky became. I was glad I hadn't lost her for good. I knew the people at Amos Cottage were trying to help her, but I worried about what kind of changes they might inspire.

Becky grew more and more excited to be with the family and energy zinged off her little body. Her quick motions were faster than usual and her flipping had a maniacal quality.

"Coffee? Yuck." I made a face.

"Does Mama Clark put sugar and cream in it? Does that make it good?" She continued to flip her ominpresent plastic toys, the red duck, and a few milk bottles.

"Do they make me eat meat? Does the Becky eat hotdogs?" Becky was bragging about her progress.

"Really? You're eating hot dogs? That's amazing! I never thought I'd see the day. How about ham? I know it's your favorite!" I teased. I knew perfectly well Becky hated ham because I hated country ham and wasn't too fond of any other kind, either. I'd even turned her against hamburgers, saying they were made of 'ham,' hence their name.

"No!!! Does the Becky hate ham? Will she never touch a bite of it?" Becky flipped my arm, a warning to quit the teasing. I settled closer to her and kissed her on the head.

"So, what else do you do?" I traced my fingers around her face until she shook herself away from me.

"Does Becky go to the Big House?"

"What's the Big House?" I wondered what she meant.

"Is there an indoor swimming pool?" She stopped flipping for a brief second and looked at me, but it was a mere glimpse. Becky never made eye contact for long.

"Wow! that's pretty cool." What kind of place had an indoor swimming pool? I pondered.

"Does she see Bang-Bang and the water babies? Do they keep the water babies downstairs in the basement?" She flipped the duck over and over while she sat on the bed and bounced.

"Who is Bang-Bang? And what are water babies?" I said.

"Is he a boy at Amos?"

"Why do you call him Bang-Bang?"

"Is that what the nurses call him? Does he bang his head all the time?" She started giggling in that looney-tune way she had.

"Oh." I tried to follow her conversation. Elaboration was a foreign concept for her. I kept at her, "What are water babies?"

"Do the babies have water on their brains?" She continued to laugh uncontrollably.

"What's so funny?"

"Why do the water babies have such big heads? Why do they have great big heads?" She sang the questions to herself, an indication I was losing her. When she was through with a conversation, her tone of voice changed. She started talking more to herself in a sing-song, low-pitched voice rather than her usual high soprano. She was retreating into her world and I didn't know how to follow her there.

I rose from the bed, took her hand, and led her back downstairs, promising her a bowl of pineapple trifle and a long, long ghost story. Our short moment of connection had ended.

That pattern—brief episodes of lucidity, then a fading away from the real world—has been part of my experience with Becky from the beginning. For an instant, Becky would converse almost as sensibly as anyone. But it wasn't something you could predict or hold onto. Those few snatches of time were what I treasured, and they brought the constant hope that somehow, Becky's true self could be excavated from whatever kept her prisoner.

After that first visit, my father wrote to the doctor in charge of the Amos Cottage program:

> We had a very enjoyable time with Becky. We were very pleased with her behavior and especially pleased with her improved eating ability. For the first time we had the pleasure of seeing her eat food that had meat in it. My mother served, among other things, beef hash and mashed potatoes, which Becky devoured with gusto. She even asked for seconds and thirds. She ate food of a coarser consistency that ever before and seemed quite capable of taking care of it. This was perhaps the most delightful part of her visit for us.
>
> We were also impressed with her calmer behavior. She seemed somewhat more reasonable than before, although there is still a distance to go in this area. We decided that it would be better if I took her back to Amos Cottage alone, which I did. I reasoned with her all the way over that if she behaved and acted right when she got back to the cottage that this would make it possible for her to visit us again Christmas. She was pretty fussy, but managed to stay reasonably calm until the actual moment of departure. I suppose she had thought when we picked her up that she would be going back home with us. They told me over the phone that she cried herself to sleep that night, but seemed normal and back in the routine the next morning. I hope this is true.
>
> …We greatly appreciated our conversation with you and the obvious interest you have in the children of Amos Cottage. We felt much more at ease over the whole situation after having talked with you. We are looking forward to continued frank conversation concerning Becky and her progress, or lack of it.

Again, my dad used his formal tone. Perhaps he was trying to sound as professional as the doctor; maybe the decade of the 60s was a time when adults took a more formal approach to important things. At any rate, the sentence about

Becky crying herself to sleep must have been hard for him to hear and then to record. He must have felt guilty and sad to think of his baby sobbing in the night. I can't bear to think of it even now—the loneliness of that little girl, the feelings of abandonment—she would never really understand why she'd been left there in that place, torn away from her family. The weight of my father's words comes to rest in my own heart and reminds me again of what's been lost.

Another month passed before Christmas brought us to Becky and North Carolina again. This time, I got to see Becky's home-away-from-home—Amos Cottage. I'll never forget the first impression the place made on me. To a fourteen-year-old girl from West Virginia, Graylyn was astonishing. I had never seen anything like it. So *this* was what my little sister called the "Big House." But we didn't go to the mansion at first. Instead, we followed the signs to Amos Cottage, a small brick building across the field.

We parked the car beneath a huge tree, and I gazed up at its bare limbs reaching into a gray sky. I noticed a single cardinal plopped on a branch; he seemed to watch us solemnly as if he were a wise sort of fellow we might ask for direction. As I stared up at him, he tilted his head, a quick nod just the way Becky worked her head when she mulled things over to herself. We walked along the brick path and paused a moment at the door, as if each of us had to prepare for what would be inside. I took a deep breath as my father opened the door, then followed my parents into what I would later remember as a hall of horrors, the kind of distorted stuff you'd see at a county fair in the "funhouse."

The smell and noise hit me like a wall as Mom, Dad and I entered the front office of Amos Cottage. The odor was highly medicinal, ammonia mixed with alcohol so potent the very air must have cleaned us as we entered the building. And the noise—strange sounds coming from everywhere at once—growls, screams, garbled words, the sound of retching—everywhere people in motion, running, buzzing around. Women dressed in white hurried down the halls as my father told them at the desk we were here to pick up Becky. We were told to wait; Becky would be brought to us.

My parents sat in the waiting area, but I couldn't stay still. Everything was too white—the walls, the nurses—it was like entering a strange, new world where nothing made sense. There were screams and cries, children making all kinds of noises, some making sounds that weren't kid-like, that didn't even sound human. I felt as if I were in the center of a very large beehive—everyone was bustling about; the noise was a steady drone—and I began to feel dizzy. I looked toward my parents to see if they, too, felt the horror of the place, but they just waited on the couch talking quietly. I wondered how they could sit there and not want to scream themselves. I felt like yelling and then I wanted to run out the door, run onto the perfectly manicured lawn and keep running. Inside my mind, the loud screeching continued, yet all the grownups were acting as if nothing was weird or out of the ordinary. I began to think there was something wrong with me, something screwy because I felt like vomiting, like falling down onto the floor. Yet, my parents still sat. They didn't seem to have any reaction to this place. Neither looked at me; they seemed frozen, zombies or something. My head started aching.

Finally, they brought Becky out. She was holding a black woman's hand, a really fat black woman who introduced herself as "Mama Clark." So this was the woman who taught my little sister to drink coffee. Her face seemed kind and Becky obviously liked her. I could tell by the tight grip Becky had on Mama Clark's hand. When Becky saw us, she ran and hugged Mother, then Dad, then me. My parents talked with Mama Clark for a few minutes; then they asked Becky to show us around.

We were going to see where Becky slept but we had to go through several rooms first. Becky led us through a room filled with cribs, except these weren't regular cribs. These beds had bars on the side to pull up, but there were bars across the top of the crib, too. Like great big white cages. Inside were children too large to be in that kind of bed—four and five-year-olds sitting or lying down, oblivious. Another smell filtered through the ammonia—the stink of diapers. Becky stopped for a minute.

"Bang-Bang," she said, pointing to a little boy in a nearby cage who was methodically hitting his head against the side of his padded crib. Again and again he hit his head, emitting a loud noise as he did so. He didn't look up; he didn't seem to know we were there. And he didn't stop hitting his head. I stared at him until I couldn't stand looking at his distorted face any longer. A strange blank screen started coming down inside my head, a black blanket that muffled the loud sounds and kept me from crying. Like a split inside myself. Rather than run around and around screaming, which is what part of me felt like doing, I followed behind my parents and acted as if this were the most normal moment I'd ever experienced.

"Will we see the water babies?" I asked, terrified they would be next.

"No," she reminded me. "Do they keep the water babies in the basement?"

Next, we passed a large playroom with children doing anything but playing. One little girl rocked back and forth while sitting on the floor staring into space. A boy stood and screamed, his voice almost gone. He must have been doing it for hours. Several nurses rushed around the room; one chased a little kid who was running naked; one held a sleeping child in a rocker; another tried to roll a ball to a boy who paid her no heed.

Finally, we came to a long room filled with twin beds.

"Is Becky's bed pretty?" Becky said, pointing to a neatly made bunk covered with a red blanket. Her clothes were folded, ready to go into the suitcase my mom brought along. Mother packed them quickly while Becky told us more about Amos Cottage.

"Can she take Gunbaby? Gunbaby and the duck?" Becky wanted to be sure Mom put all her treasures into the bag. Gunbaby was Becky's favorite doll. Made of molded plastic and looking like Daniel Boone, Gunbaby was the only toy my sister couldn't find a way to destroy. She liked taking things apart, but Gunbaby couldn't be disassembled so he became her faithful companion for several years. He wore a coonskin cap and held a long rifle, all of which were melded onto his body. His hat and the rifle were covered with brown paint and he squeaked lightly when Becky flipped him.

"Hey, Becky, can we get a tour of the Big House?" After driving by Graylyn, I was dying to peek inside.

Mama Clark, still hovering in the background, answered that we could see Graylyn next and Becky would be our guide. We made our way back through the hall of horrors and this time, my mind didn't do anything weird. Instead, my stomach growled and rolled over. My throat knotted and I could barely swallow. No one else seemed close to tears, but I was. I looked at Becky and thought about her living here, in this chaos. Every morning, she'd be greeted by the howls of the other kids. My God, I thought, if she's not crazy already, she will be when she gets out of here. But I pushed that idea out of my mind. I tried to concentrate on holding Becky's small hand in my own.

We walked the fifty or so yards from Amos Cottage to the Big House. The grounds were clipped and trimmed to perfection. The sky, winter gray, seemed huge and it was hard to believe we were in the middle of what was to me, a big city. Instead, the walk felt like a country stroll across rolling meadows, the kind you see in pictures of the English countryside. Then, Graylyn loomed before us, a graceful stone manor house complete with turrets. It was so strange to walk from Amos Cottage, that smelly, noisy bedlam, onto the calm, soothing grounds of Graylyn. I was so relieved to be outside, heading toward a beautiful place. Becky took us to the front door and a man met us. He would help Becky give us the tour.

"Can we go to the swimming pool?" she asked.

"We'll get there, Rebecca. First, let's show off some of the other rooms." The man, also dressed in a white coat, led us from the enormous entrance way into the library, a room lined with shelves filled with books—law books, medical books, books about geography and art—any kind of book you could imagine. A large fireplace with an ornate mantle was centered on one wall, while a chandelier hung from the molded plaster ceilings. The furniture was fancy and old. It looked like no one had sat on it for years. We moved on to the living room, which was about as big as our whole house. Solid walnut paneling added warmth to the room, which held three couches, a grand piano, and four overstuffed chairs. There was a musty smell that reminded me of my grandmother's attic. Still, the effect was astonishing. Seeing such opulence put the helter-skelter of Amos Cottage in the back of my mind. I was overwhelmed by the vastness of Graylyn, its quiet halls and peaceful atmosphere. I began to imagine myself as the Queen of England living here with lots of servants and lush clothes.

"Wow! Becky, this is a wonderful place." I was starting to feel a little jealous that Becky was living in this kind of splendor while I made do with our old house in Philippi. Seeing Graylyn almost made me forget the water babies and Bang-Bang, but not quite. I thought of Amos Cottage where Becky actually lived and felt guilty for my brief twinge of jealousy. How could I begrudge Becky this place when she had to be with those terrible children most of the time?

"How often do you come over here?" I asked.

"How often does she come to the Big House? How often?" She kept repeating the question, a habit that got on my nerves after a while.

"Beck, answer." I could snap her out of it with a stern-sounding voice.

"Two or three times a week." She stopped and almost flipped one of the glass vases nearby but I caught her in time.

"No flipping. You might break something. Then you'd really be in trouble."

She quit, though not without a lingering look at the vase that had, for some reason, captured her attention. The doctor was talking.

"Well, Rebecca, we can show them the pool now. I'm sorry we can't give you a more in-depth tour but many of the rooms are occupied. Lead on, Rebecca."

Becky hurried, taking the giant strides she usually took when she walked anywhere. Her gait was stiff and she reminded me of a really small Nazi soldier. Her stride was so long that she was almost goose-stepping down the hall. She didn't know how to amble, but went straight to her destination with gusto. I followed her, still reeling from the whole experience. I started to feel light-headed, as if my life had suddenly become surreal, as if I'd suddenly stepped into that painting I'd seen in our literature book, the one where a strange-looking person was screaming in horror, only I was the one holding my hands to my face; I was the one whose dull, sunken eyes had seen too much.

"Does she love swimming? Is the pool her favorite place?" Becky mumbled as she hurried down the long corridor. Finally, I could smell chlorine in the air.

The pool was amazing. Murals depicting underwater life covered the walls. Wrought-iron gates led to the garden outside through three arched doorways which were made of glass. I wondered if the water stayed warm enough in winter for swimming with all those doors.

"The pool is heated, of course," the doctor continued as he showed us the entire area. I was envious once more. I loved to swim, and it was one thing I didn't get the chance to do very often. I'd never been swimming in a heated pool in the winter. I barely let myself feel that twinge of envy, though, before I silently scolded myself—I couldn't be jealous of Becky. She was stuck here and I was at home. She was disturbed and I was normal. A strange mix of guilt and sadness settled in the pit of my stomach. I didn't know then this uneasy feeling would become a permanent part of how I would feel each time I visited Becky. I figured Becky deserved to swim every day—after all, she had to live with those weird kids at Amos. I would never deserve anything. I hadn't had to suffer the way Becky had—I hadn't been ripped from my home and forced to live in a den of insanity.

After our tour, we left Amos Cottage and drove to Mamaw's.

"Wow! Beck, that is really *some* place. I bet you like it, huh?"

"Yes." She was in a quiet mood.

"Yep, that's the most luxurious house I've ever seen. Those people must have been millionaires." I continued to tell Becky how lucky she was to be in such a place. I focused on the Big House and tried to convince us both that being there was a good thing. I had to think about the Big House because what I'd seen at Amos Cottage, Bang-Bang and the other malformed children, had disturbed me. My stomach was queasy and I had to take deep breaths to keep from gagging. Amos Cottage was horrible—the faceless nurses in white, the antiseptic smell, the noise—I hated the fact that my little sister had to stay there. The more I tried to emphasize the good parts of Becky's being at Amos Cottage, the more I knew it was too horrible, too awful for words.

But still, I insisted, she was lucky. "Becky, that pool is something else. You've got it made," I lied.

"Why can't you be lucky, too, Jet?" She asked me.

That shut me up. I didn't know why. Nothing made sense to me. Perhaps then, perhaps later, I began to question the suffering in the world. A little seed of doubt was planted and I started to wonder what kind of God could create children like the ones I'd just seen. What kind of God would hide Becky's real brain in some sort of shell, a puzzle for doctors to work? What kind of God?

The remainder of our Christmas visit was as pleasant as I could expect. I still had to go with Becky to the bathroom to make sure she didn't use too much toilet paper and she cleaned herself completely. For the most part, Becky was taking care of that herself, much to my relief. Becky was happy to be with us and no one spoke of taking her back. We pushed that thought away and tried to enjoy the holidays. I don't remember saying good-bye to Becky at the end of our time together. I remember trying not to cry in front of anyone. My parents didn't cry, at least not that I can recall. They acted as normal as ever, which made me think I was supposed to, too. I continued my prayers for Becky—those pleas were consistent, though I did ask God why? Why had He done it? All those children, the screaming, the hollow feeling of dread. And when I prayed, I cried. I knew what she was going back to, knew the ugly truth of it. I couldn't bear thinking about it, so I allowed the blanket to cover me again, smooth over the rough parts of my Christmas vacation. I thought of my friends back home, friends who would never know what my holiday had been like. I sure wasn't going to tell them. Instead, I'd put on the happy smile for which I was becoming famous and pretend my holiday had been fine, just fine.

After Becky returned to Amos Cottage, my parents and I resumed our regular life. We didn't talk about Amos Cottage. I was afraid to bring it up—after all, my parents were in enough pain. Why should I remind them of it?

Late in 1966, my father wrote the assistant director at Pressley House in Pittsburgh that my parents had placed Becky at Amos Cottage where they "anticipate she will be for several months, after which it is our hope that she will be admitted to Pressley House." They didn't want her to stay at Amos Cottage one minute longer than necessary.

I recently returned to Amos Cottage for a visit. Now, the red-bricked building that used to be Amos Cottage has become the stucco business heart of what is currently the Graylyn Conference Center, a hotel and conference facility. As I stood within the walls of what will always remain in my mind, Amos Cottage, I became almost dizzy. I could hear them still, the voices of the children, the shrill voices of the little lost souls who had suffered there. I touched the newly painted walls, partly to steady myself, partly to reconnect with those ghosts of my past. Such phantoms never really disappear—they continue to haunt us, reminding us that every choice has a consequence, a price to be paid. Sometimes, I wondered if that screaming in my own head has ever really stopped. Maybe I'd been able to blanket it for a while, but it sure grew loud again as I stood in the halls of Amos Cottage, that freak show of a place where thirty-five years earlier, I'd seen up close what hell must be.

Chapter Six

If the road goes in, it must come out.

—*The Scarecrow*

In the spring of 1967, six months after Becky had gone to Amos Cottage, I turned fifteen. Though my body had ripened into full womanhood, my heart and mind were still girlish in many ways. Not that I wasn't accomplished at certain things—I played piano very well after seven years of lessons; I read voraciously and scored high on tests, though my math scores were always lower than the verbal; I could make a pizza out of those Chef Boy-R-Dee boxes and I was an old hand at camping in the woods.

Camping was the one thing I looked forward to each year. My family didn't take long trips, just weekend jaunts to nearby parks, but I knew how to handle myself in the woods. After all, I'd been schooled in the ways of the woodsman almost as long as I'd been taking piano. Except that I liked camping a whole lot better.

When my family ventured into the woods together, we didn't have to worry what anyone else thought of us. We rarely ran into anybody we knew, so we were free to be ourselves. That meant I could try to make Becky laugh without being concerned whether she was loud and unseemly. It meant she could flip her toys and talk to herself and I didn't care who noticed—after all, I'd never see these people again. Camping meant Mom could scream and Becky and I could join her and no one cared; that is, no one cared as long as we placed our tent far away from other campers. Becky could make her wooing sound as she held her hands up to her face and if anyone heard it, they probably thought it was an owl. Deep in the woods, surrounded by towering trees and scampering critters, our family was safe from curious stares. And though I made friends easily, camping friendships were like those special flowers that bloom only at midnight—they were beautiful for their brief moment, but were conveniently gone the next morning.

I was around eight years old the first time my parents took Becky and me camping. We didn't have any equipment for the adventure, so we went with my dad's best friend, Jay, who had a trailer and other things needed to spend a few days "roughing it," as my mother called camping. Our destination was Myrtle Beach, South Carolina, and we spent the twelve-hour drive following the trailer in front of us, its red tail lights wobbling from side to side.

The first thing that happened upon our arrival was that a big, black bug bit Becky. She screamed and when I looked at her foot, I saw a dark hulk at least a couple of inches long. My dad swatted the bug and it wobbled across the sand into the grass. Mom examined Becky's foot and thought it best to keep an eye on the bite.

Jay's family continued to unpack, and moved like a precision army unit. I watched as the two boys, David and Barry, scuttled back and forth between their car and the trailer. In all the hustle, someone brought Becky and me a glass of milk. She gulped hers down and by the time everyone had settled into cooking supper, Becky was throwing up all over the place.

"Mom! She's upchucking!" I yelled as I tried to head her away from the picnic benches. But it was too late. Everything splattered on the table and I noticed her foot was beginning to swell and the redness had spread. Mom and Dad hurried to where we stood.

"We better get her to the hospital. You clean up here, Anne. We'll be back soon." They wrapped Becky in their arms and piled into the front seat of the car. I knew they'd have to find a hospital and they might be gone a long time. I slowly headed for the trailer to grab some paper towels. Jay's wife, Gin, and I cleaned up the mess; I thought this was a really gross way to start a vacation. I wasn't worried about Becky at all—I was more concerned about getting puke on my hands.

It turned out that Becky'd had an allergic reaction to the bite, but it was nothing serious. By the time she left the doctor's office, her stomach was calm and her foot had shrunk back to normal. She was rewarded for good behavior at the doctor's office with a chocolate milkshake for supper. No further accidents marred that initial foray into the camping world but, as with most of my memories from childhood, this one was marked not by what happened to *me*, but by what was happening to Becky. Becky couldn't help getting into predicaments, it seemed. And getting her out of them usually involved the whole family.

After that first trip, my dad decided that camping was the way to travel—he, too, had been bitten by a bug, the camping bug—symptoms included a desire for wide open spaces and the compelling urge to take his family on vacations at a price he could afford. In those days, the fee for tenting in a state or national park was only a couple of dollars per night. At a private camp ground, the cost might reach five bucks. The price of equipment was a one-time-deal. Who knew how long a tent would last if you took good care of it? No reason a lantern shouldn't last a lifetime, properly maintained. As he told me later, camping was the only way we could travel anywhere except to my grandparents' on his modest salary.

Beyond the economic reasons for spending nights beneath the stars, my dad also loved being out of doors. The smell of the open campfire, the crisp morning air, the birdsong and sheltering trees appealed to his musical nature. He loved to sit around the fire at night, roast marshmallows, sip wine, and tell stories. He learned to build a great fire so that the embers were still warm the next morning and the fire could easily be rebuilt. Eventually, I learned too.

My mother wasn't as enamored with the vagabond life as my father. She would have preferred sleeping in a motel and eating out. Now I understand. She had to cook most of the meals and wash dishes in cold water that had to be carried from a pump. Usually the water pumps were located far away from our tent. Camping actually made her life harder, but she was a good sport most of the time. She would often complain, though, if we didn't find a campsite close to the restroom.

"I wonder what it would be like to stay in a hotel, just once," she'd muse while frying hamburgers over the cook stove.

"You'd never notice a sunset like this one," my dad would yell while he stoked the fire. Against the backdrop of the woods, my parents and their differences stood in sharp relief. Where my mother saw rain clouds threatening our afternoon, my father saw the sunshine peeking through. Where Mom saw hard work, useless regression from the comforts of home, Dad saw the opportunity for adventure. My mother was the type of woman who screamed when she dropped a fork and jumped at any startling noise. My father once described himself as a "plodding workhorse." Once, he told me he considered my mother a "high-strung filly" and he thought I was just like her. In many ways, he was right—I, too, jump when something startles me, a characteristic that gave my sons a lot of joy in their growing-up years. Nothing was more fun that sneaking up behind good old Mom, grab her by the shoulders, then hear the rewarding scream.

One of our earliest camping photographs captures Mom, Becky and me in a less-than-perfect moment. After our trip to Myrtle Beach, Dad bought one of those huge family station wagons where the seat folds down to make a bed in the back. We were going to stuff our sleeping bags and camp stove in the car and take off for a nearby state park. The plan, as he so carefully explained it, was simple. I was to sleep across the front seat; Becky, who was about two years old and small, was to sleep at the foot of the long bed where Mom and Dad were sleeping. A beautiful plan, but like so many my poor father made, it didn't work. It's an example of his optimistic nature that he really believed a two-year-old would sleep in the designated spot with her mommy nearby. Even an eight-year-old would be tempted to crawl back to the warmth and comfort of sleeping parents.

The photograph shows Becky, Mom and me all warm and cuddly in the bed, barely awake, our eyes still puffy. There was obviously no more room in the car for Dad. The three of us had forced him out into the early morning air, and he got his revenge by snapping that shot of us, our hair wild and unkempt, grumpy looks on our faces.

Though our early attempts at life in the woods might have left something to be desired, by 1967 my family could claim a certain level of expertise when it came to camping. We each knew the Rules of the Camp and what our duties were. I had to fill the water jugs upon arrival. Then, I was expected to help Dad put up the tent. Mother took care of the cooking. I also had Becky Duty, which could be tricky because her first inclination was to wander over the new campground and explore. Of course, I wanted to investigate, too, and many times the two of us would sneak away and leave my parents with most of the work. I always had the excuse of "keeping Becky out of trouble" since we never really knew what she might do. After all, she might decide she wanted to "be" someone else and join another family, the way she'd tried to become Johnny L——. Or she might find an object fascinating and, if it was something that moved, like a butterfly or a squirrel, follow it until she got lost. I worried she would be unable to find her way back to us if something caught her attention. I also didn't want her to wander into another campsite where other people were camped. One of the Rules of Camp was that each campsite, though visible to all, was private. There should be no trespassing unless a person was invited. Never one to wait for formalities, Becky often moseyed right up to other tents if she wasn't stopped. It was my job to stop her. Though I had a few chores to do, my biggest job upon arrival at a new campsite was to keep an eye on Becky.

I loved being in the natural world and loved the friendliness of the other campers I met along the way. Since I didn't have a normal sibling, I'd become adept at making friends, and it didn't take me long to find a camping buddy, or several. I was lonely so I became very good at going up to strangers my age and striking up a conversation. If I'd had a normal sister, I might have been much more willing to stay at my own camp. Instead, I was always looking for someone else, a sort of surrogate sister. Now I realize developing an outgoing personality might have been a good thing—I've never lacked friends.

I'd hang out with these new girls, bring them to meet my folks, check out their places, then we'd have adventures. I always wanted my pals to meet my parents because my parents were cool and funny and sometimes they would hike or swim with us. I wasn't worried about what they might think of Becky; usually, she'd be in the tent with Mom or bouncing around with her toys. Sometimes, her behavior could look very normal, if you didn't try to talk to her. Besides, she was a little kid to us and easy to ignore.

During the day, we'd swim in the camp pool (most parks had one) or we'd hike one of the trails. At night, cards and ghost stories were the favored activities, always conducted around the fire. Sometimes I'd take Becky with me, especially if we were swimming. But much of the time, my parents let me wander off and play, free from any babysitting responsibilities except those first-day duties. I realize now they were very generous. They allowed me to be a child and they didn't burden me with their concerns. I felt free as I wandered the pathways through the tall pine trees, listening to the creek as it worried itself over the cobbled rocks. I could look for bluebirds or yellow finches; I could discover nests and often, because we camped primarily during the warm months, I found baby birds. At such times, I felt the trees and grasses were my heart's true home. Those weekend jaunts into the mountains of West Virginia, Ohio, and Pennsylvania taught me the lessons of the earth—the beauty of mountain views, the smell of hay fresh-cut, the delicacy of the little animals that scurry over the forest floor—and to this day, I'm my deepest self in the mountains, surrounded by the hills and clouds, the wild grasses and towering hemlocks. Spending so much time outdoors developed an unsuppressed appetite for nature in me, one that I must feed often or I become gloomy and filled with despair.

❧

At the end of my ninth-grade year, Dad called me into the living room for a conference. Mom was sitting on the couch next to him. I knew something serious was up and I dreaded hearing about it. The last time both my parents talked with me, they told me Becky would be going away. I was scared to death when I walked into the living room and Daddy started with a very solemn, logical tone to his voice, the same tone he used when he explained that Becky was going to Amos Cottage.

"How old are you, Snookie?"

I looked at him like he was crazy. Didn't he know how old I was?

"Daddy, you know I just turned fifteen."

"Fifteen. You're getting up there. Your mother and I were thinking, you'll be leaving home before you know it, going off to college. And we wanted to do something special before you go. We want to take a trip." He let a little smile slip.

He then told me that he and Mom had planned a huge summer vacation. We'd be going to the Outer Banks in North Carolina for two whole weeks, then up the coast to Washington, DC for a couple of days, then to New York City to visit my aunt and her family, and, finally, to Montreal, Canada for a week at the World's Fair. On the way home, we'd travel through the Land of a Thousand Islands and Niagara Falls.

I couldn't believe it! We'd never gone on vacation for more than a long weekend. We spent two weeks with both sets of grandparents in North Carolina each year, but we'd never had a vacation like the one he was telling me about now. The three of us were laughing, anticipating our summer as my dad continued, "We're even going to buy a trailer."

"NO MORE TENTING!!" my mom shouted.

"Can Becky come with us?" I asked.

"We wouldn't take a big trip like this without Becky. I've already cleared it with Amos Cottage. We pick her up in June."

The way they explained it to me—with me getting older, going off to college in a few short years—they made me feel like the whole thing was just for me. They had that way about them—making me feel as if their whole world was centered in me. In many ways, I guess it was. I would be the daughter Most Likely to Succeed—to marry, raise a family, make some sort of contribution to the world. Becky wouldn't be able to do those things. Her future wasn't as predictable as mine. Even though they were still hopeful for her, by this time, they must have suspected that Becky would never be able to live in the normal world.

Being the Most Likely was a mixed blessing. I felt very secure in their love, almost the way an only child might feel. Yet, there was guilt involved, too—I was okay, Becky wasn't. I hadn't done anything to be normal and Becky hadn't done anything to be the way she was. Why should I be the one without problems? Why would God give one child a normal mind, then turn right around and give another kid a brain that caught fancies on the wind, saw more than was possible in regular human experience? Maybe my own mind wasn't so normal, after all. Maybe Becky and I were closer than I knew. Our lives careened off each other, spinning us each in different directions, yet often I felt myself whirl out of control. If Becky was "emotionally disturbed," then what was I? High-strung? Too emotional? That was the message I often got as a teenaged girl. Of course, that message came mostly from my father, who, looking back, probably feared my adolescent outbursts. After all, I was smart and rebellious in a few ways—not so much in actions but in thoughts. I questioned things—the war in Viet Nam, the prejudices I found at school, the racial inequalities I observed, the place of women in the world, the existence and nature of God—anything that seemed unjust to me, I ranted about, cried about. And I could just as easily become euphoric, singing the praises of the bluets I discovered on my walks in the woods, the tiny, precise flowers that were my favorites.

Yet, through all my hormonally induced ups and downs, I never questioned that I was the adored daughter, the eldest child. I never questioned that I should be anything other than the hope of the family. It was as if I had to make up for things somehow. I had to make it up to my dad for not being a son, something he'd always wanted. My mother told me this often, though Dad never mentioned it. And of course, I had to make it up to both of them for Becky. Somehow, in my child's mind, I wanted to do that. I wanted them to be very proud of me. I'd never settle for a conventional life—I had to be *special*. I had to be the *best* because I wasn't just doing something for myself—I was doing it for Becky, too. And to lift the despair and disappointment I knew my parents felt—even though they thought they were hiding it from me, even though they gave every indication of being okay—I wanted to save them from pain, protect them somehow. Looking back, I see how sad that must have been—the strange idea that one person could ever 'make up' for someone else. I could never make the pain my parents experienced go away. I couldn't ease their lives, though I thought I somehow should. I see that now as I think of my own children. Each child is precious in his own right. One simply can't replace another. But I didn't know that then.

When I told my friends at school the next day about my summer plans, they were jealous. Dusty didn't ever travel. Her parents were older than mine and less likely to take trips. She, along with my other good friends, Mitzi and Chris, didn't have adventurous folks, as I'd begun to view my own parents. My parents *were* different. They were fun, and my dad especially had a spirit of joy that was contagious. My mom went along with him in his enthusiasms, though she had her own strengths, primarily, an appreciation for the beauty of the world. Many mornings, they would point out lovely birds that came to the feeder. Mom would name them—blue jay, robin, grosbeak—and if a bird flew in she didn't know, the whole family would try to solve the mystery of the bird's identity. At night, we'd walk into our yard and Dad would outline the big dipper in a starry, crisp winter sky. Mom never failed to mention sunsets—early on, they both instilled in me and in Becky a love of this world and a gratitude for all its fruits and pleasures.

"You are *so* lucky," Chris told me that morning I announced my trip. Chris, the head cheerleader, was the most popular girl in the ninth grade. Her blond hair she wore in a flip. She kicked her slender legs high and her big smile never failed to rouse the crowd. I would have given anything to look like her.

"We never go anywhere," echoed Mitzi, another cheerleader with bright red hair. Mitzi was cute and bubbly. While Mitzi wasn't beautiful, she was way cuter than I and her personality was wonderful. I considered myself the least attractive girl in our group of friends—I was shorter than most and had large breasts which were totally out of style during the 60s. Twiggy was the epitome of beauty and she was stick-thin. I'd never be that straight even if I weighed eighty pounds. I'd never look like Chris or Mitzi.

Dusty was the only girl to whom I could talk about Becky, though I didn't discuss her very often. Becky was away from home most of the time; during the day, I found it easy to forget about her. But at night, thoughts of Becky pushed their way into my brain regularly. I'd wonder about what she was doing right at that moment. Was she sleeping? Did she have trouble going to sleep without me to tell her stories? Was Mama Clark still nice to her? I remembered Bang-Bang and all the other sick children, the screaming, the smell—the memories surged back to me when my room was dark and the house quiet. Many times, tears came suddenly. They come now, even as I write this forty years later.

Back then, though part of me worried about Becky, the other part was trying to learn the secrets of popularity, how I could grow into one of the "in" girls rather than the offbeat girl I was, the one with dramatic tendencies and a silly giggle; the one who followed the flight patterns of birds, collecting feathers; the one who cried over newspaper articles; the one who still awoke from nightmares, then crawled into her mother's bed for comfort.

I never mentioned Becky to anyone but Dusty—out of sight, out of mind. I was already an outsider because I'd only lived in the small town for one year and I didn't have any relatives nearby. I was from the college, and that made me immediately suspect. I tried to act somewhat dumb so the college label wouldn't weigh so heavily, but all that did was make me seem ditzy. Boys were always telling me I should have been a blonde.

Though my friends and I never discussed Becky, everyone knew she was my sister. When Chris or Dusty spent the night, sometimes Becky would be there on one of her home visits, bouncing on the tramp surrounded by milk bottles, putting her palms together to "cheep" or making other odd noises. My friends might say hello, but usually we'd go about our business and ignore Becky and her strange behavior. I tried so hard to ingratiate myself to these new friends that I never considered explaining or exploring what having a sister like Becky meant to *me*. It seemed ungracious to complain about anything. After all, I was "normal" so everything must be okay with me. I'd listen to my new friends' problems and try to give advice. We'd talk for hours on the phone about boys and clothes. Never once did I disclose anything about my sister, except to answer the rare question "What's wrong with your sister?" Then I'd explain what I'd been told.

"She's emotionally disturbed. We don't really know why." My girlish conversations never went beyond this point. If an acquaintance was rude enough to pursue that line of conversation, I deftly steered the talk away from myself and back to the other person—exactly as I'd read in *Teen Magazine*'s advice on how to make boys like you. Only I discovered it worked with girls, too.

When Becky came home from Amos Cottage for spring break that year, being Becky's sister became particularly uncomfortable. A new friend, Pam, was spending the night with me. She dated a lot of boys in high school. I was excited that she'd agreed to sleep over and Mom had bought a double box of Chef Boy-R-Dee pizza mix for us to make. She also had plenty of soda on hand, even a brownie mix for dessert. I knew Pam was a gossip and if anything bizarre was going on, she'd notice it. I tried to keep her in my bedroom away from the rest of the family. It wasn't hard because I had a record player in there and we were talking about every single girl in our class, how we liked their hair, what kind of makeup they wore, if we thought they French-kissed their boyfriends. Suddenly, I heard Becky cackling in the hallway outside my bedroom door. Her laugh was maniacal, as usual—a mix between Vincent Price and Dracula. And she didn't stop.

"What's that?" Pam sat up from her reclined position next to me. We'd been going through the yearbook.

"What?" I hoped Becky would settle down and get quiet, but just when I said "what" Becky cut loose again.

"That!" Pam looked at me with a funny expression.

"Oh, that. That's just my sister. She's taking a bath." Usually, if I acted like everything was normal, my friends would do the same. It was a game called "Ignore the Weird Behavior, We'll Pretend It's Not Happening." I'd become very good at the game, but for some reason Pam refused to play.

"Why is she laughing like that? She sounds crazy!"

"Well, she just gets tickled, you know. You and I get the giggles sometimes; remember in Algebra class that time Martin Saunders farted and the teacher made him go out in the hall? We laughed our asses off!! Hey, did you know Martin made the Hi-IQ Club?" I was desperate to divert Pam's attention. I hated doing it, but I had to make up something weird about Martin. "He's also in love with Miss Krutz, the new English teacher."

The lie was enough to steer Pam away from prying about Becky. But she never spent the night again and I often wondered if she talked about my crazy sister to the other girls at school.

While I waited anxiously for the school year to end and our big trip to start, I kept busy having crushes on several boys. Since John and I had broken up at the end of the eighth grade, I hadn't attracted any other boyfriends. Not that I hadn't tried. I dreamed about several older and glamorous high school boys. But dreaming didn't exactly get their attention. The one that I most adored was Richard, a football player two years older than me. I'd think about him right before sleep, partly for pleasure, partly to keep my mind off Becky and Bang-Bang and Amos Cottage. Usually, the diversion worked.

Of course, Richard didn't know I was alive.

On Saturday nights, the girls who didn't have dates would congregate at the local Dairy King on Main Street. We'd order a large pepperoni pizza. Usually, unattached males would buzz around us, though I'm not sure whether they were attracted by us or the pizza. I spent most Saturdays at the DK, hoping to see Richard there.

Early one Saturday night, Mitzi, Dusty, and I were having a Coke to kill time before the movie started. My dad had dropped us off and would pick us up at 9:30, after the show. I was slurping ice through the straw when I saw Richard walking up the street toward us with my friend Zana.

"Oh my God, Mitz. He's coming this way," I said in a breathy voice.

"Who?" Mitzi was very interested in her hot dog. She ate all the time but never gained any weight.

"R-I-C-H-A-R-D. How do I look? Oh, I'm going to die." I felt my cheeks burn and immediately studied the bottom of my glass as if it could tell the future. By the time I got the nerve to glance up again, Zana and Richard were standing at the plate glass window in front of our table.

"Are they coming in?" I whispered to Mitzi.

"Will you relax? You're as red as my hair. Here comes Zana."

I felt the breeze as she opened the door and sat at our table.

"Richard wants to take a walk with you. I told him you had a crush on him," Zana said in a loud whisper.

"No, you didn't!" I was appalled.

"Sure I did. He wants you to walk around the block." Zana gave me a wink. "Walk around the block" was code for making out in back of the Dairy King. I'd never kissed a boy and I had no idea how it was done, though Dusty and I had practiced in her bedroom. We'd purse our lips and kiss our own forearms, trying to gauge the appropriate pressure and sexiness of our mouths. I was certain Richard would give me a peck on the cheek, but I might return his kiss full on the lips.

I gulped the rest of my Coke and met Richard out on the sidewalk. I couldn't think of anything to say.

He mumbled a greeting and steered me down the street to the long alley that cut through to the next block. It was private with tall cedar trees on each side. I could see immediately why boys liked to walk here. I tried to engage Richard in conversation.

"I saw the wrestling match last night. You did really well." Always follow the rules in *Teen Magazine*, I told myself. Those writers are experts, and they swear boys like to talk about themselves.

"I shoulda pinned the guy. I'll get him next time." He took my hand and I immediately wondered if my fingers were sweaty. His hand was large and felt square in my own. His skin was dry, no hint of nervousness. We continued to walk slowly and he talked pretty much, once I got him started. I listened and laughed when he made jokes. Suddenly, he stopped walking and pulled me to him in one swift move.

Before I could think, his mouth was all over mine. It opened like a fish. He kissed me three more times, his body holding me so tight I could scarcely breathe. My lips felt bruised after it was over.

We didn't speak much on the walk back to the Dairy King. I didn't know what to say and Richard didn't seem very happy. I couldn't wait to tell Dusty and Mitzi all about The Big Kiss. I wanted to ask them what they knew about this opening the mouth business. I was determined to get better for the next time.

While my first kiss was an important moment, a sort of hoop through which a teenaged girl was supposed to jump, something about me changed when it happened, something inside, something to do with Becky.

That kiss gave me the hope of being popular. I was already friends with a bunch of girls, most of whom were in the "in" crowd. But boys were another story. After all, boys had to like you, too, if you were going to be accepted. I decided I'd do everything I could to get boys to like me. I don't mean everything in a sexual sense—I was much too naïve for that—I mean I'd learn to flirt, talk to boys on their level. Though I wanted to do those things, I didn't really trust boys very much. After all, I'd seen how cruel they could be to Becky or to anyone they thought they could bully. I knew I could never talk to them about my sister.

I began to hide Becky away. I could bring her out with Dusty, but I'd have to keep her hidden from boys, from the girls I didn't know, from my life at school. I wasn't conscious of making this decision, but it describes the way I handled things. I'm not particularly proud of the way I managed. After all, I'd sworn to myself I'd never "deny" Becky. But somehow, this was different. It wasn't denial, exactly. I still spent a lot of time with her when she was home or when we visited Amos Cottage. But I'd learned to keep secrets, and so Becky became hidden, a nugget of a sister who fit quite nicely in a pocket.

Did she know? Did she feel hurt or rejected? Did she realize that sometimes she embarrassed me? Did she care? I don't know. All I know is that she still loved me and I loved her back as best I could.

Spring passed quickly and school ended. My dad brought home the new 14-foot trailer with a table that folded into a single bunk and a double bed that converted into small couches if needed. The trailer even had a very small toilet and shower. Of course, you'd have to turn sideways to fit in there, but such things were a luxury in the camping world. I loved all the neat tricks of the trailer—the way the drawers shut so they wouldn't jar open while driving, the way everything fit together like a puzzle, the matching curtains and soft cushions—the trailer was brand new and I liked the idea of carrying our home with us, turtle-like across the country. It seemed like my parents packed for weeks in preparation for the trip. In my mind's eye, I can still see my mother ironing clothes, then folding them precisely and placing them in the suitcase. Dad cleaned all the other equipment—the lantern and cook stove—all the utensils, while I straightened my room and talked to my friends on the phone. We planned to pick Becky up and visit my grandparents for a couple of days. Then we'd be off on the biggest adventure of our lives.

Chapter Seven

The road to the City of Emeralds is paved with yellow brick.
                                    —*Glinda, the Good Witch*

We picked Becky up from Amos Cottage at the end of June and headed toward the Outer Banks of North Carolina, the first leg of our trip. I felt like we were rescuing Becky when we packed up her stuff and took her with us. My shoulders lifted in relief as we hurried away from Amos Cottage—I had to run to keep up with Becky, who was making quick time to our car. The way her eyes sparked blue when she stole a glance at me let me know she was happy. For once, I saw her honest smile, not the gargoyle grimace she gave when Mom took family pictures, all of us saying "cheese." Becky seemed to be racing for her life, and when she reached the car, she hustled inside. Each movement was quicksilver and Becky's excitement showed in the way she flipped Gunbaby, hitting him much harder and faster than usual. I knew how she felt—free and safe. I liked rescuing her, seeing her happy. It was a feeling I would always have—as if I were stealing her away, breaking her out of jail and bringing her into the freedom and happiness of our family.

Becky loved family, and not just the immediate relatives. She was interested in aunts, uncles, cousins, grandparents, and even great-grandparents. She often asked questions about them while we rode together in the back seat of the car.

"Is Becky short like TeaCall? Does she get her height from her great-grandmother?" Becky always made connections between herself and distant relations. Becky referred to this long-dead ancestor with strange familiarity, using the nickname my aunt had coined as a child for "Grandmother McCall." You'd have thought that Becky knew Teacall intimately. Maybe she did in a strange way. Maybe the thought of another abnormally short relative gave Becky a sense of connection.

It wasn't just distant and dead relatives with whom Becky desired connection. She bragged that she'd inherited Dad's "musical ears" and demonstrated this ability by picking out tunes on the piano. She was especially proud because she could sometimes put chords with the melody and she knew the difference between major and minor keys just by listening.

"Does she grind her teeth because she got Mom's crowded teeth? Is it Mom's fault?" she'd inquire. Like most of us, Becky wanted justice. Placing blame or discovering reasons for things was important to her. As usual, her questions had a point.

"No, it's not Mom's fault. We both inherited her crooked teeth," I'd explain. The implication behind my words was that I got Mom's teeth, too, but I didn't grind mine. But Becky didn't get the underlying message. Or at least she didn't respond to it.

Finding the links between her own features and those of the rest of the family was very important to Becky. It was as if she were looking for an explanation of herself, some gene that might explain why she was the way she was, why she didn't fit in with the world. She must have hoped for some trait that would prove she was as much a part of our family as anyone.

Though Becky loved her family, I'm not sure her feelings were returned with the same enthusiasm. Both sets of grandparents adored Becky, worrying and praying for her every night. Of this, I have no doubt. But the other relatives were more difficult to understand.

I don't know if Mother's sisters ever talked about Becky or not. When we visited Gwennie and Ernie, I never overheard Aunt Margaret comment on Becky's situation and she ignored most of Becky's behavior. We saw Aunt Dot less frequently; so again, I'm not sure if any conversations about Becky took place. What I do know is that neither sister ever volunteered to give my mother a break from the grueling work of dealing with Becky each day. To my knowledge, neither offered to take Becky for a weekend so that my mother could have a day's respite from Becky's constant barrage of questions. My mother sometimes reminded me of a pecked bird when she was around her family. Birds do that—choose one of their own and peck it, sometimes to death. Gwennie didn't approve of my parents' sending Becky away from home and she didn't mind sharing her disapproval. She also criticized my mother for gaining weight and badgered her to get trim. I wonder if Mother took Becky's disorder personally, seeing Becky's disability as a reflection on her somehow, allowing Becky's problems to alienate her further from her family.

On my father's side, things weren't much better. Though Nearl mentioned working with Becky to help her learn, she never actually did so. My mother remembers one visit in particular. We stayed with Nearl one weekend to visit Becky while she was still at Amos Cottage. Nearl's two sons, Freddy and Jimmy, were teenagers at the time and loved to tease anyone within range. Jimmy was making Becky do funny, ridiculous things, then laughing at her. No matter what he told her to do, she did it. Soon, both boys were making fun of her. Becky was baah-ing like a sheep, mooing, cheeping, trying to rub her head and tummy at the same time, making faces, and generally being a willing victim of her cousins. Of course, she didn't know any better.

Mother kept thinking my father would speak up and make the boys stop. She gave him a hard stare but he remained silent. She thought Nearl would surely end the cruelty but she, too, allowed it to continue. Finally, my mother had had enough. This soft-spoken, shy woman who would never intrude on anyone reached her limit when Becky was giggling that crazy giggle of hers and the boys were doubled over with laughter. Her voice frayed with anger, my mother screamed, "Becky! Stop it! Can't you see they're making a fool of you!"

The room grew silent except for Becky who kept laughing that loud, nutty laugh. My mother was close to tears, but the boys got the message and quit poking fun at Becky. In Nearl's family, everything was a joke. Real sympathy was in short supply. I can't imagine what they must have said about Becky and our family once we'd returned to West Virginia. Somehow, having Becky ostracized us in a strange way from our extended family. No one really knew Becky the way Mother, Dad, and I did. And no one loved her that way either. Becky became the chink in our family's armor that allowed other family members to discuss all of us—where we were going wrong with Becky, how we didn't recognize good advice when we heard it—somehow, having a child like Becky made everyone else thankful for their own, normal, children. Thankful and a little superior.

Years after our Expo Trip, when I was an adult visiting both families, each had something different to say, now that I was "grown and able to understand the way things were." At Gwennie's house, Aunt Margaret informed me that Becky's problems were all my father's fault; he hadn't spent enough time with Becky and hadn't loved her enough. A week later, I drove to Winston-Salem to visit Nearl, who explained that Becky's problems stemmed from my mother's lack of energy—Mother just couldn't keep up with Becky and didn't discipline her properly. Of course, it's easy to judge people when you aren't facing the situation every day. And that's just what my relatives did—they found fault and support fell along familial lines. I'll never understand why none of them offered help, rather than criticism. It's still a sore spot with me, though my parents have never said one negative word about any of the family members who were so quick to judge them.

What I remember most about the trip to the Outer Banks was crossing the series of long, slender bridges that connect the barrier islands off the North Carolina coast. We were headed for the Cape Hatteras National Campground, and I still recall flying down the highway, few cars in sight, the trailer swerving back and forth behind us. The sky was clear and blue and enormous, so much so that it took my breath. On either side, the ocean crashed against the bridge. Gulls swooped beside the car; pelicans made a low V across the waves.

"Oh, Jet!!" Becky yelled as we started across the first bridge. She grabbed my arm and clenched it tight. Her face was in a strange grimace as she scooted away from the door closer to me.

"Don't worry; the water can't come in here. We're on a bridge," I told her. I understood how she could have been frightened. The ocean was almost at the level of the road and the bridge seemed small and untrustworthy against the power of all that water. Finally, after a few words from my dad, Becky relaxed a little.

When we drove into the camp, my mother insisted we find a spot near the bathhouse. My dad complied and slowly, carefully backed the trailer into position.

Without the tent to pitch, there wasn't much for me to do. While my parents made the beds and set up for cooking, Becky and I decided to head across the large dunes toward the beach, not to swim but just to look at the ocean, walk along the shore and gather exotic shells. I held her hand as always and helped her struggle over the sandy hills covered with sea oats. We could hear the pounding of the surf and the salt air made my nose tingle. The beauty of the beach stretching out before us made me breathe more deeply. I was always moved by such things—the mountains in the hazy dawn light, a meadow thick with flowers, the ocean meeting the pale blue sky—my feelings were intensified by seeing this deserted place with Becky, just the two of us, no parents and no other people in sight.

We ran, a clumsy sort of trotting because I wasn't going to let go of Becky's hand. If I did, she'd head straight into the water with her clothes on and Mom had told us not to swim. Holding her tightly, we ran down to the waves. Becky would have kept going if I hadn't stopped her. I knew Mother would be angry if we got our clothes wet, so I told Becky that we'd search for shells until the next day when we could swim as long as we wanted.

"Look! Seagulls!" I shouted as several laughing gulls flew overhead.

"Are they laughing at the shells? Why do they laugh? Are they people?" Becky said.

"No, they're birds—they just sound like they're laughing. I love the way they seem to stay in one place when they fly against the wind. I wish I could fly," I said.

"If she had wings, could she fly home?" Becky said. "Could she fly home from Amos?" Becky flipped a big shell she'd picked up. I pretended I didn't understand her question.

We walked, then skipped, then ran, then walked again until I heard Dad calling from the top of a dune. The sun had almost slipped below the horizon and all I could see was his dark form motioning for us. Becky and I slowly climbed the dunes heading for the trailer. I hated to leave the deserted beach, hated to stop the time Becky and I had shared. I watched as she struggled to climb in the sand, her small body about half the size of my own. Sometimes, she'd stop, pick up a shell, then flip it for a moment. She didn't want to go away from the water, though she'd heard Dad the same as I had. I let her dawdle a little, kept a looser grasp on her wrist while she bounced and skip-jumped in that way she had. She mumbled to herself the entire time, but by the low sound of it, I knew she wasn't talking to me. I knew when she wanted to talk and when she'd gone deep inside herself. Sometimes, her body would stiffen while she walked, a tense sort of response to herself, I guess. I didn't care that she was talking gibberish, out loud, a singsong way of exploring the beach. I was glad to have her back, happy to be with her, spoil her all I could. Sometimes, I didn't even want to share her with my parents. But she never felt that way, I don't think. She was always glad to see our folks, especially Mother. There was no question about her favorite—it was always Mom. I guess Mother was the one who took care of Becky more than anyone else and that's why Becky clung to her. And Mother was an easier touch than Dad—she could be cajoled into giving us our own way. She rarely punished us, especially Becky.

The next morning, Dad, Becky, and I headed for the beach. We put our towels down on the sand and dove into the waves. Becky wasn't afraid of water and loved to float, face-down, arms and legs flailing out to the sides occasionally, like a turtle except she liked to keep her head under the water. She'd flip one of the small balls she brought with her, let it bob along beside her for a while, then reach up for a brief flip. If you didn't know any better, you might have thought she was drowning. But she wasn't in trouble—she just liked to drift around like a jellyfish.

I noticed a girl about my own age nearby. I swam over to her, leaving Becky with Dad. Her name was Marnie and she was from Canada. She spoke with a slight British accent which I thought was cool. I was still in love with the

Beatles and anyone who had the slightest connection to England was top-notch in my eyes. She wore a two-piece bathing suit and was very slim. I was conscious of my breasts which I tried to hide by wearing a tee shirt over my swimsuit. The two of us became quick friends, the way young people can when they're thrown together for a short time. When we got out of the water, I moved my towel over to hers and we slathered suntan lotion all over ourselves, talking about school and boys and where we were headed that summer. I didn't have a thought for Becky once I'd found Marnie. I didn't even tell her where I was going. Nor did I remember to tell Dad I was moving my towel away from his and Becky's. I just did it.

The strange split inside me, rendered after my first kiss, hadn't knit itself back together—I still wanted to spend family time with Becky, but I could just as easily forget her, forget all she'd been through, when I was with friends. I felt guilty that I could laugh and have fun while Becky floated in the water with Dad. But I didn't want to bring her along with me. I was having a hard enough time feeling like I was okay. I wasn't thin like Marnie and my hair wasn't long and curly. Bringing Becky would brand me with a label I didn't want. I didn't want to be known as the chubby girl with the crazy sister. Besides, I told myself, we were camping and Becky was having a good time in the water. I didn't have to feel guilty. After all, Becky was with our parents, with me, and that made her happier than anything else. I smoothed my bad feelings away as easily as I smoothed my towel across the sand.

Marnie and I were at the age where we wanted to pretend we didn't *have* parents. I hadn't met hers yet and she hadn't invited me to, though I'd already introduced her to mine, very briefly. But I didn't introduce her to Becky. That afternoon, when we'd walked to my parents' spot on the beach, Becky was building a sandcastle—a perfectly normal thing for a kid to do. I didn't see the need to let Marnie know Becky wasn't exactly what she seemed at that moment—a regular little sister.

As usual, the evenings around the campfire were spent with the family. I loved this time, watching the sunset turn from fiery pink to violet, then finally to deep black. No lights from nearby cities blurred the sky at the Outer Banks. The only light blazed from campfires, mere sparks against the night. Such total darkness was scary and exhilarating and I imagined what the world must have been like before electricity tamed it. I'd create whole dramas in my head about how the Indians who'd fished along the islands lived way back then, how pioneer women had managed to survive, how cavewomen might snuggle beneath animal skins, looking up at the same bright stars that winked at me now. Dad would sit with me, drinking a can of beer. Becky would perch on the little folding stool while Mom finished the kitchen cleanup. I'd tell Becky stories and sometimes we'd roast marshmallows. Every once in a while, we'd sit without talking. That is, everyone except Becky. She always mumbled, her singsong voice low, growing louder the longer she continued with her questions. I grew used to her constant drone and it became a sort of music—the music of my family, a hollow sad sound that accompanied us wherever we went.

In the remaining time at the Outer Banks, I spent the days with my new friends, the nights with my family. Though I mostly ignored Becky once I hit the beach, she didn't seem to mind. I tried to make it up to her at night by telling stories and asking about her day. We took a couple of trips to historic towns, Manteo for one, and visited the Wright Brothers Museum. My father bought tickets for us to see the outdoor drama *The Lost Colony*.

The night we were to see *The Lost Colony*, Mom made us put on our dressier shorts. I wore a red pair with a checkered matching top and Becky donned a bright blue sun suit with a white tee shirt. Unfortunately, Becky ate a hotdog after she'd dressed. She still had problems eating meat. The hotdog bun went gooey and got stuck in the roof of her mouth. This made her gag and her hotdog came back up. She had to change clothes, almost making us late for the play. My father drove to the amphitheater in record time.

We took our seats close to the front. I could see the ocean far off in the distance. The air was sultry, the sky a deep shade of violet. We watched as a blue heron tucked its long legs and skimmed the water. The musicians tuned their instruments and the story of the mysterious settlement of the Outer Banks began.

Actors dressed as Indians stormed onto the stage, each face angry with warpaint. They held tomahawks and cried out with loud voices. I watched, fascinated, as the story of the early pioneers unfolded. Suddenly, men with muskets ran onstage.

"Are those guns? Are they going to shoot?" Becky screamed at the top of her lungs. Before my father could move, Becky struggled across the people sitting beside us to the aisle. She was yelling and crying at the same time. She scrambled out with Dad hurrying after her, trying to grab her scrawny arm, but she was too quick for him and she didn't care who she jostled.

She wouldn't shut up. Dad finally caught her and tried to calm her down, but it was no use. People in the audience turned to look at us, disgust on their faces as if our family didn't know how to behave at a play. No one could hear the dialogue. Even the actors cast dirty glances our way. Finally, Dad picked Becky up and took her out of the amphitheater.

My cheeks burned with shame as one by one the people around us returned their attention to the play. I could hear disgruntled whispers and every once in a while someone would turn to stare at us. I was glad no one knew my name.

The play had barely begun. I kept expecting Dad and Becky to return to their seats. I figured he'd get her settled, maybe buy her a candy bar or something and they'd come back. We'd enjoy the rest of the play together.

But that didn't happen. Mom and I watched the play until the intermission. Then we walked out to the concession stand and found my father and Becky had gone to the car.

"Daddy, can't you come back in?" I stared at Becky who was now playing quietly in the back seat.

"You and Mom go ahead. Becky and I'll stay here." He sounded resigned.

"I can stay with her." I really didn't want to miss the performance, but I felt sorry for him.

"No, you and Mom go back in and enjoy it." He smiled at me like everything was okay.

I looked again at Becky. She seemed oblivious to the trouble she'd caused. I was suddenly angry at her.

"Oh Becky," I said under my breath, the words carrying my anger to her. But she didn't care. All she did was talk to herself.

"Is she scared of guns? Do loud noises bother her? Is she bad for leaving the play?" She sang as she flipped the red duck she'd brought along. I just shook my head in disgust and went back inside.

Mom and I finished watching the play, but it wasn't the same. My father was the one who shared my enjoyment of things like music and theater. He guffawed at the funny parts and cried at the sad ones, just the way I did. Mom was more reserved, though she often cried at tear-jerker movies. But she never laughed out loud and she didn't like to talk about the story after it was over, the way Dad and I did.

By the end of the play, my anger had cooled a little. After all, Becky couldn't help the way she was. It was hard to stay mad at her when she wasn't really responsible for her actions. Holding a grudge wouldn't be fair. Only a real jerk would hold a grudge. I didn't want to be that jerk.

But I couldn't help thinking about the two of them stuck in the car. Becky was still in jail in a way. And Dad was in there with her. I hated to think of her returning to Amos Cottage, but part of me would be relieved when she did. Sometimes, being with Becky was just too difficult. We were all in her prison together, doing time while waiting for a change.

Chapter Eight

We're on our way to the Emerald City to see the great Oz.

—Dorothy

While on our way from the coast of North Carolina to the green forests of Virginia, my father pulled over at a lookout area. We piled out of the car and took in the view.

"A hawk!" my father pointed to a large bird flying above the hill below us. "I love to watch them fly—they don't even have to flap their wings—they just ride the wind," he said.

"Or it could be a buzzard," Mother said. "Hard to tell from here."

I shaded my eyes so I could observe the effortless flight while Becky skipped around in circles next to me. I wondered how much longer we'd have to drive before we reached our nation's capital. I grew excited when I thought about visiting Washington, DC. It would be my first trip to a big city.

There were no camp grounds inside the Beltway, so we traveled to a place called Green Acres, a well-manicured private camp about a half-hour's drive away. Becky and I loved the name of the place and Becky asked, "Is it the same farm as the one on TV? Is Arnold the pig here?" Each time we entered the camp, we'd burst into "Green Acres is the place to be/Farm living is the life for me." Becky's high-pitched voice would soar an octave above mine as I tried to get her to stick her head out the car window and join me in a serenade of the campground. She never did that. Instead, she'd sit still and sing into her hand, which she held in front of her face, palm extended outward.

We arrived late one afternoon in the heat of midsummer. Our car had no airconditioning, and even with all the windows open I could smell Becky's little girl odor. It wasn't a bad smell, slightly yeasty like rising dough. Her short hair stuck to her head and didn't seem as blond as when I'd last seen her. Though Mother had almost cried when she'd seen Becky's new cut, she had to admit combing Becky's hair was a lot easier now.

Dad pulled into a shady spot and hooked up the trailer. I was busy unloading the trunk of the car, doing whatever Mom told me. We'd seen a swimming pool on the way into camp and I was hoping to go for a swim. The blue water looked almost icy and I could already feel the relief of it.

"Can the Becky go swimming?" Becky hopped and flipped one of her dolls, hovering around Mother like a mosquito. She loved to swim. "Does the Becky need to cool off in that water?" As always, Becky flipped Gunbaby harder and harder the more agitated she became. It was an early-warning signal.

"You can go later. First, help us get the trailer set up," my father said. He believed in work first, play later.

"Aw, come on, Daddy. Let me take her. It'll get us out of your hair," I wheedled. I knew Becky's "help" could be more trouble than it was worth.

"When everybody's finished, then everybody will go swimming." He gave me a stern look. I sighed and told Becky to set up the lawn chairs around the circle of rocks that would later become our campfire. I had to give her simple tasks, one at a time so she wouldn't get confused. While she started her chore, I filled the water container from the nearby pump. Though the trailer had water hook-up, having a jug of water came in handy for a lot of things—a quick drink after a long hike; washing grimy hands; killing a late-night fire—and since I was bigger and stronger than Becky, hauling water was always my job.

"Jet, where's the bathroom?" Becky asked. We'd parked the trailer near the restroom as we usually did so my mother and Becky wouldn't have far to walk. Sometimes, a breeze would bring the rank smell of the toilets across our camp, but Mother thought it was worth it to be close to the facilities. I pointed to a building across the path about fifty yards away. Becky knew exactly where the restroom was, but asking was her way of telling me she needed to go.

"Come right back when you're done," I cautioned her. I hoped I wouldn't have to check on her to make sure she'd cleaned herself properly. She was getting so much better at that, my parents no longer insisted I go with her each time.

I filled the water jug, helped my dad unload the cooking equipment, the lantern, and other gear. We were so busy we didn't realize Becky'd been gone for quite some time.

"Where's your sister?" Mom asked as she organized the cooking utensils.

"She had to go to the bathroom," I answered. A bird with bright yellow wings had landed in a nearby bush. I'd never seen anything like it in my *Birds of the South* book so I studied it. I wasn't thinking about my little sister.

"How long has she been gone?"

"I dunno. Not that long," I said. I was busy staring at the bird, couldn't Mother see that? I continued watching the bird as it balanced on the low branch of a sapling.

Suddenly, I realized a lot of time had passed since Becky had hurried toward the bath house in that full-steam-ahead walk of hers.

"I'll go check." I sighed heavily, so that the bird flew off into the surrounding woods. I walked quickly over to the bathroom, sure I'd find Becky in one of the stalls, talking to herself. I opened the door and called her name. No reply. I bent down and looked under each of the four doors. No feet dangling. No one there.

I tried not to panic.

I knew if anything happened to Becky, it would be my fault. She was my responsibility. And I'd let her go; I'd lost my only sister. My heart was beating hard by the time I returned to the camp.

"Is she back?" I hoped that somehow we'd missed each other and she was now safe with my parents.

"No. Isn't she in the bathroom?" My mother sounded worried.

"It's empty." I started scanning the area. Several little kids were playing in the playground but Becky wasn't among them. Besides, she'd never be with other kids. She was a loner.

My dad had joined us and quickly assessed the situation.

"Jet, you go back toward the entrance of the park. Mom will head to the playground and I'll check the other campsites. Hurry now. We don't want anything to happen to her." He dispensed us with the authority of an army commander. We scattered according to plan.

I called Becky's name as I sprinted quickly over the terrain. Rocks and roots tripped me a few times. I could hear Mother's voice growing more faint as she searched farther and farther away.

Back then, the news didn't flash lurid photos of missing or abused kids each evening. I would have been shocked to discover any of my friends being mistreated by an adult, especially a parent. I'd been taught to respect my elders and I'd never been given a reason not to do so. Though I was worried about Becky being lost, I didn't have the same fears my parents must have had. I knew nothing of pedophilia or kidnapping, none of the horrors we're so familiar with now. I only knew that my sister wasn't normal and she could get into real trouble, especially if she came across mean kids who might make fun of her or talk her into doing something dangerous. I ran faster, my breath burning in my lungs.

"Becky!!!" I screamed.

I was getting close to the edge of the camp, the check-in center where the pool was located. I could hear a lot of noise coming from that area. At first, I thought it was kids playing in the water. But the closer I got, the more I realized the voices didn't sound like typical swimming-pool voices. Grownups were shouting, angry. A familiar feeling of dread started in my gut and I knew that, somehow, my sister was involved.

The sun glinted off the blue water and the crowd clustered around one end of the pool. Two men with pot bellies were leaning over the edge, pointing and gesturing wildly. Kids stared and several women had their hands on the shoulders of their children. I pushed my way to the front of the group and looked in. Becky was face down in the water doing her usual dead-man's float, her blue shorts billowing out from her thin, white legs. Her tee shirt clung to her and at first glance, you might have thought she really *was* dead. Every now and then, she'd splash her hands, come up for a quick breath, then float spread-eagled on the water's surface. She'd cleared the pool, probably by her crazy giggling and talking to herself. I'd already learned that nobody wanted to be around a weird person—they were afraid insanity was contagious. The bald man with the big gut was shrieking at her to leave the water. But she wouldn't budge. She was happy and cool and that manager might as well have been singing an aria.

"BECKY! Get out of that pool this minute!" I shouted in what she'd recognize as the I'm-going-to-kill-you voice. She looked up at me and smiled. Then she dunked her head beneath the water where she couldn't hear me. She flipped her hands against her submerged head, plashes of water sparkling in the afternoon sun.

The manager turned and pointed his finger at me. "She didn't pay. You need to get her out, girlie. Right now." His face was red, his eyes all squinted up.

"I'll get my dad," I assured him.

I ran to find my parents, who were frantic with worry. I told them where Becky was and my dad laughed.

"In her clothes?" Mom asked.

"Fully dressed," I replied.

I followed my folks back to the pool and watched while Dad commanded Becky to come out. She dunked herself once more, briefly. But something about the way Dad spoke to her clicked, and she slowly made her way to the ladder at the side of the pool. She dragged her drenched body up, her fingers held tightly against her mouth while she mumbled words under her breath.

Dad took her by the hand and together they parted the crowd, Becky dripping and sloshing water as she walked.

I knew she was in trouble, even though my dad had laughed when I'd told him where she was. She'd be punished and I didn't want to be around when it happened. Usually she'd be deprived of something she really liked for a while. For example, she might not get to go swimming tomorrow because of what she'd done today. Or maybe she'd have to give up dessert this evening. Whatever the punishment was, she'd get a lecture, too. Dad would explain in great detail why she shouldn't have done what she'd done. I hated to be around when the sermons took place because they were boring and I felt sorry for Becky. Somehow, any kind of punishment for her seemed unfair. She wasn't normal, so how could she be held accountable? But my parents didn't see things that way. She was expected to mind, just like any other little kid. And she did, for the most part. But she was also unpredictable. That was one of the things I loved about her.

Becky and my parents returned to camp, but I didn't. Instead, I took a nature trail that veered off to the left. I didn't want to be around anyone right then, especially Becky.

The sun topped the trees and the sky was smeared with pink and orange. The further I walked, the more still the air became. The screeching of the kids in the pool faded into the low cooing of pigeons. They sounded so peaceful and they comforted me a little. I could hear my shoes crunch against the rocks in the path and feel the cooling wind on my cheeks. I looked into several snake holes hoping to find something—an old skin, cold glinty eyes staring back at me. I pretended I was a Cherokee squaw and Trotting Pony, who looked a lot like Randy, a boy from school, was trying to kiss me. I'd had a crush on him almost all last year and I practiced what I wished I could say to him as I strolled along under the canopy of trees. If anyone had been watching me, they would have thought I was nuts, whispering to myself like that.

Finally, I thought about Becky.

I laughed out loud thinking of her bobbing around in the water, all those people confused and pissed-off because she'd dared come into their space—my sister, talking to herself much the way I'd just been doing, in the woods, alone. How was her talking to herself different from the way I talked to myself? Did my intimate monologue mean I was nutty, too? Where exactly was the line?

Becky was the unknowable side of the human mind, a mind that had sprung a leak somewhere. She was scary and weird, and nobody knew why. That was the most frightening part—not knowing what made her crazy and not knowing if you were going to be next.

Becky was harmless, she wouldn't hurt anyone, but she'd spooked all the grownups there in the pool. They were powerless against her, a mere girl. They weren't used to that.

I couldn't help but admire Becky for doing her own thing regardless of who was around or what anyone thought about her. At fifteen, I was sorely conscious of the opinions of others. I didn't want to stick out in a crowd the way Becky did. Instead, I wanted to be just like other girls my age. I wanted to go to parties and play Spin-the-Bottle. I wanted to kiss boys.

Even though Becky's antics sometimes embarrassed me, something about her outlandish behavior appealed to me. She did the things I only dreamed of doing—like jumping into a pool, fully dressed. She got away with things I couldn't. When Mom told her to clear her plate, she scraped all the pieces of finely cut meat into a little pile, then acted as if my mother hadn't spoken a word; or, if she didn't like something, she'd spit it out, complaining that it 'stuck to her roof.' Even when she was sent to her room because she refused to eat roast beef, she didn't seem to mind. I could hear her in there talking to herself, sometimes laughing that off-the-wall laugh she had, like Satan himself was inside her, tickling what she called her "funny bone." I secretly enjoyed the irritation she caused my parents and other adults. She did things that upset the apple-cart and I found myself admiring that about Becky.

I was a product of my time. The whole world was in rebellion or so it seemed to me in 1967. The Beatles' song lyrics, the civil rights movement, the protests about the war in Viet Nam, young women burning their bras, sit-ins, love-ins, Kurt Vonnegut and Ken Kesey—all over the country young people were speaking their minds.

I was reluctant to share my ideas about the big issues of the day. I hated the war in Viet Nam, hated the way it snatched up graduating boys almost as fast as they could walk across the stage to get their diplomas. But I could barely bring myself to disagree with my father about policy at the dinner table. I despised the silly notion that only married people should have sex—I believed in love, love, love—but I didn't dare mention this opinion to my mother. In my heart, I wanted to change society, break the rules, turn the world on its head. But I didn't have the courage. Becky did.

Part of my attraction to Becky's rebelliousness was the stoic way she took the consequences of disobedience. She was either stiff with pride or numb, I couldn't tell which. But I admired her freedom of spirit, her ability to say a big "Fuck You" to the world that I simply answered with a "Yes Sir."

Repulsion was mixed up in my feelings, too. At the pool, in that crowd of strangers, my teenage radar vision had picked out a couple of cute boys who were staring at Becky, elbowing each other and laughing. When I told her to get out of the pool, acknowledging my connection to her, I imagined them gaping at me with great disdain, though I didn't turn to face them. I was used to that look, that mix of revulsion and curiosity, that get-away-from-me shudder. Usually, I could ignore it. I knew better than to let it hurt me, but somehow, alone on a path in the Virginia woods, it *did* hurt.

In the silence of the forest, as the sun set the trees to flame, night coming all dark and ominous, I could allow myself to feel embarrassed, ashamed. I would stay there until the heat had gone from my face and I could return to my family as if nothing had happened. I stood there until the sky blurred to a dark gray. Slowly, I realized that I'd chosen Becky over strange, handsome boys. I'd gone to her, claimed her. I could have simply backed away from the crowd and retrieved my father. But I didn't. I walked up to the pool and tried to help my sister, even though she didn't want my help at that moment. I began to see that I would always have a choice and I had enough self-awareness to realize I'd choose Becky over anyone else. I was ready to return to our camp, ready to be the best sister I could.

I knew supper would be cooking and Becky's lecture would be over. My parents would joke about what she'd done, put a funny spin on it. Humor had become a friend. Becky put us in situations where the response could be laughter or tears. We tried for laughter every chance we could get.

But for this moment, I wanted to be quiet and consider all the ways Becky and I were different. And all the ways we were the same.

The next day, Mom, Dad, Becky, and I headed inside the Beltway to explore our nation's capital. We were approaching the Washington Monument when I realized I'd forgotten to wear shoes.

"I can't believe you didn't at least put on your sandals. They won't let you into the White House without shoes," Mother scolded.

"They might not let you in anywhere," Dad echoed. We'd driven too far from camp to turn back.

"They'll let me in. Don't sweat it." I wasn't really worried about not having my shoes because I went barefoot all the time in West Virginia.

Already a big group was waiting to go to the top of the Monument. The morning sun scorched the sidewalk. There were two entrances: one had an elevator, the other a staircase. My soles were beginning to burn as I stood in line, shifting from one foot to the other. I glanced at the other entry way and saw no knotted crowd.

"Becky and I'll walk up," I said.

"It's a long way," said Dad. "I'm not sure you can make it."

"We'll make it, won't we, Beck?" I grabbed her hand and she trotted along beside me. We broke from our parents and headed to the open door. A group of hippies had gathered on the lawn.

I'd never seen hippies up close before. Though only a few years older, they seemed really mature. The young men had beards and the women wore long peasant dresses that puckered off their shoulders. Long hair streamed everywhere. They were yelling and laughing and holding signs about the war. Some of the women wore wilted flowers behind their ears. They looked a little like vagabonds. There were no hippies in my hometown. But I'd seen them on TV, where they'd seemed wild and frightening. In real life, they were friendly.

"Hey, join us," one young man shouted to me while pointing at my bare feet. He gave me the peace symbol and grinned, his teeth white against his dark beard. He pointed again. "You're one of us, honey. Come on."

I didn't know what to do. Not many boys had talked to me like that before. I'd been frightened by catcalls from construction workers but no one had suggested I join them. I gave him a big smile, shook my head, and led Becky into the Washington Monument.

The stairway was dark and the concrete walls seemed slimy. The air smelled rubbery, like old tennis shoes. The narrow steps were barely wide enough for one person to climb, another to pass going down. At first, Becky and I raced up. Few people had chosen this route and we had the stairway to ourselves, so we could run side by side. After about ten steps, we slowed to a walk and a group of Puerto Rican boys clambered down, edging us out of their way. Then the stairs were empty again.

Becky was flipping her hands against Gunbaby, who went everywhere with her. The stairwell echoed any noise and the smack, smack, smack of Becky's fingers against the doll sounded almost watery. The climb grew more difficult the longer we ascended.

Becky gave out about halfway up. She plopped down on a step.

"Is she too tired? Are her legs too short to make it? Does her sister need to carry her the rest of the way?" She flipped her hands together and turned her head away from me.

"Come on, Beck. You can do it," I said as I tried to pull her up by her arm. She didn't budge.

"Dammit, Becky, I can't carry you all the way up there."

She didn't move. I stood in the stairwell. The air was dank and getting warmer by the minute. I didn't want to admit defeat and return to our parents, but I didn't want to carry Becky either.

"Get up, Becky! Right now!! If you don't get up, I'm going to spank you!" I said.

Still, Becky refused to move.

"Will the Jet carry her?" Becky said.

"Oh hell. Climb up—piggyback, okay?" I hunched down so she could clamber on.

She scrambled onto my back. I trudged up to the tiny window in the top point of the monument, my breath coming hard, my heart racing. I held her up so she could look about over the grounds. There wasn't much to see. I told her to stay still while I took a peek. On my tiptoes, I could see the green below, not much else. We went back downstairs. Going down was much easier and Becky had no trouble.

The protesters were still there and that same young man waved as Becky and I left the entrance to rejoin my parents who had opted for the elevator. I smiled again and thought to myself that I was different, too. I didn't wear shoes to our nation's capital and that made me one kind of person. I was proud I seemed to fit in with the hippies. Oddly, I felt more connected to Becky than usual. We were both outcasts of a sort, something that before had bothered me. But now, it seemed okay to be an outsider, okay to be different. I recognized I was not like most people; I might not ever "fit in." For the first time, that idea didn't scare me.

Chapter Nine

That must be the Emerald City.
—*Dorothy*

I can still see my father and Becky holding hands, her legs barely skirting the ground as they scurried from one exhibit to the next at Expo 67. They wanted to cover as much of the World's Fair as possible in our allotted week; Becky, her legs a blur, matched my father for endurance and speed. Mother and I tagged behind.

"How can she do it?" my mother would ask each day.

But Becky never tired. She seemed to enjoy the sights and sounds of the fair, the energy pulsing from the thousands of visitors.

Expo was located on an island in Montreal, Canada, and looked like a small city sprung suddenly to life. Hotels, motels, dozens of restaurants, campgrounds, and parking lots (often some local person's cow pasture) surrounded Expo, ringing it with everything a tourist might need.

There were ninety pavilions representing sixty-two different countries. The officials had allowed freestyle architecture, so each building was different. The theme was "Man and His World," and countries outdid themselves to create the most modern, scientific buildings ever made. Russia and the US, in the midst of the Cold War, wanted to impress the rest of the world with their unique contributions. People in exotic dress lined up for the exhibits: Indian women in saris; mysterious men in tall hats and long beards; women who moved like a cloud, dark veils covering their faces.

Each morning we arrived from our nearby campground in time for the opening of the gates. I found everything about Expo exciting, but Mother often complained about standing in the interminable lines and my father's quick pace.

"Can't you slow down for a minute?" she'd say.

"You want to see everything, don't you? Make each day count?" my father would reply, his expression sunny and full of anticipation.

"Not if we die trying," Mother might mumble to me.

I didn't mind my father's frantic pace. I couldn't wait to arrive at the Fair each day. The smells alone were enough to entice me back. As we made our way from one exhibit to the next, we'd waft through a dozen different scents—spicy Thai chicken, Italian stromboli, Chinese stir-fry, Belgian waffles, hotdogs—a whiff of onion, a hint of cinnamon, sweet baking bread, the sharp odor of chili peppers—just strolling was enough to whet my appetite. I wanted to sample every exotic dish.

"Can't we eat here just once, Daddy? Please???" I'd ask at lunch time.

"You know we can't afford it, Snookie. Our lunch is in the cooler. You ready for it?" he'd ask.

"But don't you want to taste all this neat stuff?" I'd continue to beg.

"Sure I do. But we don't have the money. And we don't want to waste the sandwiches your mom made, do we?"

Rather than eat in one of the exotic booths at Expo, we'd walk from the Fair back to the parking lot. My father would open up the trunk with a flourish and lift out the cooler which held our bologna sandwiches, peanut butter for Becky. There'd be apples, iced tea poured into waxy paper cups, and Little Debbie oatmeal cookies with cream in the middle. Though I longed for a taste from other countries, by the time we got to our own food, I was hungry and found the usual stuff of my school lunches satisfying.

We didn't eat in the parking lot alone. Other families had the same money-saving idea. Sometimes, I'd hear families talking in English; but occasionally, I could recognize French or Spanish. Every once in a while, strange tongues floated on the air, foreign languages I couldn't guess. At those moments, I felt as if I were really far from home. And, as always, there was Becky's own language, her mumbles to herself, the echolalia of our own words coming back to us.

Though we hurried through a lot of exhibits and I've forgotten many of them, a few stick in my mind. One of the first ones we saw was the Thai display. The building was shaped like a small Pagoda with a statue of Buddha in the middle. Ornate spires pointed skyward and statues of animals and goddesses decorated the walls. The guide told us that the items we were seeing were some of Thailand's dearest treasures, all made of real solid gold.

Becky didn't seem interested in the Thai exhibit, though, and sort of bounced in place next to my father. She tried to flip a few of the statues, but my father reached out to grab her hands before they actually touched anything.

The USSR contribution was plain-looking on the outside with an unusual convex roof. Inside, a huge ball of electricity zinged back and forth from the front wall to the back. The sphere was bright as lightning and sputtered dangerously on its journey. Becky didn't like the snap and crackle, so she, Mom, and Dad waited for me outside the display. I watched it for a long time from the second floor as I leaned against the iron railing, forgetting about them stuck outside. Being alone didn't bother me. Sometimes, I wanted to break away, go to the exhibits on my own, pretend I was all grownup and having this adventure by myself. I never actually left them, but part of me wanted to. The other part was frightened of being lost forever if I let my family too far out of my sight.

The USA building was an architectural marvel, a dome 200 feet high and 250 feet in diameter. Made of triangles on the outside and hexagons on the inside, the sphere glistened in the sunshine and glowed at night from within. Inside, there were two stories, much like the USSR exhibit. On the first floor were movie posters with life-sized Clark Gables and Errol Flynns, old-timey movie stars I watched when there was nothing else on television on Saturday mornings. There weren't pictures of movie stars I admired, like Steve McQueen or Troy Donahue. Marilyn Monroe with her cotton-candy hair was plastered everywhere, her soft, wet lips looking enormous on the wall. We made quick work of the downstairs and climbed to the second floor.

Imagine a huge maze with rooms enclosed within. That's what the second floor looked like. The light was dim, and long lines of people snaked their way from room to room to see whatever was inside. Although the rooms were walled in, the walls didn't go all the way to the floor. There was about a foot of space between the walls, which were suspended from the ceiling, and the floor. If you lined up on one side of a room, you could see the feet of the people lined up on the other side. Everyone was disembodied in an eerie way.

Becky and I got into the line, our parents in front of us. Becky tried to slip her hand out of my grip, but I wouldn't let her.

"Be still. Don't you want to see what's in those rooms?" I said.

"What's in the rooms? Does her sister want to see the rooms?" Becky said.

She settled down and stood fairly still, skipping gently in place until we reached the first room. I lifted her up so she could peek into the viewing hole. She started chuckling in a way that reminded me of gurgling water coming up from the earth.

"What's so funny?" I said as I put her down and placed my eye to the hole.

I saw a scene from the movie *Robin Hood*, with a fake-looking Sherwood Forest and a dummy dressed like Errol Flynn as Robin and Olivia De Havilland and as Maid Marian. They looked exactly like they had in the film, except they were dummies. The set was complete with trees and stuffed animals that looked almost real in the semi-darkness.

This was much better than the first floor show and I couldn't wait to see each display. The scenes reminded me of giant shadow boxes with movies stars inside.

The only problem was the lines. Like at all the Expo exhibits, processions of people curled around and around. Sometimes you had to stand an hour or more just to get into one of the more popular sites, like the Kodak building with its three-dimensional movie.

Here, at the Hollywood exhibit, the parade of folks seemed to go on forever. Though we moved very slowly, I was willing to wait, but Becky wasn't.

"Can the Becky go some place else? Is this boring?" Becky would say as I held her hand. She kept slipping her fingers away from mine, pulling, trying to run away. I circled my thumb and middle finger around her wrist. My parents had left us while they joined another line to see *The Three Stooges*. I was skipping that one since I'd never really liked Moe, Larry, and Curly. I'd headed straight to *Gone with the Wind* because I loved Scarlett O'Hara and imagined I'd handle men just the way she did some day.

"Stand still, Becky. It won't be long now," I said. I gritted my teeth, determined to hold both my place in line *and* Becky.

"Can the Becky go with her parents? Does she have to stay with her sister?" Becky danced while I tried to make her settle down. She'd begun flipping her hands together, harder and harder. I could tell she was going to get upset and I didn't want to deal with that.

"You want to go with Mom? She's right over there. Can you find her?" I said.

"Can the Becky go with Mom? Does she want Mom?" Becky said in her singsong voice.

I could see Mother's tan walking shoes below the wall on the other side and figured Becky could go to her easily without getting lost. I didn't want to walk over there with her—I didn't want to lose my place in line. I'd been there forever already, it seemed.

"You want to go with Mom, then, right?" I said.

"Yes," Becky mumbled in a low voice. Whenever you asked her something, she always gave a one-word answer. She pulled away from me before I could say anything else. I was glad to get rid of her, happy to stand in line like everybody else. She could tire a person out when she wanted to do something other than what *she* was doing at the moment.

I watched as best I could to make sure she joined Mom and Dad. My line wasn't moving very fast. Minutes passed and I didn't budge an inch. I'd lost track of my family and didn't care. I was busy staring at the boy ahead of me. He was about my age with blond hair and a scraggly mustache. Still, he wasn't bad-looking and I kept trying to force him to look my way by mental telepathy, something Dusty had told me about.

Look-and-smile, look-and-smile, I beamed my thoughts toward him.

"Have you seen Becky?" My dad touched my elbow.

"I thought she was with you," I said.

"No. We thought she was with you." He didn't seem too worried. "We better go look for her."

"But I've been waiting in this line forever. I'm almost there. Don't make me lose my place now," I said. It was true. I'd finally moved a couple of feet.

"Well, keep your eyes open for her. Mom and I'll search. Hopefully, by the time you're finished, we'll have found her," he said. He ruffled my hair. It was nice of him, I thought, to let me stay in line to see *Gone with the Wind*.

The blond boy had finally made his way to the window frame to look at the scene inside. I watched as he got into position. His parents, who'd gone right before him, hadn't looked at the scene very long and sort of smirked after they'd peered into the box. They whispered something to him as he stepped up to the viewing place. I heard him laugh out loud and I couldn't wait to see what was inside those walls. It must be really good because everyone who'd seen it laughed as they went to the next room. I figured it was that funny scene where Mammy is lacing up Miss Scarlett's bodice after she'd had her baby.

I noticed my parents searching around the area. They'd split up and Dad was looking near John Wayne while Mom circled Elizabeth Taylor. I was a little embarrassed to see them scouring the area and was glad no one knew us at Expo.

Finally, my turn at the window arrived.

The viewing space was too tall for me, so I had to stand on tiptoe. I pressed my nose to the bottom of the frame and gazed in awe at Rhett Butler and Scarlett. She wore that green dress made from curtains and Rhett was kneeling next to her.

And there, flipping Rhett's mustache, was my sister.

I couldn't believe it. She was skipping in place, flinging her fingers against the dummy and cackling. I didn't know what to do. The people behind me were getting anxious, so I moved on. I went around the corner of the backside of the room where no one could see me. I bent over and whispered loudly, "Becky, come out of there!"

She didn't act like she'd heard me. She just laughed louder and flipped harder.

"Come out of there right now!" I hissed again.

The more I whispered for her to come out, the more she laughed. I sure as heck wasn't going in after her. I decided to get my father. He was the only one who could make Becky do anything when she got stubborn like this.

I found him quickly near the *African Queen* room.

"Becky's in the *Gone with the Wind* exhibit," I told him quietly. "She won't come out." I led him to where I'd been calling her. He bent down.

"Is she still there?" I whispered.

"Yep. Flipping Rhett Butler like there's no tomorrow," he said. He squatted down low and so did I. I could see Becky's feet dancing around the dummy.

"Becky! Come out of there!" my father said in a steely voice.

Becky looked around the room as if she didn't know where that voice was coming from. Maybe something about the way my father spoke sounded different from his usual voice. Becky looked as if she thought God or something, was calling her. She froze for a minute, then resumed flipping.

"Becky, if you don't come out of there right this minute, you aren't getting any ice cream for dessert. We're going out for cones and you won't get any if you don't come out right now!" he said. Becky had finally learned to like ice cream at Amos Cottage, thanks to Mama Clark. It had become one of her favorite foods.

I could hear her inside, mulling over what he'd said.

"Can the Becky have ice cream? Will her father give her some ice cream? Does she like chocolate?" Soon, the tap, tap, tap of her feet grew closer and she ducked under the wall right next to us. My father grabbed her wrist real fast while I turned to find Mom.

"That's a good girl. You came right out when I told you to. Now, you can have some ice cream," my father said. He tried to cuddle her for a minute, but she squirmed out of his embrace.

We stopped at one of the zillion Dairy Queens along the way back to the trailer and slurped chocolate cones, like thousands of other visitors to Expo. The four of us, worn out, were ready to grill hotdogs and flop into our beds so we could hit the Fair again early the next day.

By Wednesday, we were exhausted from the dawn to dusk sightseeing. That morning, I awoke to the sounds of rain hitting the tin roof. Inside, the trailer was unusually dark and when I peeked out the small window slat, clouds hid the sun and everything looked gray. Instead of my father's usual wakeup call, I heard gentle snores from both my parents behind the curtains that separated their double bed from the rest of the trailer. Becky was sprawled on her mattress situated directly beneath my bunk. Her bed served double duty; at night, the table and seats spread out to make a single cot; during the day, we reconstructed the table for eating our meals. On nice days, we ate outside at the picnic table centered in our campsite, but on days like this one, the indoor table was a luxury we weren't used to having. Back in our tenting days, we'd learned to eat, cook, and live in the rain.

I looked down at Becky, her small arms and legs flung in every direction. Her blond hair had turned from golden to a very light brown in the year she'd spent at Amos Cottage and, of course, now it was cut short. Since I'd never had curls, I missed Becky's as if they had been my own. But I didn't miss her screaming whenever anyone tried to comb her hair. She preferred her hair short—it was easier for her to take care of and much less painful. I noticed pale streaks of blond running through the strands, glimmering even in the dimness of the trailer. I thought once again about how different we were. At fifteen, I still felt clumsy and big, especially when I sat next to Becky. I continued to be embarrassed by my breasts—I hadn't adjusted to having them or the attention they drew.

"Hey, why don't you show us them big titties? I bet nobody here's got a better set," said Kathy, a popular girl who was also a bully. We were in gym class. She used to stuff people into the big garbage cans in the dressing room. Usually, she picked on poor Agnes, but once she'd stuffed me in there. Yuck. I never knew what she might do next and I never felt safe when she was around. For some reason, she seemed fascinated by my body and was always making a suggestion about me showing off some part of it. I tried to laugh right back at her and dress quickly. Her comments made me feel clumsy and unattractive.

Becky, on the other hand, was far away from the changes puberty brought. Her features looked almost like a porcelain doll's—big blue eyes, button nose, soft pink skin and blondish-brown hair. I loved watching her sleep, her mouth open slightly, her body still baby-like.

"Look who's awake! I don't believe it," said my father as he pulled back the curtain to reveal my mother still sleeping behind him. He had on his usual white tee shirt and pajama bottoms.

"Isn't it time for us to get going?" I said as I turned over so he'd have privacy for dressing. We were used to living in close quarters and I knew when to turn my face away without being told.

"Well, we thought we'd sit this one out. Your mom and I are tired and I'll bet you are, too. I know Becky is—she never sleeps this long. So, let's just hang out here today since it's raining. We'll hit Expo again tomorrow," he said as he made coffee.

I closed my eyes and listened to the familiar sounds of coffee being brewed on the camp stove. My mother was still snoring softly, as was Becky. I savored the moments of quiet and peace. Before long, I'd gone back to sleep as the rain poured down and my father prepared his breakfast.

On rainy days like this, we found fun things to do. Becky and I would crawl into Mom and Dad's bed after they vacated the premises. We'd play Slap Jack and I'd tell Becky stories about Snow White and the Seven Monkees or Cinderella and the Leather Boot. We would sometimes work on the alphabet or her numbers. Every once in a while, we'd have a real conversation.

"What's it really like at Amos, Beck? Do you like it?" I might say when I sensed Becky was in the mood to respond to me. When she was in such a mood, she seemed almost normal. These glimmers continued to give me hope. Even today, when we have our special moments of connection, I see the hope for normalcy flitter near me, delicate as the wings of a hummingbird. But it disappears almost immediately, darts away.

"Does the Becky miss Mom and Dad? Does the Becky miss Jet?" she'd say. "Why did they send me away? Why did Mama Clark go away?"

"I don't know why Mama Clark went away. But Mom and Dad sent you to Amos to help you learn things. They miss you very much. So do I," I said, trying to explain.

"Why can't the Becky learn things at home?" she would say, flipping Gunbaby gently.

"I don't know. I guess because they have special people to help you at Amos Cottage," I'd say. The questions were hard because I didn't really know the answers myself. Sometimes, Becky would ask me about God and why God made her "emotionally disturbed." I didn't have the answer for that one, either.

"Want me to draw your face? I'll make you the Scarecrow, like in *The Wizard of Oz*," I'd say. I was tired of the difficult questions and I wanted to get us both to safer ground.

"Does she like the Wicked Witch better? Does she want to be the Wicked Witch?" Becky would respond as she lay still on the pillow while I pretended to color her skin green, give her a crooked nose and scraggly gray hair. I didn't forget the black hat, either or the long, bony fingers.

Sometimes, the entire family would play a game when it rained as it did that day in Canada. Of course, we had to select a game Becky could play, so we usually were limited to Candyland or Old Maids. Sometimes, we'd work on her numbers by playing UNO. Becky's games weren't as challenging as Casino or Cribbage, but my parents were good sports and didn't seem to mind playing those silly games. We'd break for lunch—peanut butter and jelly sandwiches, Oreo cookies and Red Delicious apples. Becky still liked her baby food, vegetables and beef from Gerber. But since her time at Amos Cottage, she was also eating other things like peanut butter and jelly, occasionally pieces of meat and even ice cream. And now, thanks to Mama Clark, she drank coffee.

After a good day of rest, we were ready to return to Expo for our last two days. We hadn't been to the best part, the part I'd been waiting for—the rides.

The amusement park at Expo had the usual array of thrills—rollercoasters, Ferris wheels, bump cars, and a merry-go-round. But Expo had something else, something that appealed to everyone in those early days of space exploration. John Glenn had circled the world just a few years earlier but the US had not yet landed a man on the moon, though there was talk of it. Expo offered a ride for the new Space Age—the Gyrotron. This ride was supposed to simulate a flight through space first; then, riders plummeted to the center of the earth where a monster was supposed to appear. I'd read about the Gyrotron in the Weekly Reader in social studies class that year. I couldn't wait to experience the Rocket Ship, as I called it when I told Becky about it.

My mother wasn't fond of rides or carnivals. She would go on the more tame amusements like the merry-go-round or the giant swings. But my father loved them all, especially the rollercoaster. And Becky enjoyed anything that had a gentle, rhythmic motion like the little kids' boats and trains.

The amusement park was huge. People milled around everywhere, laughing, screaming, eating cotton candy and ice cream cones. Everyone seemed happy, even our little family.

We started with the merry-go-round and then took Becky on the rides for small children. Dad and I got on the rollercoaster while Mom took Becky on the train. We decided we'd save the Gyrotron for the grand finale.

At last, we were ready to hit the Gyrotron. Another long line snaked up an inclined platform that looked like the rocket platforms I'd seen at Cape Kennedy on television. The line moved very slowly and over and over, we heard the blastoff sounds. Becky put her hands over her ears each time the rocket took off.

"Are we *ever* going to get in?" Mother complained. She could read stories repeatedly to Becky, prepare thousands of meals in a year's time, but she never could stand single file with any grace.

"Be patient. We're moving. See?" Dad would reply to try to soothe her. We moved maybe one step.

"Let's just forget it," Mother said.

"No, Mom! This is the one ride I've been waiting for! Please don't make us miss this one!" I begged. "Tell her, Becky. Tell her you want to ride the Rocket Ship."

"Why can't Becky ride the Rocket Ship? Is Mom irritable? Is she tired?" Becky bounced in place by my side. She didn't like queues, either.

"I am a little tired. But we'll wait. I guess we'll get there soon enough," said Mother.

I kept my fingers around Becky's wrist so she wouldn't skip away and disappear in a flash. Though she'd turned nine that January, she looked more like six. Her face had the innocence of a three-year-old, especially around her eyes. It would be easy to lose her in this crowd.

Finally, after almost an hour, we boarded the Rocket Ship. Unlike the rollercoaster, the Rocket Ship didn't strap you in. There was only a bar that fastened across the whole seat. Mom, Dad, Becky, and I sat on one bench and the bar clamped down in front of us, but not tightly.

Without warning, the Rocket Ship started its blastoff, that loud boom vibrating up through our bones. Becky panicked and jumped up off her seat.

"Sit still!" my father screamed. He grabbed her and held her in the seat with a firm grip. She squirmed for all she was worth. For such a small child, Becky could wiggle and escape from just about anyone's grasp. We were at least fifty feet off the ground and Becky was struggling to get out of Dad's hold. She had no idea of how high we were lifting or how dangerous her actions were. The whole car was beginning to tilt with her movements, the way a Ferris wheel cab does when you're stuck at the top.

Becky tried, but she couldn't break away from Dad's strong arms. He held her in place, tight up against him as the ride progressed. It was too late for us to get out of the car. Becky screamed and kicked, crying until she turned red in the face; still, he gripped her but she continued to fight him.

Though I had eagerly anticipated riding the Gyrotron, what I remember about the experience is the fear on my father's face as he struggled with Becky. No matter what we did or where we went, Becky messed things up one way or another, or so it seems to me now as I write this. I didn't feel that way, however, at the time. Maybe I was used to life with Becky, or maybe I empathized with her so much that I didn't resent her for ruining things. Only now do I recognize the patterns of that early life. Somehow, Becky taught me to take life as it comes; there's no real control; there are no easy answers. As I remember the Gyrotron, the ride itself disappointed me. The monster wasn't very scary and the car moved too slowly to ever be mistaken for a space ship. Riding the Gyrotron wasn't the thrill I'd expected. I don't know if I was disappointed because of the actual ride or if I couldn't experience it completely because of Becky. At the time, I was only glad no other people were riding in our car; I was happy no strangers witnessed the spectacle of my family.

Though I was sometimes embarrassed by the way my mother acted in lines and the way my father bobbed along practically dragging Becky behind him, and though I was especially sensitive to the stares of other people as Becky flipped and talked to herself, often I would be washed away with waves of love for each member of my family. Looking back, I realize these surges of emotion were a normal part of puberty. My hormones were turning me from a girl-child into a woman, even though I wasn't quite ready for such a change. My intense feelings were the result of a combination of things—my own nature, puberty, the way I'd been raised to care about the world, and my relationship with Becky. During those formative years, I learned to empathize with my sister, to communicate with her in ways no one else could. By listening to Becky and trying to see the world the way she saw it, my own imagination was stimulated. Trying to figure out why God created Becky the way He did and what my role was in all of this, led me to what would ultimately become my passion and vocation—writing. For when I write, I am always asking these questions: What is the nature of reality? Why is there suffering? How much of ourselves do we owe others? Can love save the world? If not, what then?

Our grandparents: Gwennie and Ernest Ballard, Maude and Walter Clinard

Mother in high school

Mother and Dad at their wedding, 1951

Mom, Dad, and Becky in 1959, the year after Becky's birth

Me at age seven, Becky at age one in front of Huntington house

Me and Becky at age eight and two respectively

Becky and I in flannel red and white striped PJs my father made for us, 1964

Becky and I around 1972 – me 20, Becky 14

Dad at choir rehearsal

Becky, Mother, and me, around 2002

Chapter Ten

Poppies…poppies…now they'll sleep.
—*Wicked Witch of the West*

We drove home by way of the Thousand Islands of Canada and enjoyed the green husks of land scattered like seeds across the huge expanse of water. The beautiful scenery continued for so long I became used to seeing all manner of water birds and breathtaking vistas from my front-seat window. I'd viewed pelicans and gulls aplenty and couldn't wait to search the woods of home for familiar jays and wrens. I had changed places with Mother somewhere along the trip because I tended to get carsick and the air seemed fresher up front. The front seat also afforded a better view. Mother took the back seat with no complaint, but I can still see her in my mind's eye holding her large purse, sheltering her face from the air blowing from my window. Some cars were airconditioned in those days, but not ours; such luxuries were reserved for the rich.

After six weeks on the road, I still tingled with excitement. To know the world was so full of marvelous things—exotic people, unusual customs, new foods—these discoveries were eye-opening for me. Suddenly, what happened in Philippi, West Virginia didn't seem as important. My life didn't seem quite so dramatic. The world was waiting for me and I couldn't wait to run into its arms.

How can I explain the heart of that young girl? How can I explain the way it felt to believe in everything, to be filled with longing so that your body vibrated like a plucked string? Even now, I cannot explain what I might have been longing for. Perhaps romance? New experiences? Or maybe I was simply longing for new life, something bigger. I imagined myself becoming famous; I didn't know what I'd do to garner fame, but I was sure that somehow I would be transformed into someone glamorous. As I sat in our red Galaxy, I daydreamed about becoming, becoming, becoming…

The whole time we'd traveled, I'd given no thought to friends back home. I hadn't thought about starting high school in the fall or about Becky leaving again, going back to that horrible Amos Cottage. Her year at Amos Cottage had helped her in some ways. The best part was she could wipe her own bottom. Becky had also learned some basic words, numbers, shapes, and colors. At Amos Cottage, she'd developed a terrible case of poison ivy and had received several shots to clear the rash away. So, Becky had also learned a rabid fear of doctors and especially "shot needles." Perhaps she had learned something about the slipperiness of life, too. How trusted loved ones could betray you, send you someplace alien and cold, even if they did it for your own good. I didn't blame my parents; I knew they were doing their very best for Becky. They had hopes for her eventual recovery, and they knew they didn't have the skills to help her achieve it. I was a part of that betrayal, though I hadn't had any say-so about the decision. But I would have done something, anything, to help Becky come back home if I could, especially since I knew she was unhappy away from the people who loved her.

I hated to think about returning her to Amos Cottage, even though I believed such a return would be what was best for Becky. In my head, I understood and agreed with my parents' plan; but in my heart, I was haunted by the image of Becky alone with all those water babies and Bang-Bang, alone with the smells of institutional life rather than the sweet scent of home, alone and crying in her bed the way I cried in my bed for her.

When we finally pulled into the short driveway in front of our house on Faculty Row, I felt tired and a little let down. Our glorious summer had come to an end, and now the time had come for new beginnings. I would start high school, and who knew what would happen.

The first thing I found out when we arrived home was that Becky would not be going back to Amos Cottage. She had been accepted into Pressley House! The only hitch was waiting for a vacancy before Pressley House could take her. The vacancy was expected in September or October. My father had known the encouraging news before the trip but had waited to tell me until there were more details. Earlier that year, he'd written to Dr. Alanson Hinman at Amos Cottage:

> We would appreciate very much your sending us a report on Becky as to how she is progressing. Also, I was wondering if it is time yet to send a report to Pressley House in Pittsburgh? As you know, we are concerned about Becky

not getting any education and we would like to move her just as early as they will accept her. Of course, we will abide by your decision as to the best time for Becky to make the change.

Later, after our trip to Expo, my father wrote to Dr. Roger Elser, Director of the Division of Special Education at the West Virginia Department of Education:

Again, may I express our deep gratitude for what our state, through the work of your office, is doing for unfortunate children such as our Rebecca, and many others... Late in June we made an appointment with Pressley House in Pittsburgh for an interview with Becky... Upon completion of her interview, they informed us that she was now ready for acceptance into their program.

I can hear the relief, the joy, the hope my father must have felt as he wrote those victorious sentences. After searching the country, at last, here was a place where Becky could get the treatment she needed. Here, she could come out of whatever was blocking her learning and step into the light of normalcy. At Pressley House, surely her emotional disturbance would be healed.

The next question my father would address would be, of course, how he could pay for Becky's extra schooling. The state of West Virginia had helped pay for Becky's year at Amos Cottage. But would further funding be available? My father made his case for Becky's stay at Pressley House as follows:

Dr. Eigenbrode of Pressley House estimated that Becky would need to be there between two and three years, at the end of which time she should be able to come home and attend public school. As I understand it, the basic charge will be $16.99 per day, or $5840 per year. This will be an increase over the $12.50 per day at Amos Cottage, but we feel that the large increase in professional supervision will make it well worth the difference. There are two other distinct advantages. She will be able to begin her formal education which, at the age of nine, is so long overdue. Secondly, the reduced distance from home will make it possible for us to visit her much more often than we were able to at Amos Cottage.

As I told you earlier, we are prepared to do all that is in our power to keep Becky in Pressley House as long as she needs to be there. Unless we have help, however, I cannot see how we can possibly keep her there more than eighteen months, perhaps less. Even this would place a terrible financial load on us. Therefore, we are hoping and praying that there will be further help forthcoming from your office. We understand that you can do nothing until after the 1968 legislature meets, but we do request that you keep us in mind at that time.

I cannot imagine my father asking for help, especially asking for money. Quick to lend money, no questions asked and generous to those he loves, his independent spirit must have balked at having to make such a request. He told me once that he halfway resented the fact that Gwennie made most of my clothes as I was growing up. He confessed to being relieved on the one hand, because her contribution meant his small salary could be spent on other things, but he was also envious because he wanted to provide those things for me himself. Writing letters to the state, to various foundations and charities must have rankled. But he wrote them anyway.

Letters like this, appealing for help to pay for Becky's special needs, appear throughout the file my father has kept over the years regarding Becky's situation. The file itself comprises two overstuffed folders about four inches thick, all totaled. Thin, yellowing sheets, these papers are carbon copies of the originals. Stacked together, they represent a lifetime of careful, steady concern. I have a hard time reading them as I write this memoir. They break my heart.

But in the summer of 1967, I knew nothing of such matters. I only knew that my parents were happy about Becky's new opportunity, and I was, too. We were glad she would be closer so we could see her more often. I continued my prayers for Becky, for God to heal her forever. I prayed for her without ceasing, as I'd been taught in Sunday School. I didn't realize it then, but my parents were praying for her, too. I know this because I watch them now, starting the day with prayer time and Bible study, thanking God for each meal, for all good things—the pretty bird's nest in the hanging fern, enough money to live on, work to give purpose to life even in old age—I know them well after all these years. And I know that I, whose faith isn't as refined or strong as theirs, pray for my own sons in just that way, as if their lives depended on it. How much more so must my parents have prayed for Becky? For her safety. Her mind. Her future.

❧

Starting tenth grade at Philip-Barbour, the new, all-county high school, was exciting and scary, much the way starting first grade had been, except hormones and boys were now thrown in the mix. I hadn't seen or heard from Richard after that unsuccessful first kiss but he'd be at Philip-Barbour, a senior while I was a mere sophomore. I dreaded the thought of running into him in the halls, but was also thrilled by the idea, hopeful he might smile or say hello.

Once I'd returned from the dream world of travel, things seemed much the same as before. It was almost as if Expo had not been real at all, except for that longing that sang in my head. Sometimes, the singing was so quiet I barely heard it; but other times, usually on moonlit walks when the air was still, I could hear my longing burst forth in an operatic voice, booming and throbbing all along the edges of my skin. On those nights, I knew I'd been somewhere, done something that no one at Philip-Barbour had done. I was different, only this time, it wasn't having Becky as my sister that made me so; it was my whole family. This time, I was happy to be different, special. I sensed important things about to happen and I would be in the middle of them. Life was taking me on its silvery wings to some enchanted destiny where I would be cherished by one and all, a marvel, a mystery.

But this future marvel went to football games, screamed her lungs out with the other fans. Each school day was like running the gauntlet. I'd hustle down the halls to class, always worried about being late to Band, my French horn banging clumsily against my legs, books halfway sliding from my other arm. I was never a picture of grace the way Chris was. Of course, she didn't play the French horn; she played clarinet, a much more feminine and easy-to-carry instrument.

I'd only been playing French horn for one year. I wasn't very good at it and neither was Nancy—we both played fourth chair. One day, our director looked at us and said, "You girls! Take those horns and practice in the girl's restroom. You're making me ill."

Nancy and I looked at each other, then picked up our horns and made our way through the row while the rest of the students snickered. We walked down the long hall, twittering with embarrassment, our ears ringing with the director's final instruction, "And stay in there until you can play something!"

The restroom was large and well-ventilated with no seats except for the obvious ones and no doors on the stalls. Nancy and I plopped down on a toilet, drained the spit from our instruments, and proceeded to blow our oompahs in unison loud and, well, not necessarily clear. Eventually, we came to enjoy our time together in the restroom, oompahing for some of the hour, gossiping for the rest. I knew the feeling Becky must have often had, the feeling of being an outcast, a reject. Though I had a companion for my prison sentence and we had a good time, I was marked once again as different and had become the object of much joking, just like Becky.

While I struggled with boys and dating and high school, Becky spent the days at home with Mother, jumping on the tramp while the other kids were in school and practicing the things she'd learned at Amos Cottage. My parents worked with her, especially my mother, because they were worried that while she waited to go to Pressley House, she might lose some of the skills she'd gained at Amos. Now, though she took care of herself after using the potty, she often got carried away with toilet paper and would stuff enormous wads into the commode, stopping it up. This habit didn't endear her to my father who was forced to take a plunger and bring the entire mess onto the bathroom floor. When I was home, I became a card-carrying member of the toilet paper police, another chore I didn't like. But regulating paper use was much better than my previous duty, bottom-cleaning.

That fall and into the early winter, Becky and I waited. I was waiting for boys to notice me, while Becky was waiting to go to Pressley House. The spot she'd been promised was not forthcoming as quickly as my parents had been told originally. While she was at home for those few months, even though part of me was concerned with the usual teenage dilemmas, the part of me that loved Becky was happy. The family seemed right for a change, and I didn't have to worry about whether Becky was being cared for and loved. I didn't have to imagine her being miserable around kids like Bang-Bang. She was back safe in the nest, and something in me relaxed.

When I walked from the bus stop at the campus library to our house on Faculty Row, I usually found Becky outside bouncing on the trampoline. Surrounded by her collection of milk jugs and balls, Becky would be sitting in that odd way she had, on her knees but with her feet splayed out at a wide angle. I never could make my legs do that; Becky must have been double-jointed, because for her such a position was easy and comfortable.

When she was on the trampoline, Becky would sit and bounce gently, bobbing up and down while flipping the bottles with her small fingers. Sometimes, I'd join her, make her remove the bottles and the two of us would jump the way you were supposed to jump. We'd run through our routine of tricks with me calling out the order: Knees! Sit! Tummy Flop! Backwards Flip! Every now and then, one of us would get the huge bounce, fly up into the air thrillingly high before we returned to earth. Becky loved it when she got the big boost, and we each flew so high I held my breath. Once we started to jump on the tramp, the rest of the neighborhood would filter into our yard and we'd all take turns. Becky didn't like to take turns and I had to force her to get off. Once the yard was full of kids, Becky usually went inside. She didn't like being in a large crowd of raucous children and didn't have to be told to go to her room. The agreement was understood: when the other kids were in school, Becky could have the tramp; when they returned home, she had to give it up.

With Becky gone, no one hogged the tramp and those not bouncing amused themselves with freeze tag or Red Rover. Every now and then, much to my embarrassment, I'd hear my mother yelling at Becky. I suppose every child cringes when a parent screams, but I really hated it when my mother cracked and her voice erupted and spewed all over the neighborhood. At such times, I wished she were more like my father—logical, self-contained, aware of other people and what they might think. I never knew what Becky did to get such a blasting. Usually, her constant questions threw Mother over the edge. I understood how that could happen but still, the sound of Mother's screams bothered me.

Chapter Eleven

Experience has taught me that I can do anything
if I but take time to think it out.
　　　　　　　　　　　　　　—The Wizard

In the basement of our house, in the room my father built himself over the course of several summers, a yellowed billboard hangs on the wall near the pool table. On it, four young men with crewcuts pose, each wearing a white dinner jacket and a bow tie. Printed across the top in bold black letters is THE HARMONEERS. Three of the young men are wearing their straw hats, but my father is holding out his arm with hat in hand, looking as if he'd come straight out of vaudeville. In the photo, my father's wide grin reminds me what a ham he is. He's good-looking, and I can understand why women have always loved him. From gray-haired ladies at church to his college students to members of the soprano section of the church choir, women have always gathered around my father, ooh-ing and ah-ing over his singing, his conducting. I can still recall old women hugging me in their floppy arms, the sweet smell of their powder and the scratchy feel of their hat brims as they leaned down to me and said, "You're a lucky little girl to have such a fine daddy."

The Harmoneers was the name of the barbershop quartet my father belonged to while he was a student at the University of North Carolina. One year, the quartet won the Horace Heidt contest held in Raleigh. Horace Heidt had a national TV show much like Ted Mack's *Original Amateur Hour* or, more currently, *American Idol*. To win was quite an honor. Unfortunately, the trip to California to appear on television was beyond the budgets of four college boys attending school on the GI Bill. Though my father had ambitions to become a singer of national reputation—an opera singer, no less—he became instead, as he put it, "a big fish in a little pond."

When I was a girl, my father was the Minister of Music at a series of bigger and bigger churches. I remember sitting with my mother in a cushioned pew every Sunday. My father would glide into the choir loft in his flowing robe and sit in the special director's chair. I slumped against my mother's soft body, the peppermint smell of the candy she'd given me clearing my nostrils. In the dark sanctuary, I gazed at the stained-glass window above the altar. I stared at a picture of Jesus holding out a shepherd's rod while the air was still and hushed. Then, at the perfect, mysterious moment, my father would rise, face the choir, signal for them to stand. His arms would lift and sway with the precision of a bird in flight. Though everything was quiet, I could sense the coil of energy in my father, the way he stood on the balls of his feet, ready to spring into music.

The organ would begin, vibrating the pew against my leg. I'd hear a wonderful swell of voices, each blending into a chorus that would lift up to the very realms of heaven. Or so I imagined. I learned early the power of music and words, a power that can move the spirit.

The choir would sing so softly I had to sit forward and strain to hear them. Then they'd grow louder and louder until the sound made me dizzy and I buzzed down to my bones. Each choir member stared at my father as they sang and I watched as he gestured for the cut-offs and the correct expression. After the music stopped, my father and the choir would freeze in place for a silent moment, as if we were all in a magic spell together. Then he would motion for the choir to be seated and everyone breathed again.

Sometimes my father sang a solo in church. He would stand quietly, face the congregation, smile, then nod to the accompanist to begin. The tones came out effortlessly, or so it seemed. I didn't know about voice lessons and proper breathing, though each morning I could hear my father vocalizing, singing "mee-maa-mah-moh-mooo" as he showered and dressed for work.

My father didn't believe in merely singing a song well, especially a church song; he wanted to convey the meaning of the words. To him, church music was an integral part of worship, and he considered it his duty to provide that by interpreting a song so that his entire body became an expression of the music. Nothing got under his skin more than a singer or a choir that was sloppy with language.

Once my father moved from church work to college teaching, he continued to be in the spotlight. At the college, his energy and enthusiasm drew students from several surrounding states as well as from the West Virginia area. His choir soon gained the reputation of being the best in the state; indeed, among the best in that part of the country.

The college concerts each year were different from the church choirs. The Tour Choir was much larger than most church choirs, around fifty students, each voice selected from a number of tryouts. Sometimes, they sang with an orchestra. For these performances, my father wore tails and carried a baton, which he would tap against his music stand before a number. Members of the audience from the town dressed up in satins and silks, while the college students wore jeans and sweaters. Mother and I always arrived early because she didn't drive, so we had to ride with my father. If Becky was visiting, she came with us. Becky didn't enjoy the long wait for the concert to begin, but she loved the music itself.

When the house was full, the lights would dim and the low murmuring of the audience would stop. The choir marched in straight, dignified lines from the wings and took their places on the risers in the center of the stage. The accompanist, dressed in a long flowing black gown, would get situated at the piano. The orchestra tuned up until the first violinist gave the signal. Then my father would sweep onto the stage, his tails flying out behind him. The audience burst into applause as he took his place on the podium. He ignored the clapping, except to give a quick nod. Everyone grew silent, with the possible exception of Becky. When Becky was with us, Mother spent most of the time elbowing her or threatening to spank her if she didn't quit "woo-ing" along with the choir. Sometimes, Becky enthusiastically directed from her seat.

My father raised his arms. In the dim auditorium, he reminded me of an eagle, full of power and grace. With a quick upbeat, the music began. Soon, I was no longer aware of him standing in the front. All I knew was the music, the way it wove around, harmonies and melodies, chords crashing and voices blending, the strings bringing tears to my eyes, the kettle drum beating like blood. Until the very end, you forgot about the short man in tails waving his arms, mouthing words, and shaking his hair like a mane.

But then, when the last note was sung, he turned to face the audience and bowed, a long gentlemanly bow as if he were offering to fling his coat across a puddle so the audience could trample through. People clapped, harder and harder until soon, they were on their feet. "Bravo!" I heard. "Encore! Encore!" Becky would clap her hands, too, very hard and for a long time. Mother had to give her a mint to get her to stop.

At that moment, my father shrugged his shoulders, smiled and gave the audience a little more of what they wanted.

I learned at a young age the difference between the public persona and the private self. When he was onstage, my father always seemed to be smiling, happy. He wasn't always so at home. Though he was by nature optimistic and pleasant, he demanded order, routine.

My father woke me each morning with a song. On sunny spring days when the first hint of warm air swirled through our mountain town, my father would break forth with "Oh What a Beautiful Morning!" in his operatic tenor. My first response was to bury my head more deeply into the covers. But his good humor couldn't be resisted for long. If that rendition didn't get me out of bed, he might try his favorite—"See the fairies dancing on the lawn/Calling 'Wake up, wake up, Sleepyhead.'" I believed in fairies and left bits of food for them in the backyard. I always clapped my hands when Becky and I watched Mary Martin trying to save Tinker Bell on the *Peter Pan TV Special*. My father knew that if he invoked the fairies, I'd have no choice but to get out of bed with a smile on my face.

Sometimes, he would march into my bedroom blaring "Seventy-six trombones led the big parade!" until I couldn't stand it any longer and would roll out of bed, my feet on the cold wooden floor, my eyes bleary. On those mornings, all I wanted was peace and quiet. I loved sleeping, and the older I got, the more I hated getting up. By the time I was a teenager, I dreaded the morning ritual, my father singing and being resolutely cheerful, me starting off the day irritated, but finally cajoled by my father's smile, his silly jokes. Who could have the heart to be angry with such a man? Who could bear to rain on his parade?

I remember one morning when my mother woke me in her no-nonsense voice.

"Anne, you better wake up. Your bus will be here in about fifteen minutes."

"Why didn't Daddy call me?" I said.

"He left already. Honestly, you'd have thought I committed a cardinal sin," my mother said.

"Why?" I said.

"I forgot to make the orange juice. You'd have thought it was the end of the world," she mumbled more to herself than to me. That's the way my father was. He loved for his world to be predictable and under his control. He must have been very frustrated with Becky's condition, an area in which he did not have domination.

Though my father liked order, he also had an adventurous streak. He approached each day like it held a secret just for him. Forward-looking, a positive-thinker, he believed in possibilities. This optimism kept him hopeful about Becky.

I climbed trees because he'd done so as a boy—the higher, the better. I learned to love a challenge, the sense of conquering something new, whether it was traveling to a new camp ground or paddling a canoe across a lake, or making my way across a raging river, rock by slippery rock. When my family hiked to places like Grandfather Mountain in North Carolina, I edged my way to the very last foothold of the precipice and felt the giddiness from standing so close that a strong wind could have pushed me into the waiting trees below. I often imagined jumping, dreamed about the whoosh of cool air as I fell through it, and pictured the soft landing I'd make into those mossy boughs that seemed ready to catch me. Sometimes the urge would become so strong I scared myself and my knees wobbled. I didn't want anyone to know I was afraid, especially my father, so I'd sit down right where I was, my feet hanging over the rough, scratchy ledge. Usually, Becky would be right beside me. I don't know if Becky was a daredevil or whether she was used to following me everywhere. I sometimes felt as if my hand was a flesh-and-blood handcuff, always circling her small wrist. She never showed fear.

On our Big Trip, we camped near Niagara Falls and my father drove us to a park above the falls. I immediately took Becky's hand and crept to the very edge of the riverbank. The water looked like it was boiling. Gray and white, deep charcoal and mud-colored, blue in spots with a green tinge, the colors swirled and careened around and around, whirlpools and choppy waves bubbling up, then whirling out of sight. My foot was on the bank less than twelve inches from the chaos. I knew one slip would land me in that water, and Becky, too. I turned to wave at my parents.

Both of them were watching us, not saying a word. They looked frozen. Then, casually, my father waved for us to come to him. I felt a rush of exhilaration as I pulled Becky along with me to join our folks. I could feel the blood pounding through my body.

"I was too scared to say a word to you girls," my father said in the car. "I thought I might startle you and you'd go into that water. I knew I couldn't save you if you fell." He stopped the car and turned to me in the back seat. "Don't ever do that again, Anne. Don't ever take a chance like that."

❧

Ministers of Music and college professors didn't make much money in those days, so my father was always on the lookout for ways to increase his earnings. He decided to take a mail order course in electronics.

Every so often, a bulky package would arrive at our house. My father would unwrap it, folding the paper into a neat square before he tossed it into the garbage. Then he'd assemble the various parts on his work table in the den. Wires, batteries, flashlights, tubes, and my favorites, resisters, were placed carefully into little boxes. He would read the directions, then put together all the stuff and presto, he'd have a radio. Or an oscilloscope.

Sometimes, he used his electrician skills to fix the tiny electric cars and pieces of race track I got in my stocking at Christmas. I never asked for a race track, but for several years, I'd empty my stocking and mixed in among pieces of candy would be brightly colored racing cars. My dad would get them, too, all wrapped up in ribbons and bows. Together, we'd set up the track and race like mad all Christmas Day.

I always felt my father and I were on the same wavelength. I knew what he was thinking and he knew what I was thinking, too. We laughed at the same jokes when my mother only smirked. We got misty over movies together. Music could move us.

I can remember sitting next to my father on Sunday afternoons, the smell of his Aqua Velva faint but recognizable.

"Can you hear how scary the big, bad wolf sounds? Ah, there's Peter. He'd better watch out," my father explained as we listened to *Peter and the Wolf.* I closed my eyes. He told me the story, identifying each melody representing a different character—grandfather, Peter, the wolf, the duck, the cat and the bird.

"Listen. Can you hear it?" he'd ask.

Chapter Twelve

You must remain in the palace for several days...
—*The Emerald City Soldier to Dorothy*

When my mother screamed, the curdling sound raised the hairs on my arms and brought blood to my cheeks. When she raised her voice, it sounded as if she'd lost complete control. Perhaps she sounded that way because her regular speaking voice was soft, whispery almost. And she bore with Becky's endless questions calmly until, unexpectedly, her frustration would boil over into a murderous yell. Her angry voice seemed to shake even my father, who would jump up immediately to investigate the cause of such caterwauling. Who knew what my mother might do in such a rage?

Besides that, it was embarrassing. Once Mother got going, she didn't care who heard her. When I was fifteen, much of what my parents did embarrassed me. I was keenly aware of how they appeared, or at least how I *thought* they must have appeared. On the rare occasion when my mother yelled at Becky, I was beyond humiliation because every one of our neighbors could hear her. Of course, no one else's mother shouted like that. Or so I thought at the time. But then, no one else's mother had a child like Becky.

From August until January of 1968, while we waited for the Becky's spot at Pressley House to materialize, Mother had responsibility for Becky twenty-four hours a day, seven days a week for almost six solid months. She got no breaks. Why she didn't get a sitter and take some time away, I don't know. Maybe she didn't feel she could afford such a luxury. For the most part, she did her housework and dealt with Becky with patience. But Becky knew how to get my mother going. Becky would badger Mother with questions, a barrage of nonstop verbiage that would challenge the patience of Job.

Since our move to Philippi, Becky and I no longer shared quarters. From my room, I could hear the whole episode, from the first innocent questions through the repetition that could go on indefinitely, as far as Becky was concerned.

"Why do they use shot needles? Do shot needles get the medicine inside? Am I afraid of shots? Is there another way to cure poison ivy?" Becky would start.

"The shot needles get the medicine in faster than other ways. You had such a bad case of poison ivy, the doctors at Amos Cottage wanted to help you as quickly as they could," Mother would answer.

"What are shot needles made of? What kind of medicine makes the poison ivy go away? Is the Becky allergic to poison ivy?" Becky said, her voice rising ever so slightly. I could hear her flipping something, probably Gunbaby. Her feet tapped against the wooden floor of the den in that skip-jump, skip-jump way. I could hear Mother ironing my father's shirts, the soft thud of the iron against the ironing board constant, steady. Becky's habit of referring to herself in the third person had improved since her stay at Amos Cottage, but if she became agitated, the old way would return.

"I don't know what kind of medicine they used. And yes, I'd say you are very allergic to poison ivy," Mother said.

"Why does she get poison ivy? Is it because her mother gets it? Is her mother allergic, too? Is it her mother's fault she gets poison ivy?" Becky would mumble the series of questions over and over, under her breath but loud enough for anyone to hear. Then, after Becky had mulled the question over long enough, she'd ask Mother directly.

"Is it your fault? Does the Becky get poison ivy because you get it?" Becky said.

"Maybe. I guess such things can be inherited," Mother said.

The flipping grew faster as did the sound of Becky's feet hitting the floor. She was starting to get upset. I didn't know whether to finish reading my history assignment or rescue my mother. I decided to stay out of it for the moment.

"Why does poison ivy itch? Why do people get poison ivy? Why doesn't Daddy get it? Did Daddy ever have to get a shot for poison ivy? Did Jet ever get a shot?" By now, Becky's words were coming out in a steady stream, faster and faster like water flowing downhill.

Mother's voice was still soft as she addressed the questions. She never could master the art of appearing to listen and grunt once in a while in response to what Becky was saying. I tried that sometimes, and every little while, Becky would let me get away with it.

"I don't know why people get poison ivy. Mamaw never got it and I guess that's why your daddy doesn't get it so bad. Maybe he inherited her resistance to it. I don't think anyone has ever had a shot for it except for you and me. We're the unlucky ones!" said Mother.

"Why are we unlucky? Is it God's will? Why do some people get poison ivy and others don't? What is lucky? What is lucky?" Becky said.

I decided not to intervene and tried to read about the events leading up to the American Revolution. Becky and Mother's voices blurred into background noise, as usual. I was used to blocking them out sometimes.

"I CAN'T ANSWER ANY MORE QUESTIONS!! YOU ARE DRIVING ME CRAZY!! DON'T ASK ME ANOTHER THING!"

Mother's shout shook me out of my reading and my heart jumped in my chest. Becky was flipping like crazy and her feet tap-danced across the floor. She broke into zany laughter, the roaring-back-your-head kind that made Mother even angrier. The ironing had stopped and Mother's voice seemed to rattle the walls. I slammed my book and ran into the den.

"Come on, Beck. Let's go out on the tramp," I said.

"Take her out of here. Just take her out!" Mother said.

I grabbed Becky's arm and yanked her toward the back door. I felt sorry for her, getting yelled at like that. As usual, I thought it didn't seem fair for anyone to yell at Becky. She couldn't help herself. She was bound to ask questions. But I felt sorry for Mother, too. She took the questions for as long as she could, longer than my father ever did. And then, as if Mother had hit some sort of wall, she simply couldn't tolerate one more question. I understood, but I wished she could find another way to deal with Becky other than yelling. I hated to think the whole world would know about our problems.

Becky and I hurried out to the tramp. Becky was still giggling, cutting her eyes to look up at me in that demonic way she had. When Mother lost her temper, Becky always laughed. Predictably, that made Mother even angrier. I never could figure out why Becky responded that way, especially to Mother, who was so patient ninety-five percent of the time.

"Want me to tell you a story?" I asked her as we bounced up and down.

"Does she want a story? Does she want the Jet to tell a story? Will the Jet tell the Wizard of Oz? Will the Jet tell about Dorothy and the red shoes?" Becky said.

That was her way of saying she wanted me to tell *The Wizard of Oz*. The film had become one of her obsessions since she'd seen the old movie on TV last Thanksgiving while we were visiting her at Amos Cottage. She loved the very end of the story and she would repeat Dorothy's lines over and over—"There's no place like home. There's no place like home."

Finally, the long autumn spun itself out and winter arrived. The seemingly endless reprieve had come to an end for Becky. The excruciating wait for my parents was finally over. Pressley House had the opening they had promised and Becky was scheduled to leave after Christmas.

My long wait had come to an end as well. I was no longer the lonely girl on Saturday nights. I'd caught the attention of an "older man," nineteen-year-old Danny, a boy already out of high school. At first, my parents didn't allow me to date him. The rule was I couldn't go out in cars with boys until I turned sixteen. But he came to the house several times and finally won them over. My curfew was eleven o'clock, sharp.

I was happy about the way things were going after being without a date for so long. My confidence returned and for the first time, I had a real boyfriend. However, Becky was not happy about the results of her long wait. She'd be going away again to another new place and she had learned earlier than most children that there really is "no place like home".

My father was busy corresponding with the necessary people as we readied Becky to move to Pittsburgh after Christmas. He wrote to Dr. Hinman at Amos Cottage about her situation:

> Just a word to bring you up to date on Becky. She finally got into Pressley House. It has taken from August until now for them to place another little girl in the Chicago area and make a bed available for Becky. She did very well during the interim between Amos Cottage and Pressley House, but did not make any advance that was noticeable to us. I felt that there might have been a slight regression in certain areas, but not to an alarming degree... I would greatly appreciate it if you could send her medical records to Pressley House. Unless they have your medical records, they will give her a complete round of boosters, etc which may not be necessary. Knowing her intense dislike of shots, I would like to spare her these if possible in order that she not associate them with Pressley House in the way she did with Amos Cottage.

My father also wrote to the West Virginia Department of Education once more requesting funds to help defray the cost of Becky's schooling. Though I was at the time still oblivious to the fact Becky's presence in a special school continued to take a financial toll on my parents.

> I am both pleased and relieved to finally be able to advise you that Rebecca is now at Pressley House in Pittsburgh. We took her there January 12, which happened to be my birthday. Needless to say, it was the finest birthday gift I ever received. We are so thrilled that she now will be able to not only receive

help for her emotional problem, but also education which she has sorely needed. The cost for keeping her there will be $16.00 per day, totaling $5760.00 per year. We are grateful for what your office was able to do for us last year and we hope and pray that such aid will be forthcoming this year. As I think I told you, we are meeting payments now by borrowing on my insurance...

Eventually, the state would respond to my father's pleas for money but not before he'd borne the brunt of the financial pressure for several months. Then, as now, the wheels of government roll slowly. While my father waited for confirmation of state assistance, he figured out ways to pay for Becky's care himself. I am still amazed that my parents were able to finance such a venture. When you consider my father's salary was around $8,000 per year, the monetary picture becomes more clear. Yet, I was blissfully unaware of any unusual stresses or strains. I ate. I was clothed; sometimes, there was even spending money for movies. Best of all, I got to see the world, at least see more of it than any of my friends.

I didn't go with my parents to take Becky to Pressley House. They thought it would be better if I stayed with Mitzi. But I watched as they packed Becky's clothes and some of her precious toys—Gunbaby, *The Wizard of Oz* book she'd gotten for Christmas, the "Green Ghost" game. The night before she left, I tucked her in. After an hour's worth of stories, we talked.

"I guess you'll be heading to Pittsburgh tomorrow, Beck. I sure will miss you," I said.

"Do I have to go? Do I have to go to Pressley House?" Becky said.

"Yeah. I guess you do. Teach you stuff. And we'll come to see you—it's a lot closer than Amos. I'll write to you, too, and when you learn to write, you can send me a letter," I said.

She grew oddly quiet. I rubbed her back and traced the silly rhyme "Going on a Treasure Hunt" across her small shoulders. Her soft snore alerted me that she'd drifted off to sleep and I slipped out of her bed, tiptoed across the room and closed the door.

Later, alone in my room, I cried. I buried my face in my pillow so no one would hear me. I begged God to help Becky, to cure her so she would never have to leave home again.

That winter, I fell in love; at least, I was in love with *having* a boyfriend. I was not in love with Danny, the person, though I wore his class ring on my finger, making it fit by wrapping angora yarn around and around until the ring grew fat and soft, sometimes itchy. I matched the yarn each day to the outfit I was wearing and flung my fingers about at every opportunity to show off the fact that I had a boyfriend. Not only did I have a boyfriend, but he was older; he had a car and he took me to the movies.

Danny and I dated on Saturday nights only. No matter how early we went out, it was always a struggle to make my curfew. If we went to a movie, we had to drive to Clarksburg or Grafton, each town a half-hour away from Philippi. Often, we were forced to leave a picture before the ending. That gave us about fifteen minutes to park up at Cherry Hill, one of Danny's favorite activities.

One time, his penchant for parking got me into big trouble. We were exactly five minutes late. I figured five minutes wasn't too bad and surely, I wouldn't get into trouble over such minor tardiness. A half-hour would qualify as flagrant rule-breaking which would bring dire results. But five minutes?

Five minutes was nothing to me but to my father, five minutes must have been an eternity.

"Anne, tell Danny to leave immediately. I want to have a word with you," my father said the minute Danny and I walked in our front door. Clad in his pale-blue cotton pajamas and bright red bedroom shoes, my father bounced on his toes, his body tense. Danny mumbled a quick "goodnight" and hurried outside.

"You are five minutes late, young lady," my father said in a serious tone.

"I know—I'm sorry. The movie was so good, we didn't want to leave," I said. My tone was flip—though my words didn't say it, I thought my father was being ridiculous.

"You are grounded for two weeks," my father said. He paused to let his words sink in.

"That's not fair, Daddy! It was just FIVE MINUTES!" I said.

"Late is late. One minute, five minutes, two hours—it's all late," he said. He turned to go to bed, then faced me once again. "Since your mother and I are going on choir tour for one of those weekends, you'll have to go, too."

"I can't believe you're going to make me go on a stupid choir tour!" I said.

"Don't blame me—you're the one who was late," he said as he turned, once more, to amble to his bedroom.

I fumed and stomped to my own room, flung my clothes down to the floor and fumed some more. The few minutes I'd spent with Danny necking on Cherry Hill wasn't worth this! Now, I'd have to explain that I was grounded—it sounded so babyish! I bet Danny didn't even have a curfew!

Making-out was okay, but I was never sure how far to let things go. I was learning to kiss, but Danny often stuck his tongue in my ear which I thought was totally gross. Of course, I never told him I thought his technique made my ear hurt. Sometimes, his hands would start to roam, but I was quick to put a halt to that. He never pushed the issue.

While I was learning about dating decorum, Becky was straining to adjust to life at Pressley House. Her regular routine consisted of morning and afternoon classes conducted on the campus. She walked from her house across the yard to the school with several other girls of various ages. Some of the children attended public school and caught the bus from Pressley House. After she'd spent her mornings learning to read and write, she returned to her house for lunch. Usually, lunch consisted of soups and peanut butter sandwiches. Becky told her house parents she didn't like meat, so bologna was out. After lunch, she returned to the school for ballet classes, which she loved. Her teacher, Mrs. King, allowed students to select the music they used for practice, and Becky was full of ideas about which songs she wanted. After ballet, the children had recess on the nearby playground, where Becky often played on the swings and sliding board. There was a little store on-campus where the children could buy candy bars, Cokes, popsicles, and small toys. Good behavior earned tokens which could be spent at the store. Bad behavior took a certain number of tokens away.

Before supper, Becky had a few chores to do around the house. She had to make her own bed and straighten her room. Certain days, she dusted the furniture and other days, she dried and put away the dishes. Chores were new to Becky. At home, she'd had few. Sometimes, my father would ask Becky to bring him something to drink or pick up her toys. Mother rarely asked either of us for help.

After supper, Becky would bathe and put on her PJs. Her house parents didn't tell any stories, nor did they tuck her into bed. When I asked Becky recently about her experiences at Pressley House, she said, "At night, I would get homesick sometimes. I missed Mom and Dad. Did they think Pressley House would help me? Is that why they sent me away?" As an adult, Becky no longer phrases all of her conversation as questions, though the interrogative is still her favored method of communication.

But I didn't know what Becky was experiencing at Pressley House back then. I only knew that she was gone and our family didn't feel complete; a hole had been torn in us that I tried my best to ignore. If I focused on boyfriends and school and dancing and the Beatles, maybe I could patch that hole just a little.

Danny wasn't handsome and he wasn't a rocket scientist. But I enjoyed the benefits of having a boyfriend. He sent me a huge, heart-shaped box of candy for Valentine's Day, my first gift from a boy. The box, covered with red satin, was edged with white lace. Inside, chocolate treasures clustered together. I shared the candy with my parents, and receiving such a gift made me feel treasured.

But as the winter progressed, things began to go wrong between Danny and me.

First, that song came out, "Young Girl," by Gary Puckett and the Union Gap. Danny seemed to take that song to heart—"Young girl, get out of my mind/My love for you is way out of line/Better run, girl/You're much too young, girl." He kept telling me I was not right for him because of our age difference. But he said he loved me and he didn't want to break up.

I answered the charge of being too young by allowing him to touch my breasts.

Soon after, Danny got drafted. The war in Viet Nam was escalating, so more and more boys were called up. Even in remote Philippi, the war reached its bloody fingers in to grab local sons who weren't lucky enough to be in college. Danny was among those and he was scheduled to ship out in June.

His response to being drafted was strange. He would make a date with me for our usual Saturday night. I would select the right outfit, roll my hair on spongy pink rollers and put on heavy eyeliner and thick globs of mascara with pale pink lipstick. My hair was cut shorter in the back than in the front, a precursor to the "wedge" cut. The sides turned under except for one big spit-curl on each cheek.

For the first of these dates after Danny got drafted, after spending most of the day in preparation, I waited in the living room for him to pick me up at 7:30 PM. At 7:45, I called Mitzi to see if she'd heard of any car wrecks or anything. By 8:00, I was really worried and asked my mother what I should do. She told me to be patient, maybe something unforeseen had happened. By 9:00, I realized he wasn't coming so I called Mitzi to commiserate.

Sometimes, I cried out of anger and frustration because this behavior continued for several weeks. I'd get a call of apology around Wednesday.

I forgave him. Over and over. After all, Jesus said to forgive seventy times seven and I was trying to live the Christian life. If I treated Danny the way I wanted to be treated, he would surely behave properly. I don't know if having a sister like Becky had anything to do with my tolerance of Danny's rude behavior or if I was merely inexperienced. I knew from living with Becky that sometimes, you had to make allowances for people; nobody was perfect. I put up with a lot of bad behavior from Becky because she couldn't help it. Maybe Danny couldn't help it, either.

By the time Easter rolled around, our relationship was stranger still. I had his ring but rarely saw him. He promised to go to church with me Sunday and I ignored rumors about him going out with another girl.

Easter was an exciting time because Becky would be coming home. I'd be going to church with a boy for the first time. Mother decided it was high time I had a real Easter outfit, so we drove to Clarksburg to shop at Kresge's, the big department store right in the middle of the downtown area. We had plans to eat supper at the new Burger King.

That day, I tried on a lot of dresses but finally settled on a bright yellow sheath with large polka dots. Mother insisted I have a spring coat, so we picked a royal blue with slit pockets. She bought me gloves to match my dress and a hat made of netting with small, yellow velvet ribbons on it. Blue patent leather shoes and a matching pocketbook completed my outfit.

I was thrilled with my new sophisticated look. I must have been sophisticated because it was store-bought and everything matched, just like in the fashion magazines. I would look wonderful when I went to church with Danny and my family.

Oh, my family. I had forgotten about them. I wasn't worried about my parents; Danny had already met them. But I hadn't told Danny about Becky. I hadn't even mentioned that I had a sister, much less any details about what sort of sister. Danny and I didn't share such things. I didn't think we should. After all, he was my steady beau. I wore his ring, helped him spend his money, received his gifts, and let him kiss me while we were lying down (yes, things has progressed that far, what with his draft notice). I couldn't let him know anything about me, my life. I certainly couldn't begin to explain Becky.

I hate to admit it, but Danny was nothing more to me than an accessory, much like my new hat and gloves. I had no feelings for him, except the pride I felt when I showed off my ring to my pals at school. Although I understood that "All You Need Is Love," I had not idea what love was. I loved Becky and my parents. But Danny? Well, Danny was sort of a figment of my imagination. But I didn't want the figment to find out anything about my real life.

I decided for just this once, I'd leave Becky completely out of my conversation. Danny and I wouldn't be sitting in the pew with my family, and he was taking me to lunch at Mellie's Restaurant afterward. We would miss Becky altogether.

On Good Friday, the whole family drove to Pittsburgh to pick up Becky. I was excited about seeing Pressley House and Pittsburgh, a big city. After Expo, I'd fallen in love with big cities. Everything seemed possible in such places. The skyscrapers, the intricate streets, the people walking in a hurry—I loved all the sights and sounds. And, even though Pittsburgh was ugly and dirty-looking back then, visiting a new place invigorated me.

Pressley House looked very different from Amos Cottage. There were no water-babies for one thing. And the children lived in normal-looking brick houses at the end of a court. When we got there, Becky met us at the door dressed in a plaid dress and ill-fitting sweater. She hugged Mother, then Dad, and me last. Her hair looked as if it had been chopped with a blunt knife but other than that, she seemed okay. We walked to her room and found two beds made up neatly. Her house parent told us Becky had made the bed herself. I was impressed. Becky's roommate, Roberta, wasn't there. I was disappointed I didn't get to meet her, but both Becky and I were happy to make our getaway from Pressley House as soon as we could.

My father grabbed Becky's suitcase and we left quickly. I guess Becky and I weren't the only ones ready to hit the road. The ride home took a couple of hours with my father driving a little over the speed limit. We were in a hurry to get Becky home with us, to her own room, her own things, and her own people.

Back at home, snuggled in my bed, Becky and I talked late into the night. For the first time in her life, she didn't make all of her comments in question form. I found myself in what was almost a real conversation.

"So Beck, what's it like at Pressley House? You said your roommate has red hair, right?" I said as I lay next to her.

"Yes," she answered in a flat voice.

"Do you like her?" I said.

"She's okay. Why does she hit me? Why does she crawl into my bed sometimes? Can my house parents keep her away from me?" Becky said.

"If she's bothering you, you should tell them. Are they nice?" I'd met her house parents, a middle-aged black couple. The house mother was very fat and the house father was tall and slender. Neither said much when we picked Becky up. I was careful to be polite for lots of reasons. I knew if we weren't nice to them, they might take it out on Becky after we'd gone. Also, though there were no black people at the high school in Philippi except for Charlie and Louie, I'd watched the civil rights marches and sit-ins on TV. I'd heard Martin Luther King and believed in his words. I remember shocking my history teacher by saying I believed it was perfectly fine for people of different races to marry and rear families. I'd been the only one in class who thought so.

During many suppers, while Walter Cronkite droned in the background, my family discussed the civil rights movement. My father, though raised in the South, had served in WWII, that great leveling field. That experience, along with his ideals wouldn't allow him to be much of a racist. He was considered quite liberal by some members of our extended family, but his arguments made perfect sense to me. My own ideas about justice told me in no uncertain terms segregation was not fair. A simplistic view, yes, but I honestly didn't see any differences between the races. I knew, perhaps more than most kids my age, judging someone on the basis of appearance or skin color or bizarre behavior was wrong.

I still remember seeing the movie *A Patch of Blue* starring Sidney Poitier. In the story, a blind girl (played by Sandy Dennis) falls in love with a man she's met in the park. Both are happy until the girl's mother, played with a vengeance by Shelley Winters, realizes her daughter's new friend is a black man. As I sat in the darkened theater and watched the cruelty of that mother, I began to sob uncontrollably. My friends, Paula and Mitzi, tried to shut me up but I was quickly becoming hysterical. I recall shouting at the movie screen, screaming for the lovers to be left alone. By the end of the film, I was shaking all over and my eyes had smeared black liner over my cheeks. Though my behavior was bizarre, I didn't lose any friends over it. But I wonder what they must have thought. I wonder if they thought I was crazy just like my sister.

When I think back on that event, I might have seemed unbalanced. I was near hysteria over a movie, talking to the screen, unconcerned that I was in a public place surrounded by people who *weren't* shouting and crying. I had more in common with Becky at that moment than with the people around me.

Though I would never have admitted it then, I was disturbed by Becky's house parents. They were different and made Becky's foray into the world seem more dangerous somehow. The fact that Becky was living with folks of a different race emphasized one more way in which Becky's experience was different from my own.

"Does it make you want to eat eggs if they smear them on your face? What good does smearing the eggs do? Why did my house father smear the eggs?" Becky mumbled to herself.

"What are you talking about? Smearing eggs on whose face?" I said.

"My face!" She responded.

"Who did? Why? Why would anyone do that?" I said.

"Was it because I didn't want to eat my breakfast? Was it because I don't like eggs?" Becky said as she flipped her hands into the air above us. Her motions were speeding up and I knew she was becoming agitated.

"Your house father smeared eggs on your face? Because you didn't like them? How bad did he smear them? Just a little bit?" I asked, my own temper starting to rise.

"No. Did he rub them all over my whole face? Did he say if I wouldn't eat them, I could wear them," Becky said. A loud chortle erupted from her throat, that low cackle that slipped out at the strangest times.

"He shouldn't have done that! I'm telling Mom and Dad in the morning. Let's go to sleep now, okay?"

"Yes," Becky said, again her voice a monotone. "Is it wrong to miss you, Jet? I miss my family. Is it because of my mental disorder? Does that cause it?"

"No. It's not wrong. We miss you, too. I miss you a lot," I said.

I let Becky stay in my bed that night, even though she slept like a wild child, kicking and wiggling in the darkness, fighting with the covers and grinding her teeth in her sleep. I worried about her and wondered what else was going on that my parents and I might never discover.

Chapter Thirteen

Brains do not make one happy and happiness is
the best thing in the world.

—*The Tin Woodman*

That Easter Sunday, I skipped Sunday school so Mom, Dad, and Becky would be out of the house when Danny arrived. He wouldn't see Becky because he had to spend the afternoon visiting his grandparents. He had only six weeks to ready himself for Viet Nam. I intended for him to leave the country with no knowledge about my family; he would have nothing from me except passionate kisses.

Earlier that morning, Becky and I had checked our Easter baskets to see what the Easter Bunny had brought us. Jelly beans, marshmallow chicks covered with yellow sugar, a chocolate rabbit with a hot-pink hat, and chocolate marshmallow eggs lay on top of the crinkly plastic grass that nestled in the pink wicker baskets. Becky picked out the black jelly beans from both our stashes of candy, her favorites both in color and flavor. She flipped the chocolate bunny and the cellophane wrapper made a slightly tinny sound. I went for the chocolate marshmallow eggs first and had already stuffed two in my mouth when my parents motioned for me and Becky to follow them.

"I wonder what's on the patio," my mother said as she led the way out the kitchen door. My father followed her and the air was jumpy between them.

When I got to the back door, I saw a cage. Inside was a tiny white bunny with floppy ears and pink eyes. His whiskers twitched as we slowly approached him.

"Look, Becky! The Easter Bunny left you a baby rabbit," my father said.

Becky didn't seem to care much about the new rabbit. She was too busy flipping a plastic egg and eating black jelly beans. Her tongue was dark gray and some of the dark color had stuck to her teeth. She ignored the bunny altogether.

I could see that my parents were disappointed with Becky's reaction.

"Hey Beck, check it out!" I said, trying to get Becky to pay more attention to the rabbit. She gave the animal a quick glance, then resumed her flipping.

"Would you like to hold the little bunny?" my mother said.

"Yes," Becky replied, her voice without inflection.

My father opened the mesh wire door and reached in to grab the rabbit.

"Easy there, little fellow," my father whispered as he petted the rabbit's ears. "Here, Becky. Pet your bunny."

Becky was hopping and flipping in place and she jump-skipped over to him. She touched the rabbit with two stiff fingers, then pulled away quickly.

"Don't you like the rabbit, Beck? If you don't like him, you can give him to me," I said. I didn't want to think of that poor rabbit belonging to Becky. I knew Mother would feed and water him, but I also knew he'd get no attention from Becky. I, on the other hand, would have been very happy to have my own rabbit. I would have held it and cuddled it until it was tame and gentle. I knew I was too old for such Easter gifts. After all, I'd gotten the Easter clothes, but I couldn't help being envious of Becky and her new pet.

"What are you going to name him?" my father said.

Becky flipped the plastic egg faster and harder. She now hopped in circles around Mother, like a hummingbird flits around a feeder.

"You should name him something cool. Got any ideas?" I said.

"How about Blackie?" Becky said, still flipping the egg, not even looking at the rabbit.

"But he's white," I said as I took the rabbit from my father's arms and held him. "Think of something else." The bunny trembled at first, but I held him close to my chest and soon, he was nudging me, exploring.

"Easter Bunny? Could she call him Easter Bunny?" Becky said.

"I've got it! Let's name him Pumpernickel!" I shouted. "It's perfect!"

"Becky should pick out the name herself," my mother said.

"Okay. How about Pumpernickel, Beck? You like that?" I said. I'd learned early on Becky would go along with me on most everything, as long as it didn't have to do with eating meat or crossing the street or loud noises.

"Yes."

"See—she likes Pumpernickel. Pumpernickel it is!" I moved closer to Becky so she could pet the fuzzy ears once more. I was pleased with the name—it sounded like something the Beatles would use in a song. Cool.

Becky patted Pumpernickel clumsily a couple more times, then she was back to the candy in her basket. I held the bunny for a long time before I got ready for church. I wanted my parents to know at least someone appreciated their gift. Though I was a teenager, I still liked the idea of being their "good girl." I wanted them to notice I was kind to Becky and others. I wanted to make my parents proud.

By four o'clock that afternoon, Danny had returned to his house, Becky was bouncing on the trampoline, my father was asleep in the living room while Beethoven's Fifth played in the background and my mother was reading the Sunday paper in the den. I sat on my bed, looking at my Easter gifts from Danny. First, he'd handed me an enormous chocolate egg, decorated with pastel pink, purple, and yellow icing. Then, he gave me a small gold watch that hung on a golden chain. The watch cover had flowers painted on it and you slid it over to one side to see the time. That watch was the most beautiful piece of jewelry I owned. I was thrilled to read the words 'genuine gold-tone' on the back side in tiny print. That morning, I had immediately asked Danny to fasten the necklace around my neck, and he did so with a big smile on his face.

As I held the watch between my fingers, his ring wrapped in bright yellow angora to match my Easter dress, I dreamed about our future. I didn't think about Danny going off to fight in Viet Nam. Somehow, the fact of his going to look death in the face hadn't touched me. He'd write to me and I'd write back. Our love would last through the war and who knew? Maybe someday I'd be Mrs. Danny...

In the middle of my daydream, I heard a commotion outside.

"What the heck you doing?" a kid's voice yelled.

"You're gonna hurt it! Don't do that!" another voice screamed.

I jumped up from my bed and ran to the back door. Becky was on the patio with Pumpernickel. She'd gotten him out of the cage and was flipping him the way she did her toys. She tossed him up, flung her fingers at him a couple of times, then caught him as he fell. She grabbed him by the back leg, pulled him up again, then started the whole process again.

"Don't Becky! Don't flip him!" I screamed as I flung open the screen door to rescue Pumpernickel.

I don't know if my scream startled her and broke her rhythm or if she just lost her concentration, but for some reason, she didn't catch him this time. Pumpernickel fell to the concrete with a thudding sound. He didn't move.

"Mom! Dad! Come quick! I think Becky's killed Pumpernickel!" I yelled. The small crowd of children became very quiet, but no one moved. My parents came out in a rush. My father jumped down from the porch and checked the rabbit. He carefully cradled Pumpernickel in his hands.

"He's gone. His neck's broken," my father said. "You kids go on home now. Go on home."

My mother took Becky into the house while my father buried Pumpernickel. I could hear my mother's soft voice.

"You must be easy with little animals, be gentle like this. I know you didn't mean to hurt the bunny. But next time, try to touch it ever so gently," Mother cooed to Becky.

I was too furious to speak to Becky. I couldn't believe she'd done it—murdered an innocent rabbit. I stomped to my room, threw myself on the bed, and sobbed. I cried for the rabbit; I cried for Becky; I cried for my parents; most of all, I cried for myself. Why, oh why, couldn't my sister have been normal? What kind of a kid kills a rabbit? Deep down, I knew Becky didn't *mean* to kill Pumpernickel. I knew her flipping was her way of discovering new things. She flipped everything. But even though she hadn't intended to kill Pumpernickel, she remained unaffected by his death. She hadn't even cried or shown a flicker of feeling. She hadn't loved the rabbit and that was just weird—a kid her age not caring for a new pet. I couldn't figure it out. I couldn't figure out why she was the way she was and why God didn't fix her. He could have if He'd wanted to—what was stopping Him?

❧

As the end of the school year drew near, Danny's departure for the army seemed anticlimactic. The night before he was to leave, we made out for what seemed like hours. I allowed him to move his hands underneath my shirt for the first time. It was my going-away present to him, but when I'd returned to my room that night, guilt hit me right in the gut. In the late 60s, though the sexual revolution was happening among grownups in places like Los Angeles and New York City, in small towns like Philippi, virtue was expected, especially the chastity of middle-class girls. There were no such expectations for the boys. This double standard was the first of many injustices I saw around me that would eventually change my life. Maybe seeing the unfair set of circumstances in my own family predisposed me to be sensitive to such things, but I, like Becky, hated inequity. She couldn't stand to see any of the children at Pressley House punished, unless the offense was violence against another child. For minor infractions, Becky counseled mercy. I, too, hated seeing a bias, especially society's bias toward males as I understood it in the dating arena. In spite of the rules, I was curious about sex. But it also scared me witless.

I knew Danny could be killed in Viet Nam. I'd watched the news and attended a couple of funerals for older boys in our community. I hated the war, didn't believe in it, though later my distaste would turn to active protest. Though Danny had shipped out, not many weeks passed before I was hanging out with Chris and Mitzi, going to ball games and dances, continuing to be a typical teen to any casual eye. Danny and I exchanged a few letters; but soon, I had moved on to other infatuations. Danny had become a memory as I realized he'd never been right for me. If I couldn't share my true self with a boy, no amount of dating could replace such intimacy. It was an intimacy I didn't believe possible with any boy I knew. How could I share the pain I couldn't even put into words? How could I ever trust anyone enough to let him into my heart, into the chamber where Becky lived?

As spring moved into summer, I would turn sixteen; Becky would be ten. Though distance separated us, I felt bound to her by invisible strands of worry and love; I wondered what the summer would bring.

Chapter Fourteen

There's no place like home.
—*Dorothy*

What I remember most about the summer of 1968 was the way my mother seemed to have changed. Almost overnight, she had gained a lot of weight and she didn't keep house the way I thought she should. She had a listless quality about her, an attitude I didn't understand. At the time, I didn't connect Mother's mood with the fact that Becky was spending the summer at Pressley House, but looking back, I realize my mother was in a sort of mourning, grieving over her child, saddened by thoughts of Becky alone and misunderstood by everyone in faraway Pittsburgh. My mother must have had the same feelings I did—sorrow, anger, frustration—except she was having these feelings with the intensity and depth only a mother can reach. I know that now.

But that summer, all I knew was the sound of Mother's voice as it filtered through the wooden floor to my bedroom, dipping and curving about in the air, much like the road that led to our house at the top of College Hill, the asphalt hugging the mountain in that same haphazard way. I couldn't understand any of the words, but I recognized the tunes; hymns, mostly—"In the Garden," "The Old Rugged Cross."

Her singing jarred me, tipped me over to the edge of my bed. I hated how her thin trill imitated the women who performed solos at church. I couldn't tolerate the way Mother's sound lingered in my brain, the echo of her whiny voice following me to the pool with my friends or out onto the trampoline. I especially detested the way she woke me up on Sundays. I'd hear her shift songs on her way up the stairs, going from "Blessed assurance, Jesus is mine" to Handel's *Messiah*, a wispy rendition of "Arise, shine, for thy light is come." She was pleased with her wit, but after what seemed like a thousand mornings, the joke got old.

That summer, everything became a song with her; at least, that's how it seemed to me. I don't remember exactly when the singing started, maybe when Becky went away the first time or maybe before that. Most of the time, Mother stuck to the familiar hymns. But every once in a while, she'd launch into a Beatle's song—"I Want To Hold Your Hand" or "She Loves You." She'd increase the volume on the "yeah, yeah, yeah" part until it was all I could do to keep from telling her to shut the hell up. I'd never actually say those words to my mother, but I could think them with impunity; and each time I thought such a thing, I got a tiny thrill.

It seemed forever since my mother actually spoke to me, except to remind me to clean my room or tell me to get off the phone. I could keep track of her easily by listening for her song, and could gauge the exact moment she'd be at my door to see whether I'd hung up or not. The system worked well, allowing me plenty of extra moments yakking with Mitzi or Chris.

When I came downstairs for a snack, I could see Mother bending over the table in the living room with Pledge in one hand, my old underwear in the other, singing "This is my story, this is my song/Praising my Savior, all the day long." At that point, I was so relieved to see her cleaning instead of spending the whole day watching her soaps that I didn't mind the hymns so much. Over and over she'd sing, a crazy litany, her weak soprano scraping along, marking each hour of the day.

I figured mother's sudden love affair with notes and measures would pass like some exotic flu bug, the kind that hits you hard for the first couple of days, but by the end of the week, you're back to normal. But the singing didn't go away. Rather, it grew; and by most evenings, my mother's voice sounded hoarse and ragged. I spent as much time away from home as I could.

I explored the woods behind our house, discovering things I'd never noticed before: the tiny bluets, each bloom smaller than my fingernail, yet perfect, the blue darkening at the edges, a yellow star at the center of each blossom; the mountain laurel with heavy white and purple buds hanging against dark waxy leaves, making shadowy habitats for rabbits and ground squirrels. I watched the mountains turn from new April green to the deep green of July.

I was happy to skip along the trails made by the neighborhood kids and watch the sun streak through the trees, splotches of light and dark that fit together tight as puzzle pieces. I liked puzzles. They made sense to me. Sometimes, puzzles were the only thing that did make any kind of sense, and I felt better after having put together a jigsaw alone in my room, like I'd somehow improved the world by taking the jagged parts and linking them to create a beautiful picture.

But Mother's singing often disturbed the peace I'd created for myself, irritating me the way a mosquito bite will itch its way under your skin and go all red and puffy. I still recall how my muscles would tense up each time I heard her. Even now, when I hear "All You Need Is Love" on the Golden Oldies station, I think back to what it was like then, growing up with my mother's voice lifted in song and my little sister torn away from us.

Sometimes, just to remind myself what Becky looked like, I'd get out the tattered box of pictures my mother kept in the hall closet. Though we visited Becky at least once a month over the summer, during the in-between times, I'd lose the exactness of her features and needed to see her again, at least photos of her.

In my baby pictures, I had sprigs of brown, straight hair poking out in odd directions. My cheeks were fat and round, very shiny because the photographer rubbed them with Vaseline, according to my mother. The kids at school used to call me "chipmunk" because my cheeks looked stuffed full of something. I hated the way they bulged out, but I consoled myself with the thought that I made mostly As on my report card.

But Becky looked like an angel in her snapshots. Her hair was thick and rich-looking. Her clear blue eyes and finely drawn features attracted the viewer immediately. She was dainty-looking where I was big and gangly.

My one consolation was that I was smart, normal. However, in the looks department, there was no contest. Becky was clearly the beauty. I'd rather have had Becky's delicate face and blond hair, but no one thought to ask me.

Maybe she paid a price for her good looks. Maybe my brain cost me, too. We both gained something, lost something. I didn't know who was keeping tabs, but balancing things out seemed important to somebody.

Most days, I'd spend the mornings at home, reading the fairy tales of Hans Christian Anderson or rifling through my parents' books to find something of interest, like *The Concubine*, by Norah Lofts. After lunch, I might go to the pool with Mitzi or Chris. Sometimes, I'd go to the "climbing tree" at the end of the college president's huge front yard. Someone had built a tree house in the oak at the farthest edge of the yard, and when you scrambled up to the five or six planks wedged across the limbs, the view was magnificent. You could see the Tygart River meandering through the hills and the covered bridge that crossed it. Philippi never looked as beautiful up close as it did from the mountain. All the coal dust that had settled on the old buildings wasn't visible from on high.

The tree house provided many hours of time alone as well as time for talking with the other Faculty Row teens, secret talk. Sometimes, Dusty met me there when she wasn't with her steady boyfriend. Jo Clair and her brother, Jimmy, my next-door neighbors, were frequent tree house occupants, as was Mike, another "faculty brat" who lived across the street. All were slightly younger, but that didn't matter. We discovered friendship in the branches of that old oak, and I found in Jo Clair a kindred spirit. Her long blond hair was enviable and she was thin, with blue eyes edged by blond, curly lashes. Her brother Jimmy had those same intense eyes. Mike, the youngest, had dark features and a sharp mind that made him seem as old as the rest of us. Any of these fellow tree-dwellers was a welcome respite from the boredom that summer sometimes brought.

When I came in from my afternoon adventures, I'd find Mother at the kitchen table, stirring supper or writing a letter to Becky. Becky was learning to read, and when she was at home, Mother worked with her diligently on recognizing words. When Becky was away, Mother still tried to encourage her by writing to her with carefully printed sentences that Becky might read herself.

One afternoon, I'd been given a chore—clean my room before I left the house again. Though I protested with as much vehemence as I dared, I really didn't mind the assignment. I enjoyed going through my stuff.

As I unloaded the middle bookshelf, I rediscovered a doll I'd kept from long ago. My Tiny Tears. If you fed her a bottle of water, she would either cry "real" tears or wet her diaper. I loved that doll. Sitting in my room, holding Tiny Tears in my arms, I recalled the time I'd raced home from school when I was in fourth grade to catch a special rerun of *Bonanza* on TV, the episode where Hoss finds the Leprechauns. I'd missed it on Sunday night. *Bonanza* was on TV too late for me and, even though I pleaded and begged, my parents had sent me to bed. But the story had been so popular, the local station had decided to run it again at a time when kids could see it.

I took the stairs two at a time so I could change into my play clothes and plop in front of the old black and white set in Mother's bedroom. When I opened the door to my room, I couldn't believe what I saw. Scattered over the floor were doll parts. Arms, legs, heads, torsos. Standing in the middle of the mess was Becky, sort of jumping in place and flipping the head of my bride doll. The bride doll's golden hair was crumpled in Becky's hand while Becky flung her small fingers against Bridey's face. Bridey's eyes blinked open, then snapped shut with each new blow.

"Mom!! Mom!! I'm going to KILL Becky!!" My voice tore from my throat and I stepped quickly over the mutilated toys to save my Bridey, or what was left of her. I screamed again at Becky but she didn't do anything. She just stood there and looked at me, that wacky grin starting at the corners of her mouth.

"What's the matter?" Mother said as she hurried up the steps. When she reached the doorway, I noticed her hands were covered with flour and she was wiping them on her apron.

"Oh my God." Mother's face turned white and for a minute, she didn't say a word. Her eyes reminded me of caged birds, wild and looking for a way out. Then she put her arms around me and whispered.

"She didn't mean to... she just doesn't know any better." She stooped over to retrieve one of Bridey's legs and picked up her torso where the other leg was poking out of her wedding dress. "Your daddy can fix all these dolls." Mother patted my back for a long time. Finally, she turned to me, her hand still on my shoulder and said, "Don't be mad at her." She left the two of us there and I heard her humming softly as she went back to the kitchen.

"Stay with Becky. Don't leave her by herself," she called from the stairs.

I stared at Becky, the fury still in me. She looked down at her hands and started that crazy snicker. When Becky laughed that zany laugh of hers, my grandmother used to say she was "full of the devil." At that moment, I thought she was, indeed. I was ready to push her out of my room. But then, before I could give her a shove, she started talking to herself in that strange melodic way she had, referring to herself in the third person once again.

"Is her sister mad at her? Does her sister want to kill her? The Jet is angry... Why is her sister angry?" Over and over she muttered the phrases, as if she were trying to figure out everything in the world, as if nothing made sense to her. As she mulled things over, I felt my heart soften, go to a sort of mush.

"It's okay, Beck. I'm not mad. I'm not." I pulled her to me and she stood stiff while I hugged her.

Soon after the doll incident, I decided to give Becky what was left of my old dolls, all except for the Barbie and Tiny Tears. Within a day, each doll had been decapitated and had lost all its limbs.

Remembering those lost dolls, I cradled Tiny Tears in my arms for a few minutes, then swaddled her in a blanket the way my mother had taught me. I thought about Becky and what she might be doing at Pressley House. I wondered if her house parents had smeared eggs on her face again. Or if they'd done something even worse. I so desperately wanted Becky to be like other little kids. I kept that picture of her in my mind, of us growing up together, me giving her advice about boys, discussing our weird parents, laughing in our room after we'd been told to settle down and go to sleep. Part of me knew that life was impossible, but another part believed in miracles.

I'd taken to praying for Becky for so long, always with the hope of an instant cure. I don't mean just occasional prayer spoken off the top of your head. I mean "deliberate petition." I'd learned about tenacity in Sunday School when the teacher told us about the widow who kept bugging a certain judge for justice until he finally gave in, just so the widow would shut up. That's the kind of praying I'd done for Becky.

I begged God until my throat hurt and my tears made wet spots on my pillow. My ears clogged with those tears and my hair was damp from them. Still, I prayed. I imagined my prayers rising up to heaven, a silver stream of words washing over the ears of all the angels, then trickling into the very Ear of God. My prayers would sound like the sweetest music and His Ear would lap them up. He wouldn't refuse me—the melody of my prayer was too perfect for that.

I didn't let up because Becky's life depended on it. Most nights, I prayed myself to sleep.

But that was when I had had an unshakable faith in God. At sixteen, doubts were beginning to creep in. Every evening on the news and every morning in the paper, pictures of dead soldiers and burning villages met my eyes. I'd heard George Wallace spew his hatred, and I burned with shame that I, too, was white. I'd been inspired by Dr. King's message of brotherhood. But then, I'd watched Dr. King's funeral on television, much as I had watched President Kennedy's a few years earlier. War raged, annihilation threatened, people hated. I was sixteen. It was hard to keep the faith.

And, though I'd prayed faithfully and with confidence, not much about Becky had changed. She still flipped her doll heads; she still ground her teeth and chattered to herself in her special way. But maybe Pressley House would be the answer, just like my father had said.

Later that summer, Dad, Mother, and I packed up the camper to visit Becky for the weekend. I didn't know what to expect. Though we'd picked her up before and I'd seen her room, we'd never spent any time in Pittsburgh. And, since January, Becky had only been home once, at Easter. My father had explained that no matter how hard it was for us to leave Becky at Pressley House, no matter how much we missed her, we had to give the group home a try, for Becky's sake. At first, the doctors didn't allow much visiting. They thought Becky would never adjust to Pressley House if she went home all the time. My father was very careful to do just as they prescribed. And, he explained, when you really love someone, you do what you think is best for that person, not what feels best for yourself.

I kept wondering what it would be like to leave home, to be without my family. The thought of going away kept changing for me. Some days, I couldn't wait to go off to college in a big town with lots of things to do and people to meet. Other days, the idea of leaving my parents would make me feel so lonely that tears welled up in my eyes. On those days, I imagined I'd even miss my mother's singing.

I didn't dare try to put myself in Becky's shoes.

On the morning of that first real visit to Pittsburgh, Mother woke me early. As usual, she sang, but on this special day, she veered from her routine and wandered into new territory—Negro spirituals.

"Are you ready for the kingdom? Oh, yeah."

She stuck her round face into my room, her mouth pretty with bright lipstick. She snapped her fingers in rhythm to the gospel song.

"I'm getting up. Give me time." My anger seeped out everywhere and my voice clenched up its fist. That year, I sometimes had a hard time controlling it.

"Do you have to sing?" I mumbled this last part, afraid I'd hurt her feelings by mentioning the weird habit. Usually, I gave no thought to my mother's feelings, but I didn't want to spoil the weekend. I wanted everything to be perfect for Becky.

Once Mother left me to myself, I slipped on the black skirt I'd chosen with a matching striped blouse. Though the skirt was longer than I liked, I wore it anyway because black was Becky's favorite color. Besides, Becky wouldn't care whether my skirt was the fashionable length or not. All she cared about was seeing me, seeing the whole family.

I looked forward to spending the night in the trailer again. My father had found a state park right outside of Pittsburgh, and I imagined myself in the top bunk with Becky below, just the way it had been last summer on our big trip. Each night, I planned to tell Becky her favorite stories—the Wizard of Oz with nothing but flying monkeys and evil witches, Snow Black and the Seven Elves. My words would weave us together somehow and we'd laugh at my lunacy, my offbeat yarn-spinning. Becky still liked scary ghost stories and anything about dentists. With each new saga, I'd try to outdo myself and I'd thought all week about new stories for Becky. I'd include the very spooky "Who's Got My Talee Toe" and I'd been working on one about dental hygiene, "Plaque, Floss and the Out-Of-Control Hygienist." Becky was just entering what she called her "dental fascination" phase and found great pleasure in contemplating oral care.

While we packed the car with the big black camping box my father had made from plywood to store our cooking utensils and cutlery, my parents both acted as if we were going to an amusement park or some other wonderful adventure. We *were* planning to visit Kennywood Park where there was, supposedly, a huge rollercoaster. Becky loved those, though you might have thought she'd have been afraid to ride one. She'd scream and scream, leading a stranger to believe Becky hated the whole experience. But the minute we hopped off, she wanted to get right back in line for another turn. I couldn't wait to try the one at Kennywood.

My father told me there was a great zoo in Pittsburgh and promised a trip there later in the summer. When we'd gone to the French Creek Animal Farm in West Virginia, Becky really loved the petting zoo. I wasn't as fond of it as Becky seemed to be. I hated to see the birds caged, hawks and eagles with their wings clipped, forced to perch on the fake limbs of an artificial tree. Their feathers were scraggly and their great golden eyes seemed sad. Something about the cages reminded me of Becky and the children at Pressley House and Amos, children forced into routine and regimentation.

The last time Becky had gone to the French Creek Animal Farm, she followed a billy goat around forever, flipping behind it and pulling its tail down every chance she got. She wanted to cover its butt. She liked a sense of order, everything in its place. I knew the Pittsburgh Zoo would be a lot bigger and better than French Creek, and I couldn't wait to see what Becky might do when she saw exotic animals like elephants and lions.

Though we planned these outings for the whole family, I knew the activities were mostly for Becky. My father said seeing different things would stimulate her mind and help her to learn. I was along for the ride.

I couldn't understand why my parents were in such jovial spirits. I guess they'd missed Becky and were excited by the thought of hugging her and being with her. I felt that way, too, but for me, the trip also meant a knot in my stomach and tears threatening to erupt at odd moments. My throat stayed tight and achy. And, as always, there was the dread of saying goodbye to Becky once more.

Becky was waiting at the door when we arrived, her hair choppier than I'd recalled. Her face was red and roughened by the sun, her shirttail out on one side and the plaid skirt she wore hiked up in the back. She'd never liked skirts, but I guess she, too, wanted to dress up for the occasion. Or maybe they made her.

A fat woman dressed in a white uniform stood guard beside Becky, one large black hand on Becky's shoulder. I suppose the woman was one of Becky's house parents, but I'd seen her so briefly during our last visit, I couldn't be certain. Becky started toward us the minute she saw us walking in from the parking lot, but I saw the hand restrain her. When we reached the door, the woman in white could no longer hold Becky and she rushed to us, throwing her arms around my mother. Mother held her, the longest hug I'd ever seen. Then Becky embraced Dad and, finally, me.

The woman led us to Becky's room which she still shared with Roberta. Becky's weekend bag was packed. Gunbaby poked out from the top of the zipper. He was still all of a piece and looked as much like Daniel Boone as ever with his molded rifle and coonskin hat. Becky had flipped the brown paint off of his breeches and now he was flesh-colored all over; even his gun was shiny pink.

Other kids gathered at Becky's doorway. They watched us, their eyes wild and strange, as we picked up the suitcase and started to leave.

"Where going? Where?" said one little boy with bright orange hair. I watched, stared, even though I knew it wasn't polite, as his head jerked to one side over and over. The big girl behind him sucked her thumb and drool oozed down her chin. Becky introduced this girl as her roommate, Roberta. Roberta didn't say a word; she just kept her thumb in her mouth.

"Home? Becky going home?" said a black girl who looked about sixteen. My age. Her hair was matted into short pigtails and she wore a striped shirt with plaid slacks. I cringed at the combination.

Suddenly, I wanted out of there. The air was too hot, too thick with people. Becky seemed to disappear, blending into this strange collection of mutants. It was hard to tell her from the others. I didn't want her to be a part of this gang of weirdos. I wanted her to be with Mother, Dad, and me. I pushed through the little cluster and Becky followed.

She ignored their cries of goodbye and didn't turn back to give anyone a wave. She didn't even notice when the boy with the nodding head grabbed my hand. She hurried for the front door, full speed ahead. My hand was gooey from where the redhead held onto me, gripping me tight until the nurse made him let go. I brushed my sticky fingers against the new skirt and ran with Becky to the car.

That night, we ate supper at the Golden Arches. Mother worried about what Becky might find to eat there because she still refused to eat most things with meat in them. Her eating habits had been peculiar for a long time and we were all surprised when she said she wanted French fries and a milkshake.

"I didn't know you liked French fries, honey. That's great. I'm glad you're trying new things," Mother said as she smiled at Becky. Dad tussled Becky's hair with his big palm. She and I dipped our fries in ketchup and slurped our chocolate shakes. I watched as hope bloomed across Mother's features while Becky gobbled up real food. I, too, felt hopeful. Maybe my prayers were being answered after all.

"What do you do at the group home, Beck?" I wanted to know if she was getting better or if it was just my imagination.

"Does her sister want to know what she does? Ballet? Does she take ballet?" Becky answered me like usual, but I knew what she meant.

"Ballet, huh. Wow! That's cool. I've always wanted to dance. Can you show me a dance?" I didn't mean for her to demonstrate in the restaurant. That she might do so hadn't even occurred to me. But before we could stop her, she was pirouetting around the place and every eye was on her. She didn't care. On and on she spun, bumping into people, spilling drinks, collecting stares until Dad caught her by the elbow and pulled her back to our table.

Mother tried to settle her down and Becky began to cry. The fries I'd eaten sank like cement in my stomach.

The weekend passed quickly and soon the time came to say our goodbyes. I had learned that the time always came.

Dad swung into the lot in front of Becky's building and parked in the visitor slot. Seeing that word "Visitor" printed in white on the curb made me feel funny, like we weren't a real family. My lunch sloshed around in my gut. Becky begged me for another story as Dad turned off the engine.

"We don't have time for any more stories, honey. Gotta get on the road. I want to get us home before dark," Dad said. His thin brown hair fell across his face when he turned to talk to us in the back seat. He pushed the strand away with his hand and I noticed his skin was grayish, the color of dust balls under my bed. Mother was quiet.

"Just one more. Pleeeease? I can make it short," I said.

"No, not this time," he answered in his no nonsense voice. I realized I'd lost this skirmish. I grabbed Becky's hand as she pulled on the door handle near her.

"Come on, Beck. Come with me," I said as we scooted out together. I wanted to keep hold of her somehow.

We walked behind Mother and Dad. Both of us dawdled, dragging our feet, stopping to smell the flowers that lined the sidewalk. I didn't want to leave her, not here, not with all those loonies. She didn't belong. Why couldn't anyone see that but me? She was smarter than those other kids and so much prettier. She didn't drool.

My stomach tightened.

Becky led us to her room where Mother put her clean, folded clothes away in the dresser drawer. While she worked, she and Becky sang silly songs. This time, Mother's singing didn't bother me. I even joined in and did the motions with Becky for "I'm a Little Teapot" and "The Itsy Bitsy Spider." Becky showed us some of her drawings and told us about her ballet lessons and her teacher, Mrs. King. She demonstrated the positions she'd learned.

"Is ballet her favorite thing? Does she love to dance?" Becky said.

"You do it very well," said Dad. Becky's face glowed with pride.

Mother finally finished with the clothes, snapped the lid of the empty suitcase shut and shoved it under Becky's bed. Mother's cheeks looked sunken and even her red lipstick didn't do much to brighten her face. She spoke in a whisper.

"That about does it," she said, soft as a lullaby.

Dad wrapped Becky in his arms, hunched over her like a sheltering tree.

"Give me a big hug."

Becky held on long and tight. She'd never been one for hugs and kisses but she'd learned to allow them, even the really extended touches. Now, she made a show of her kisses, stretching her arms open wide and embracing us stiffly, her arms tense; she smacked her lips with a loud, wet noise.

After Dad was finished, Mother cupped Becky's small cheeks in her hands. They gazed at each other.

"When can Becky come home, Mommy? Becky wants to come home." Becky's eyes teared up and Mother stood speechless. Dad reached to take Becky into his lap. He didn't look at Mother, who seemed unable to move.

"They're trying to help you, Becky. Help you learn. You work hard and you'll be home soon, I promise," he said. His voice broke just a little. Mother turned her back to us.

Finally, it was my turn to say goodbye. I held Becky, my eyes squeezed together hard.

"Bye, Jet," she yelled into my ear. I felt Dad's hand on my shoulder, the signal to let her go.

By the time I'd curled myself into a ball in the backseat of the car, my head pounded. Dad backed out of the parking space and I unrolled myself to wave at Becky one last time. She stood inside the storm door of the building, that same fat woman beside her, that hand again on her shoulder. Dad began to drive away very slowly.

Suddenly, Becky broke loose, opened the door and ran after the car. She was all arms and legs flailing in the air. I stared, unable to believe she was following us, unable to tear my eyes from her small body framed by the rear window.

"Dad! Stop the car! She's running after us! Stop!!"

I heard him suck in his breath; then he looked in the rearview mirror. His throat made a loud sound as he swallowed. Mother hunched her shoulders just a little. She stared ahead.

Dad didn't respond. He kept driving the same slow pace as when he started. I watched as the woman lumbered after Becky, caught her and bound her in those huge, black arms. We drove on.

No one spoke. We didn't utter a word for the whole trip home. We were wrapped in silence, egg-shell thin. A sound would have broken us.

Chapter Fifteen

Toto did not really care whether he was in Kansas
or the Land of Oz so long as Dorothy was with him.
—*The Wonderful Wizard of Oz*

My junior year at Philip-Barbour, the big song was Otis Redding's "Sitting on the Dock of the Bay." Though I still loved the Beatles, real life had taken precedence over my enthusiasm for them. However, Becky had discovered a fantasy group for herself—The Monkees. She, too, collected cards, books, posters, and albums. She, too, had begun to feel the call of her hormones and found a safe way to answer that call. Though she was only eleven, Becky had already started her period. Because she'd been around Mother and me, she was better prepared in some ways than I had been. Mother didn't explain the facts of life to Becky; she couldn't; Becky was in Pittsburgh. But Becky adjusted to the changes, though she wasn't as discreet as Mother would have liked. If she needed the proper equipment, she'd say in a very loud whisper, "I need some pads. For my period." No matter that we were gathered around the dinner table; Becky made no distinction between table talk and toilet talk. However, she *was* learning to speak in declarative sentences, rather than questions. For some reason, whenever she tried to whisper, she spoke in a more regular way.

I'd noticed on our last visit that Becky had developed small breasts, enough for training bras. My little sister was growing up, and I wondered how that might affect her. I couldn't imagine her coping with boys. Her burgeoning maturity unsettled me. Becky was attractive, and her beauty made her an easy target. Rape could be added to the list of worries I carried on my shoulders for Becky.

Not that she showed any interest in boys her own age; she clearly did not. But she was a big fan of the Monkees and carried around their pictures. Her new interest gave me another opportunity to tease her. I'd pretend to snatch away the Monkee cards, sending Becky into a frenzy. At first, her favorite Monkee was Mickey Dolenz, the drummer. Even after we'd grown up, Becky, a more faithful fan than I, remained enamored of Mickey until she attended a Monkees reunion concert with me. That night, she switched her allegiance to Davy Jones because he had held up the best under the siege of time; he was now the most handsome of the group.

Today, Becky treasures a couple of her Monkee cards above the rest; both are pictures of Davy in a swimsuit. Modest shots of beefcake, no doubt, but enough to tantalize Becky.

"Will you look at that sexy chest? Whoa, Beck, what a man!" I whisper to her when I visit her at her adult group home. She smirks and then points to another pose.

"Is he sexy in this picture? Do his legs show?" she says.

I put my hand over her eyes.

"Don't look, Beck. He's too hot!" I say, continuing to block her view.

"Let me look, Jet! Let me look!" she says as she tears my hand away and holds the card close to her face. "Handsome, so handsome," she croons, singing herself a love song.

Becky's all-time favorite photo of herself is one in which she's standing next to her idol, Davy. At Rouse's Group Home, one of the caretakers procured tickets to another Monkee's reunion concert. After the concert, Becky met Davy backstage and had her picture made with him. Jones is short, under 5'4"; this endears him even more to my sister, who, in the snapshot, is tucked beneath his arm with a grin that looks as if it might split her cheeks.

The Monkees have stood by Becky for a long time, serving as reminders of home and family when she was living elsewhere. I was glad she started her card collection and happy she could sleep with them while she lived in Pittsburgh. Those tattered cards might ease her pain. At least, I hoped they would.

But I didn't think too much about my sister's growing up, especially while I was hanging out with my friends, something I did as often as possible. I can still remember turning up the car radio as loud as I could stand it while Mitzi, Chris, and I explored the one-lane roads that crisscrossed Barbour County. My father was generous with the use of his Ford Galaxy and he'd taught me to drive himself, so he had confidence in my abilities. If he'd known all the places we'd roamed in our family's only vehicle, he might not have been so open-handed.

One afternoon, the three of us picked up a couple of boys who were hitch-hiking into town. Mitzi, Chris, and I didn't think there was anything odd about seeing young men hitching a ride, and when we knew the boys, even vaguely, we'd give them a lift. That day, we picked up Jimmy, that charming boy-next-door, and his friend, Glen. Glen was in our class, though not a close friend. But Jimmy and Jo Clair formed part of the "faculty brats club." Jo and I climbed the tree house, played basketball in the early autumn evenings and talked about boys. Jo loved rock and roll music and I went to her house when I wanted to listen to the latest sounds. Jimmy was also into music and was getting a band together. From my house, I often heard him playing his guitar—usually loud and funky music, but sometimes, I could hear him pluck a melody that was soft and beautiful. He was skinny with a thick head of brown hair and his eyes were shaped like Jo's with those same curly, blond lashes.

Jimmy and Glen scrambled in the back seat of the Galaxy and told us they were heading up to the college.

"Cruising for college girls, huh?" said Chris.

"Not really. But I wouldn't turn it down," said Glen.

"Ha ha. Why don't you guys come riding around with us?" Mitzi said.

"Where ya going?" said Jimmy.

"Where the road takes us, I guess," I said.

"What the hell," said Jimmy.

We headed out of town, singing to the songs on the radio—"Heard It Through the Grapevine," "Love Child," "Hey Jude." The girls sang along while the boys made fun of us in the backseat.

Jimmy lit a "cig," as he called it, and Chris and Mitzi took one when he offered.

We drove around on the two-lane highway for at least fifteen minutes before taking a dirt road that looked like it might be worth exploring. Though the sign said "Private Property," we didn't heed it. We'd violated such signs before and nothing bad ever happened.

The trees had begun their annual change of clothes and the branches overhead were red, yellow, brown, with tinges of greens dappled throughout. The sky was that wonderful clear blue that happens only in the fall of the year, not a cloud visible anywhere. On each side of the road, nothing could be seen but mountains covered in a cloak of trees, garnished by a few green meadows. No houses, no other cars, just us and the mountains.

"It's beautiful," I said as I rounded a curve.

"Look! A deer!" shouted Mitzi.

I slammed on the brakes just in time to avoid a large stag who had planted himself in the center of the road. Somehow, my back tire slid into the ditch on the driver's side. The deer leapt to the far side of the road and disappeared into the darkening woods. I gave my car some gas, but all I heard was a whirring sound.

"Great. We're stuck," said Jimmy.

"Well, get us unstuck," I said.

Glen and Jimmy got out and pushed. All the wheels did was spin us into the mud even deeper. They told me to put the car in neutral and they began to rock it back and forth. No good. The wheels sunk in deeper than ever.

"Oh my God, what am I going to do? My dad will *never* let me have the car again," I said.

"Don't worry. We'll get out. It may take a while," said Jimmy.

"Born to Be Wild" blared on the radio and Chris, Mitzi, and I started singing along. I felt wild, out in the middle of nowhere, the mountains surrounding us and the bright sky above. It seemed dangerous somehow, to be so far from town with just ourselves and the boys to depend on. Part of me was worried about my dad's car and getting home late. The other part wanted to live like this forever, exploring wild places with friends, taking lovers the way I'd read Lord Byron did, and writing wonderful, sexy, romantic poems about it all. In my CP (College Prep) English class, I'd fallen in love with the Romantics and had done a paper on Byron. I loved the way he thumbed his nose at societal conventions. Women swooned over him. I read that he'd had something like nine hundred lovers, and I spent hours figuring out how many different women per week that would have been. I'd estimate when he might have lost his virginity and count from there. That he died young made him even more attractive, much like Keats and Shelley. I dug that tragic stuff. But waiting for these boys to dig my car out of the mud wasn't quite as romantic as the poems I'd read. I was beginning to get nervous. The minutes ticked by slowly and after Mitzi, Chris, and I had sung along with the radio for what seemed like forever, the singing lost its appeal. The light had shifted and the afternoon was going fast. I needed to get the car back soon before my father noticed exactly how long I'd been gone.

Finally, the boys found a piece of flat wood and slipped it beneath the tire. We slowly rolled out of the ditch and I drove home with a car full of yelling, singing teens. I dropped my friends off quickly. We were glad we hadn't had to call our parents to come get us. My dad saw the mud that covered the rear end of the car as I drove into the drive.

"Next time you borrow the car, clean it up before you bring it home," was all he said.

Though he was generous with his car and jovial most of the time, my father was busy with his duties as Chairman of the Music Department at the College, frazzled by making choir tour arrangements, and sometimes worn out by the many voice lessons and classes he taught. On top of the usual duties of fatherhood, he was also constantly wrangling ways to keep Becky in Pressley House as long as possible, so she would get the most benefit from their program. He wrote to Pressley House:

> Please pardon my delay in sending the check for Becky's care for the month of January. We have nearly used up the funds we received from the state of West Virginia and I found it necessary to arrange some further loans on my insurance... I shall mail you a check as soon as I receive the (loan) money.

Later that same year, he wrote to the Division of Special Education of the West Virginia Department of Education requesting further help with the high cost of Becky's care:

> I am writing both to bring you up to date on Rebecca's progress at Pressley House and to advise you of our continuing need for aid in maintaining her there. Rebecca has now been in Pressley House for a little over a year and has shown marked progress in several ways. She is considerably calmer and less excitable than before. Her eating habits have improved considerably in the period that she has been there. Although on a one-to-one ratio, she is doing first grade work. In addition, the span of time spent in schoolwork each day is gradually increasing. Though they are encouraged by her progress, the people at Pressley House are very careful not to show undue optimism about her future. They are unwilling at this time to make any prediction concerning her length of stay needed there or the amount of adjustment she will have made when she is ready to leave there. We simply wait and hope, rejoicing with each new step forward.
>
> We are still paying at the rate of $16 a day, which amounts to $5,840 per year. As of this date, we have exhausted all of our financial resources except that which might be borrowed from personal friends. Since it appears most likely that Rebecca will need two more years at Pressley House, we obviously need all the help we can get. We hope that your office will be in a position to give us maximum consideration.
>
> If you would like an official statement from Pressley House concerning Rebecca's progress, I shall gladly request it for you. Again may I express the gratitude of our entire family for the help from your office. We shall never forget what it has meant to us.

Again, weeks passed before the state responded to Dad's letters, but what he'd written about Becky was right. Even I had noticed Becky didn't bounce around as much as she used to. And though she didn't request meat, sometimes she ate it without pitching a fit. Plus, she'd learned to like ice cream and candy, making her much more like other kids.

While I tried to look cool and fit in with the "right" crowd at Philip-Barbour, my father shouldered the cares of his world. Though I thought of Becky frequently, my thoughts were private, never shared with friends or my parents. I'm somewhat ashamed to admit it, but sometimes I was more concerned with being popular than with what my sister or my parents might be going through. Other times, though, I worried about Becky, worried what might happen if she never became normal. Would I be responsible for her? Would her care fall to me someday? Would I be able to take care of her?

At that point, I was convinced I could easily care for Becky, give her a home with me and the family I hoped to have some day. If she didn't get better, I'd have to, right?

❧

That year, all anyone at school could think about was the Junior/Senior Prom. Prom night was packed with events lasting from dusk to dawn.

Back then, school activities were carefully supervised by parents. No one thought about renting a motel room to drink or drug themselves into a stupor. For us, staying out all night was exciting enough. First, there was the prom itself, where we dressed in our formal gowns. The boys wore tuxedos and we hired a popular band to play. The theme was "Beneath the Sea" and Chris, Mitzi, and I spent hours decorating the gym for the big event.

Girls started worrying about getting a date in September, though the prom wasn't scheduled until late May. But if you didn't have a steady boyfriend, a date was as necessary as your gown. And, like selecting just the right dress, you hoped to have just the right prom date, too.

I worried along with everyone else. The subject of how to get a boy to ask you to the prom was dissected in ongoing conversations. Flirting techniques, endless analyses of a boy's behavior, what other girls were doing to get attention, every bit of minutia we could dream up was discussed in great detail. Luckily for me, not exactly Miss Popularity, a new boy came to school in the middle of the year. His name was Roland.

Roland was tall, well-built, had a ready smile and seemed friendly. He was the object of unending female adoration, and wherever he went, a pack of girls gathered around him.

170

Except for me.

I watched Roland. Every now and then, he'd catch me and smile. I'd smile and look away. Very coy, very cool. Somehow, I knew the attention from that gaggle of girls didn't please him. Oh, he enjoyed their flirting but he also seemed overwhelmed and almost shy at times. After that first smile, I decided I'd entice Roland to ask me to the prom.

Snaring Roland was the first time I'd made conscious use of my womanly charms. But I made a plan, tailoring it to lure him from the other girls who were throwing themselves all over him. Each day, I'd look at him, return his smile; and, after a week of anticipation, I started a conversation with him in the hall. He asked to walk me to class. Walking someone to class was a bold statement of affection back then.

Even when Roland started escorting me around school, I remained aloof some of the time. Other times, I was warm and flirty, touching his arm when we talked, gazing into his eyes. I don't know where I learned this behavior; it seemed to come naturally so it would be hard to call it contrived, but I was aware of my power. Roland gave me confidence in my ability to attract a man, and I was the one in power this time, unlike the situation with Danny. By the time I met Roland, I was determined never to be in a vulnerable position again.

While I explored my female power, Becky dealt with her own problems regarding sexuality. One night, while she was visiting, she crept into my room for a story.

"So Becky, are you liking Pressley House any better? You're learning a lot of new things," I said, hoping to find out if the house parents were treating her right. I didn't want to hear about any more eggs on her face.

"It's okay. Did someone suck my breasts?" she said softly.

"What?" I sputtered. Then I forced my voice to calm. "What do you mean?"

I had visions of some disgusting boy forcing himself on my baby sister. Anger boiled in the pit of my belly. Becky giggled.

"Did she come into my bed? And put her mouth here?" Becky pointed to her nipple.

"Who? Who came to your bed?" I thought Becky must be confused; surely, she'd meant to say 'he.'

"One of the girls in my house. Did she crawl into my bed late one night? Did she suck my breast?" Becky laughed nervously.

"What did you do? Did you tell her to get out?" I said.

"I didn't do anything. Then she went back to her room," Becky said.

"Did you tell your house parents?" I asked.

"No!" Becky said.

"Why not? Why didn't you tell them?" I asked.

"Did she not want to get into trouble? Is she afraid to tell her house parents?" Becky said.

"But you should tell them about this. This isn't something that should happen. What's the girl's name? Was it Roberta?"

"No. I don't know her name. She's gone now," Becky said.

"Did you tell Mom and Dad?" I said.

"No," Becky replied.

"Do you think we should tell them? I mean, maybe they could do something about it. Can I tell them tomorrow?" I said. I didn't know what to do; my parents would be very upset about this, I expected.

"No! Don't tell them, Jet!" Becky almost shouted the words.

"Okay, okay. Don't get upset. I won't tell," I said.

Soon after, Becky drifted off to sleep. I tossed and turned, wondering whether or not to tell my parents. Becky had trusted me with a secret, her first. I finally decided not to tell. I wanted her to be able to share anything with me and I knew she had to be able to trust me so I kept quiet.

಄

After all my plotting, Roland finally asked me to go to the movies. When he drove up in a pale blue convertible, I was impressed. His clothes were crisply pressed and he smelled clean and piney. We kissed that night, just one quick goodnight smooch but it was enough to encourage Roland to ask me to the prom. I accepted on the spot.

As the date of the prom grew closer, my mother and I drove to Clarksburg to find the right dress. After agonizing about whether a gown made me look too fat, too thin, too pale, too flushed, we decided on a pale-pink chiffon dress with an empire waist.

I knew some girls lost their virginity on prom night and often, if a girl didn't go all the way, there would be a lot of heavy petting. I decided that I'd go to the prom with Roland, but I wouldn't give him one kiss. It was an exercise in power once again. Poor Roland—he was a victim of circumstances—things were so out of control with my sister, I desperately wanted one area where I called all the shots.

Roland ushered me to the car and opened the door for me. Someone had taught him the right manners and I liked it. He talked mostly about football, which was boring, but I acted interested. I didn't talk to him about much at all, especially not anything important, like Becky and how I missed her, even though my life was busy with school and trying to be popular.

The kiss-less evening had gone just as I'd bragged to my girlfriends it would. I felt my power and relished thinking Roland liked me so much that my kisses weren't necessary.

When I think back on that time, I don't remember much about Becky that year, except for her unsettling disclosure. I'm sure we visited her often and brought her home for holidays. Maybe I'd grown accustomed to leaving her, or maybe I had too much of the world to ponder. I didn't forget her; of that, I am sure. But after the day she chased our car, I couldn't bear to think about her too much. And, though I still prayed for her regularly, I was slowly losing my faith. Prayer seemed futile, so I concentrated on good times and making out with boys. But only on my terms. That year, so important in many ways, marked the first time I'd used my power as a woman. Becky and I were blossoming into women, though thinking of Becky that way bothered me. I thought about the strange girl who had entered Becky's room and molested her. Though the girl was no longer at Pressley House, I worried what else might be happening to my little sister. When I imagined someone mistreating her, I could feel my blood pound in my chest. I would kill anyone who bothered her. I could do it, my pumping veins told me. But I'd never know about anything like that if I told my parents about Becky's secret. So I convinced myself never to tell.

I ended my junior year successfully, at least on the surface: I made decent grades and had done well on the ACT college exams; I'd gone to the prom with a handsome boy, the envy of the other girls; my piano lessons continued going well and I was slimming down. Looking at me, no one could have known I harbored violence in my heart when I thought of anyone hurting my sister; no one could have known I worried what insanity may lurk deep within, craziness to go hand in hand with Becky's; no one could have known the well of sorrow buried in my soul.

Chapter Sixteen

When you go around picking on things weaker than you are,
why, you're nothing but a great big coward.

—*Dorothy*

The summer between my junior and senior year, my family did its usual thing:
we picked Becky up from Pressley House and trekked to North Carolina to
visit my grandparents. At Lincolnton, I remember days spent on the front
porch, perched on the rail, my younger cousins and kids from the neighborhood scattered across the large space, playing cards on the old wooden swing
as it moved slowly back and forth. A few kids might be lying on the newly
painted slats, fresh for the summer from my grandfather's paintbrush. Sometimes, Becky would join the group, especially if I told ghost stories. I was the
oldest of the girl cousins and frequently took the gang outside for
story-telling. My grandparents didn't have airconditioning (few did back
then) so the front porch and the yard offered relief from the heat indoors.

With the kids gathered around me, waiting for a scarier-than-anything
tale, I caught a glimpse of Becky flipping her newly budding breasts. She
would rub her hands over herself, then do a quick flap. She didn't seem to care
whether anyone was looking. I figured she was surprised by the changes in her
own body and was learning about her new self the same way she learned about
any new thing—by flipping it. I tried to get her attention, willed her to look at
me. I was going to give her a stern look and shake my head, NO. But she didn't
turn my way and after that first touch, she plopped down with the other kids
and looked toward me, ready to listen.

Later that week, Gwennie came to fetch me while I was swinging on the
front porch with the grownups. Aunt Margaret had just asked me about my

plans for college, and I was explaining that I hadn't yet applied but would be doing so soon.

"I'd like to go to Salem College in Winston but Dad already said no. We couldn't possibly afford an out-of-state school," I said. Since I was headed for my senior year, every adult I met asked me about my future plans. Such inquiries made me feel good—I was being taken seriously. But another part of me got tired of answering the same old questions.

I was getting ready to tell Aunt Margaret about my dream to become a writer when Gwennie hurried onto the porch, making a beeline towards me.

"Anne, you've got to go help your sister take a bath," she said, her breath coming fast as if she'd run some sort of race. She took hold of my elbow and didn't give me a chance to say "boo" to Aunt Margaret, much less finish my conversation.

She dragged me into the living room and whispered, "You've got to go in there and do something. Rebecca is touching herself...you know...*down there.*"

I didn't move immediately toward the bathroom. I sure as heck didn't know what to do if Becky was touching herself. Was I supposed to make her stop? How?

"Go on, now. Make her stop," Gwennie said, pushing me to the bathroom door. "The child probably picked that up from that horrible place in Pittsburgh," she said as she turned and walked toward the front porch. "Never should have sent Rebecca there..." she mumbled.

I opened the bathroom door to find Becky in the tub. She was, indeed, exploring herself, but not in depth.

"Cut it out, Becky! Don't touch your privates. Gwennie's about to have a cow," I said.

"How can I wash then? How can I get clean if I don't touch myself?" Becky said.

"You can wash all you want to. Just don't...well, don't linger!" I said. "Especially in front of Gwennie—she's about to have a hissy!"

"Why is her grandmother upset? Is her grandmother old? Is that why?" Becky said, flipping the water.

"Who knows? Just don't do that again, okay? I don't want to have to monitor your baths from now on," I said.

Becky didn't answer. Often, when she didn't want to do what someone wanted, she would refuse to acknowledge she'd even heard you.

"Beck! Beck! Did you hear me? Don't touch your privates anymore! Okay?" I said.

"Okay, Jet," she finally replied.

I left the bathroom to return to the porch. I didn't know what else to do. I didn't want to help Becky finish her bath—I didn't want to be the one keeping her from her own private self. I don't know why my grandmother picked on me to solve her problem. But I felt strange about the assignment; I'd done my own exploring. Who hadn't? It seemed to me Becky should be allowed to do so as well. The difference was I knew enough to search for my body's mysteries in private; but with Becky, there was no such concept. Whatever Becky did, she did in front of God and everybody.

We left for home soon after, and by the time we'd arrived in West Virginia, my throat felt like razorblades were slicing me each time I swallowed.

My parents took me to the doctor the next morning to discover I had a bad case of mono—the kissing disease. My father made plenty of jokes about *that*, but I didn't find my situation funny.

I blamed Roland for my illness. Where else could I have gotten mono? My interest in him, slight at its apex, was going down fast.

"But he's so handsome," said Mitzi. "I can't believe you're going to break up with him."

"He's got a car and everything," said Chris.

"The chemistry just isn't there," I said. I had no idea what chemistry was, but I'd heard the line at the movies and I said it with as much flair as the actress in the movie had said it. That cracked us up and Chris kept saying the phrase over and over in a mock-dramatic tone—"No chemistry, Dahhhling. Just no chemistry!"

For most of those long days of summer, I slept. The doctor had been very strict about my regimen, which was to eat healthy foods and rest, rest, rest. It was a good thing Becky had returned to Pressley House right after vacation was over. I wouldn't have wanted her to catch mono, and if she'd been home, I wouldn't have been able to get as much rest. I'd have had to rescue Mom if Becky badgered her with too many questions, and if I didn't feel well enough to intervene, I'd feel guilty when I heard Mom scream at Becky. Instead of peace and quiet, Becky would be hopping and talking to herself, disturbing any sleep I might need. Plus, Mom would have read to her and I wouldn't receive the "treatment" as often as I did. The "treatment" was orange juice and ginger ale on demand; medicine brought on a tray with a snack; abundant TV, watching exactly what *I* wanted all day. It was definitely better to be sick all summer without Becky around.

While I was suffering through mono, my father was becoming more and more desperate for financial help. Though my dad must have been worried, that summer I was too sick to notice anything out of the ordinary. So far, for the school year of 1968/69, my father had made all the payments to Pressley

House, borrowing from his insurance and using what extra cash he could find. In June, he wrote to the financial officer at Pressley House:

> Funds for Becky's care are getting harder to find each month. I know that, in an emergency, I can go to my parents or my wife's, all of whom are retired and eking out a living on Social Security, but I do not want to do so except in an emergency. Therefore, I have sought funds elsewhere. I have a friend who has money loaned out which has been promised by June 15. If it is repaid on time, he will be in a position to make me a loan. If not, I will then turn to my parents. In other words, I can assure you that Becky's bill will be paid. If I may have until June 20, I will greatly appreciate it.
>
> So far, I have not heard from our West Virginia Department of Special Education this year in reply to our request for aid. I have written a second letter asking for some indication of their intentions. I assume that Dr. Eigenbrode has forwarded the information to them which I requested in my letter of May 14. If for any reason he has not, I hope he will be able to do so with all haste. A report from you people is very important to the deliberations of the Department of Special Education.

I remained blissfully unaware of the continuing struggles my parents faced. For the most part, my father seemed upbeat and cheerful. My mother, though she didn't get much done in the house, put on a serene face for me. She tried to maintain a happy atmosphere in our home and she cooked every meal we ate. Each outfit I wore, my mother washed and ironed. She made sure my homework was done, and when I'd gotten a D in algebra last year, her only comment was "I've always hated math, too. Don't worry about it." My parents never shared their concerns with me, financial or otherwise. I can't imagine the three of us sitting down to discuss how Becky's condition affected us, nor can I envision us talking about the pain of her absence. That's not the way my parents operated. Instead, they tried to make life as "normal" as possible. As a result, I remember my childhood as being happy. There were no scenes of my mother crying her heart out, no fights over money or anything else. My parents remained polite and pleasant most of the time.

Though they must have talked to each other about their troubles, I never heard such conversations. I tried to emulate what I observed. If they didn't cry over Becky, then I shouldn't either—at least, not in public, not in front of them. I did my best not to cry each time we left Becky. But I couldn't help tearing up when we said goodbye. I never boo-hooed or sobbed. I had more control than that. Instead, all my emotion went directly to my gut and I felt sick on the car trips to and from Pressley House.

I've often wondered what would have happened if we'd all had a good cry together. Would such a thing have been healing or would it have made my life more difficult, more confusing? As it was, our shared silences have bound us together much the way I imagine a cry would have. We are bonded tightly—partly because of our love but partly because only we know what it was like to live through having a child like Becky in our lives.

By early August, my father's money worries were over—at least for a while. That fall, Becky remained at Pressley House because the State of West Virginia had awarded her three thousand dollars for the 1969/70 school year. They also reimbursed my father for most of the money he'd spent in 1968 on Becky's care. Though I never knew about these machinations, I can imagine the enormous relief my folks must have felt to have one more year of help for Becky. My life remained the same, financially, whether my dad was stretching our budget to the limit or whether there was a sudden influx of money. I didn't get an allowance but did get unlimited use of the car, gas included. When I wanted to go to the movies with Chris and Mitzi, my father gave me enough for the movie and popcorn. We didn't eat out except on yearly shopping trips to Clarksburg. But we still camped at state parks on weekends and we still traveled to North Carolina to visit my grandparents. No matter what was happening with Becky, my life remained stable and secure. Though I never thought of my life that way then, I often considered Becky's life, what she must be going through so far from home. Part of me was glad I was the only one at home—the focus was on me, or so it seemed to me at the time. But the other part felt very guilty that I was safe in the bosom of my family while Becky had to deal with house parents who put egg on her face.

When I lay sick in bed that summer with mono, I didn't give Becky's situation much thought. All I could think about was how lousy I felt. I remember thinking how lovely sleep was, almost a person, almost a best friend. Sleep would wrap me in his dark arms and cradle me for hours on end. Even when I was awake, I could feel Sleep calling to me, wanting me to return to my bed.

Though I'd been inside for most of the summer and could only communicate with my friends by phone, I'd kept up with what was happening. Those last days of summer, the tail end of August when the cooler air of fall tinted the mountains a duller green, I was able to hang out with my campus gang. Jimmy, Jo Clair, and I spent a lot of time in the tree house and over at their house. I was no longer contagious and a strange thing was happening—I was talking to

Jimmy more than I'd ever talked to a boy before. And we didn't just talk about football.

Jimmy had big dreams, and so did I. He wanted to play music and his band practiced at least twice a week, though some of the band members lived in Grafton, a half-hour away.

I wanted to be an actress and star on Broadway. Or a writer. Or a singer. I knew my voice wasn't great, but I hoped it might grow deeper and more mature-sounding as I grew into adulthood. After all, my father had a wonderful voice, a big, booming tenor. Surely, my genes would kick in and I, too, would be able to stand before a breathless crowd and belt out songs like "There's No Business Like Show Business" or "I Could Have Danced All Night." I wanted to look as fresh as Julie Andrews had looked in *The Sound of Music*, and I dreamed I could sing as lightly as she. I'd grown up in the golden age of musicals and those great melodies helped me get through what I considered my "tough times." "When you walk through a storm, hold your head up high" and "Climb every mountain" became my philosophies of life. I clung to those words when I felt discouraged or when doubts about the future crept in. My doubts began to edge their way into my consciousness when I thought about having children of my own someday. I wondered if I might have a child like Becky; I worried that whatever was wrong with her was inherited and I knew I couldn't have borne such a problem—one in the family was enough. So, I'd sing to myself in bed when the doubts came—"At the end of the storm is a golden sky and the sweet silver song of a lark."

I adored old movies, too, like *Wuthering Heights* with Laurence Olivier as Heathcliff. My mother and I had watched that movie one Saturday afternoon and both of us sobbed our hearts out. I could be a drama queen; just give me a chance and I could make it to Hollywood.

I loved pretending and carried on numerous conversations in my head all the time. Sometimes, I'd be so busy acting out a scene in my mind that I'd forget I was in public and someone might be watching me. If anyone did catch me in my make-believe world, I just smiled and went on—it didn't occur to me then that *me* talking to *myself* might be viewed as a little strange. People considered it bizarre when Becky talked to herself, but it didn't occur to me that my own mutterings might be thought odd. Such an observation would have upset me at the time—I didn't want to be compared to Becky in any way. Even now, when we're together, I position my body so it becomes evident I'm her caretaker; I'm the normal one.

I remember when I made faces in the mirror and posed in every outfit I wore. I even pranced around in my pajamas, flinging my arms over my head the way I'd seen the girls in *Playboy* magazine pose. I considered myself almost pretty in an old-fashioned way, sort of like one of those actresses from the 40s. I had full lips, a straight nose, and a round face. I looked like a cross between Elizabeth Taylor and Cher, an odd combination but one I thought had possibilities in the world of Hollywood. But an acting career was good for a few years, not one's entire life. Same with singing. The voice would go, the looks would go.

As always, there were times I seriously considered helping people like Becky. If I kept a house full of such folks, my sister would have a place to live and someone who loved her nearby. But I wondered how I could manage such a thing; and inside, I knew that wasn't my true calling. I was too much in love with stories to be called to a life of service, though I might wish it otherwise. Though I had fantasies of becoming all these things, I knew I was good at one thing—writing—and that one thing wouldn't deteriorate with age.

I decided to become a writer by default.

But before I could become a writer, before I could pursue life with a capital L, I had to *experience* it. I can still remember walking through the woods on the way home from the bus stop. The September sky was clear and the leaves had already begun to change from green to yellow and red. The birds flocked together, whirling across the sky like dried leaves. I was talking in my head, praying really. And I asked God to let me experience EVERYTHING—I wanted it all—love and passion and tragedy and horror, everything! It seems silly now, a reckless wish. But then, I couldn't foresee many consequences. Then, I was just waiting and my skin seemed to shiver and shake with longing.

Jimmy was the kind of boy who could understand all those mixed-up feelings because he had them, too.

That fall, I spent more and more time with Jimmy and Jo Clair. Sometimes, Mike joined us for long tree-house talks and games of pool in Mike's basement.

I didn't mind running around with a younger crowd on Faculty Row. Dusty, my former best friend, was too busy being in love to hang out. All she ever did was date her boyfriend, Pete. I was jealous and hurt that Dusty preferred Pete's company to mine, but I didn't know how to tell her that.

Riding the bus home from school, the foursome, Mike, Jimmy, Jo Clair, and I, became good friends. We hiked down to Suicide Rock, climbing all the way to the top of the huge granite stone where a college student was said to have killed himself over the love of a girl from town. Just the sort of romantic tale that appealed to me. Jo Clair was quickly becoming my best friend, and Jimmy, Jimmy was becoming something, but I wasn't quite sure what.

I'd never had a friend who was also a boy. I hadn't been around boys except in a dating situation, which always felt forced and unnatural to me; I hadn't cared for the boys I dated. They served a purpose, though. They made me appear popular and made me feel attractive. They took me places and paid for everything. I didn't talk much to them but listened a lot. And for the most part, they bored me silly. I was smarter than they and I knew it. I had spunk, and I knew it. I was headed for great things, while most of them hadn't even wanted to go to college. I knew nothing about romance except for what I'd seen in the movies; and so far, no one had made me feel the least bit romantic. I simply hadn't met my match.

But Jimmy changed that. For months, we hung around together, the four of us. A few scenes I can still remember and remembering brings a smile to my lips, even now.

The winter before, a deep snowfall hit Philippi, so deep school was canceled. Jimmy, Jo, Mike, and I bundled up in our warmest clothes and took our sleds to the back road atop of College Hill. The road was full of huge potholes, but a heavy blanket of snow covered the gravel. By the third trip down, we must have been going thirty miles per hour, maybe more. We hit those potholes and left the ground. Airborne, Jo and I screamed. We could hear Jimmy and Mike whooping and hollering all the way down. We spent the whole day sledding, until the sun cast its final rays on the snow and the pewter sky darkened.

Most evocative of my memories is the time we spent in the tree house. Sometimes, only Jo and I would be there. She'd complain about how her mom made her do all the chores while her older sister, Carol, had none. I'd share my insecurities, how I hated my hair and the way my hips flared out. We laughed at each other and encouraged each other to shape up and have wonderful adventures. Other times, Mike and I would watch the clouds from the branches of the oak and try to spot a hawk in flight. Once in a while, Jimmy and I would find each other there, but with just the two of us, the silences became too full and clunky. We didn't stay there long on those days. We needed a third person to ward us off the strange direction we were heading.

When I think back, I can't remember exactly when I fell in love with Jimmy. But I do remember our first kiss.

We were in Jimmy's house and his parents were at work. Jo, Jimmy, Mike, and I sprawled on our bellies, playing Hearts in the living room. Jo and I were winning and, as I usually did when I won anything, I ran my mouth.

"Not good at Hearts, huh?" I said as I played the queen of spades on Jimmy's king, giving him thirteen penalty points.

"Game's not over yet," he said.

"Might as well be—no way you can beat the women. Why don't you just give it up?" I said, staring him in the eye.

"That'll be a cold day in hell," he said as he took another trick.

"Yeah, we'll see," I said as I tossed off a heart onto his six of diamonds. "Take that!"

On we played, me tossing down gauntlet after gauntlet and Jimmy making threat after threat.

Finally, in a frenzy, I grabbed the cards away from him.

"Give me those!" he said. By this time, I was sitting up, holding his cards behind me. He reached over and pulled me to him so that I was almost lying on him.

"Give me those or I'm going to kiss you!" he threatened.

I just stared at him.

"I mean it—if you don't give me my cards, I really am going to kiss you!" he said.

I continued to peer into his eyes, daring him. I didn't think he'd actually do it. Before I realized what was happening, he'd pulled my head down close to him and I felt the softest, fullest lips touch mine very gently, very tenderly.

Though I'd made out with boys before, for hours even, I'd never been kissed like that.

"I warned you," Jimmy said afterward.

I couldn't speak. All I could do was run my fingers over my lips in a sort of unbelieving way.

The next day, Jimmy asked me to go to band rehearsal with him. We drove to Grafton, to an old Victorian house where Steve, the bass player, lived. I met the other guys: Fred, the lead singer, and Jeff, the drummer.

In the late 60s, everybody had a band. Even the monotone boy with greasy long hair and a bad complexion could be transformed into a rock-and-roll wonder if he could scream and play the guitar. I hadn't expected Jimmy's group to be any good—most of the local bands I'd heard were terrible. But I went along because I wanted to be with Jimmy. That one kiss had changed things between us and I wanted to hear what his music sounded like.

The boys in the band were decent enough. Fred kept in the background with his long brown hair curled down over his collar. Jeff was short with a square-shaped body that looked solid and Marine-like. Steve had a little paunch, making him look older.

They started out with "Light My Fire" which Fred belted out with enthusiasm. Jeff had a girl with him and so did Steve. I felt like Yoko Ono, hanging out with the Beatles. Then the band played "Knock on Wood" and "Born to Be Wild." The other girls and I started dancing and I glanced at Jimmy as I moved to the music. He was watching me, smiling. I smiled back.

By Christmas, Jimmy and I were deeply in love the way only the very young can be. We spent our lunch hour standing in "Lover's Lane," the special hall where all the "steadies" gazed into each other's eyes, held hands and stole kisses when the hall monitor wasn't looking.

I told him about Becky being at Pressley House, though I didn't let him in on my feelings regarding the situation—I couldn't have shared those with anyone. But just being able to let him know about her helped me feel like I could be a real person and have a real relationship. He already knew she was "different" because he'd seen Becky bouncing on the tramp, flipping plastic milk jugs. He knew how she talked and he knew about Pumpernickel. But he didn't seem to think I was weird, too, as I feared some people might. As if Becky's condition were somehow contagious, like mono. Some people acted scared around Becky; sometimes, even those who were supposed to love her behaved as if she had the creeping crud.

I don't know what Jimmy really thought about Becky. But I do know he listened to me talk about her and he was kind to me, understanding. He was always nice to Becky once he and I started dating. Prior to that, I think he ignored her completely.

That Thanksgiving, as surprising as it may seem, Jimmy traveled with my family to see Becky. That's how close we were. I couldn't imagine allowing anyone else to go to Pressley House with me, not even Mitzi or Chris. But with Jimmy, I wanted to share who I was, and Becky was as much a part of that as anything.

Becky was scheduled to dance in a ballet recital that Wednesday evening and she was very excited. We were going to the performance and then taking her back home for the holiday.

I was a little nervous about taking Jimmy to Pittsburgh. Becky had made improvements there, but she was a long way from normal. Her reading skills were growing rapidly and she could write in very primitive-looking script. Her jitteriness had settled, unless something unusual was going on—like a ballet performance. I was afraid Jimmy would laugh or make fun somehow, though he'd never done anything like that. Plus, we had to spend an inordinate amount of time with my parents, which was enough to make me uneasy by itself. Add Becky to the mix and, though I tried, I couldn't get the nervous feeling out of my stomach.

The two-hour ride wasn't bad, considering I was with my parents and my boyfriend in a very small space for what seemed like two years. I don't know what we talked about. I suspect my dad and Jimmy discussed music, something they both loved. My father usually called rock and roll "noise," but he was on good behavior during the trip.

When we arrived, we parked in the visitor slot in front of Becky's cottage as usual. I couldn't rid myself of the sick feeling I got when I came to Pressley House. My stomach tightened and I could feel my lunch gurgling around inside. I couldn't help but remember the last time we'd come.

Becky didn't rush to meet us this time. Instead, we went inside and Jimmy was introduced to both sets of Becky's cottage parents. I'd been introduced to them before but hadn't bothered to remember their names. But this time, as I heard my father ticking off the list, I wondered which of these two burly, tall men had smeared my sister's face with eggs. Barbara and Dick were both large and fat while Faye was stocky and muscular. Her husband, Fred, must have been well over six feet with hands that could easily palm a basketball. Evidently, another house parent had been replaced; this seemed to be the pattern with group homes; Mama Clark had left during the last two months of Becky's stay at Amos, a devastating blow to Becky.

"I'm glad to meet you, young man. If you will step this way, we'll wait for Rebecca in the den. She's getting into her dance costume. She's very excited about this recital. It's the Fall Festival and all the children are performing in some way. I suppose she told you all about Mrs. King, the dance teacher. Becky adores her," Barbara said as she led us down the hall. I could see children of all ages in their rooms, slipping costumes or dress clothes over their heads, having their hair combed by an adult. Some were brushing their teeth.

"If you'll excuse us, we have a lot of children to get ready," said Dick. With that, the four house parents left us to ourselves. I heard someone crying softly down one hall and watched as Faye hurried in that direction.

I looked at Jimmy and smiled. I wondered how he was taking all this. I was sort of used to it by now—the odd noises a few of the kids made, grunts and groans that could startle you if you weren't on guard. I was accustomed to the way some of the children held their bodies, hunched over or arms at unusual angles. And I was no longer shocked by the sight of someone my own age sucking her thumb or smiling a vacant smile. But Jimmy had never been any place like this. I wondered if he was up to it.

He smiled back at me, a very small movement on one side of his mouth. I could tell he wasn't comfortable.

"Nice den. Got a TV and everything," he said.

"Yeah. Becky gets to do a lot of stuff. Like these dance lessons," I said as I took his hand.

"Cool."

We heard a loud scream and Jimmy gripped my hand tighter. Then silence. Finally, Becky rushed into the room.

"Hi Mom. Hello Father. Hi Jet," she said in a louder-than-usual voice. She hugged each of us, quickly and with vigor.

"Becky, you remember my boyfriend, Jimmy, don't ya? He came to watch your recital," I said.

"Our next door neighbor? Hello Jimmy," she said, perfunctorily.

She was dressed in pink tights with a matching tutu. A little skirt flared at her waist and pink ballet shoes completed the outfit. Her hair was shiny and had grown out a little since the severe cut she'd had earlier. Someone had applied pink lipstick to her lips and had shaded her eyes with blue shadow. She looked beautiful, delicate, and happier than I'd seen her in a long time.

"Is her dance costume beautiful? Is she so pretty?" Becky said as she hopped around the room, flipping her hands together.

"Wow, Beck, that's a great costume. You really do look pretty. Are you nervous?" I said as I fluffed her hair a little.

"Her sister wants to know if she's nervous. Is it scary to dance on stage? Is she scared?" Becky continued to move around like a butterfly, flitting from one person to another.

A slender woman with long dark hair entered the den. Becky hopped over to her immediately, and she pulled Becky close and hugged her. Becky squinched up in her usual "hug response," but she made no effort to remove herself from the embrace.

"I'm Mrs. King, Becky's dance instructor. She's going to be the star of our show tonight," said Mrs. King, her long-fingered hand outstretched toward my mother.

"She is? That's wonderful," my mother said.

"She's the best little dancer I've got! And she's worked very hard to learn all the steps to her routine. This star's going to shine tonight!" said Mrs. King, smiling.

Becky's face seemed radiant and she jumped more excitedly by Mrs. King's side. She was grinning a real smile rather than the forced grimace she sometimes used. Energy seemed to bounce off her and into the air. Her enthusiasm infected the rest of us and we couldn't wait for the performance.

"Does she have to take her costume off? Will she put it back on later?" said Becky when Mrs. King kissed her goodbye and told her not to eat too much for supper.

"Yes, honey. Take it off for now. It'll just be a couple of hours before you can put it on again," said Mrs. King.

Becky dressed quickly and then we went out to eat at the new Arby's, where we munched roast beef sandwiches and French fries. I picked at my food; back then, I didn't want Jimmy to think I ate much. I thought it was more feminine not to show relish for food.

All Becky talked about over supper was Mrs. King and the different dances she was going to be a part of. Then she explained about her special dance, a solo.

"Is she going to dance to 'Somewhere over the Rainbow'? Did Mrs. King pick out Becky's favorite songs? Will all the kids dance to 'Follow the Yellow Brick Road'?" Becky said in between bites of fries and spoonfuls of chocolate shake.

"Wow! You'll be doing a dance to your favorite songs from *The Wizard of Oz*? How'd you wrangle that, Beck?" I said.

"Did Mrs. King ask us what our favorites were? Did she like *The Wizard of Oz* the best? Were the boys a little angry because Mrs. King picked that one? Did the boys want her to pick music from The Beatles?" Becky said.

"So, Mrs. King picked your choice. I think she really likes you!" I said.

Becky flipped her fries and mumbled to herself. "Does Mrs. King love Becky? Is Becky her favorite?"

We hurried back to Becky's house after supper so she could have plenty of time to get into costume. Mrs. King was waiting for her and helped her into her outfit. We drove to the school auditorium and were early enough to get good seats, fifth row center. The auditorium was filling fast with families of all types. I wondered how many had kids like Becky and how they managed.

I studied the program to see when Becky would be performing. First, there was a brass band and then a couple of gymnasts. Becky came at the halfway point.

"Do you think she's nervous?" Jimmy whispered to me. "I mean, this is a load of people. I'd be scared shitless."

"I don't know if Becky gets nervous or not. She's never really had reason, I guess. I hope she does okay," I said.

"She'll be fine. She looks really cute in that costume," Jimmy said.

"Yeah."

We listened as the brass band struggled through "America the Beautiful." It sounded like me and Nancy in the girl's room with our French horns. We watched as a group of kids did forward rolls and crooked cartwheels across the stage. Finally, it was Becky's turn.

The lights dimmed. A single spotlight focused on Becky at the center of the stage. Everything was quiet. The record player started and Judy Garland's voice began to croon. Becky arched her arms over her head and rose to her tiptoes. She began to glide gracefully to the right.

Suddenly, a loud bang! erupted. Becky screamed and ran offstage. More pops echoed through the auditorium. The lights came on. Mrs. King ran from behind the curtains to see what was happening. Moments passed. Then Mrs. King reemerged, holding a couple of boys by their ears. They each held a balloon in hand, ready to pop it. Evidently, the boys had discovered Becky's intense fear of loud noises and had planned to ruin her solo. Ruined, it was.

"Little bastards," Jimmy said softly.

My parents, Jimmy, and I made our way backstage immediately. The show continued after the pandemonium had settled down. Becky was crying and hopping in the dressing area while Mrs. King tried to calm her.

"Did the boys pop balloons to scare her? Did they know she hates loud noises? Did they do it on purpose?" Becky was letting loose a torrent of questions and she didn't wait for Mrs. King to answer.

Mom and Dad put their arms around Becky and spoke softly to her. I joined them.

"You were doing really well, Beck. The dance was beautiful. I'm so sorry those brats ruined it," I said.

"Yeah, man. You were the best one," said Jimmy.

No matter what we said, nothing seemed to comfort Becky. She'd missed her opportunity to show us all that she'd learned, even though we insisted she do the dance backstage so we could see the whole thing. If I had been able to find those boys, I would have hurt them. I'd never been more angry.

We left late that night and drove back to Philippi. Jimmy held my hand the whole way home and I could see in his eyes that he really understood how much I loved Becky, how much I wanted her to be happy. I never thought anyone would be able to understand me in that way. Becky had brought us closer than I ever dreamed possible. Somehow, by understanding about Becky, Jimmy had reached a place in me I didn't think anyone could reach. Strange that my sister could have such an effect, one I could appreciate and be thankful for. I was beginning to learn what having Becky for a sister meant to me.

Chapter Seventeen

A place where there isn't any trouble…
Do you suppose there is such a place?
—*Dorothy*

My senior year, I lived in a cloud of love. Jimmy and I spent all our free time together, doing homework at his house, playing Spades with Jo Clair and Mike, going to the races with Chris and Randy, and driving to Grafton once a week for band practice. When the band had a gig, I'd ride along and sip mixed drinks at a table near the front where I could watch Jimmy play his guitar. Sometimes, I'd dance with one of the other "chicks" who belonged with the band. I liked to dance in front of Jimmy while he sang or played his saxophone. I didn't know anything about having a "private dancer" back then, but that's what I was—I was Jimmy's girl and I danced for him with all the passion I knew.

One reason I was allowed to spend so much time with Jimmy that year was that my father had moved to Morgantown to attend West Virginia University to study for his doctorate. He'd rented a little one-bedroom apartment, and every so often, Mother and I would visit him or he would come home for a weekend.

At Thanksgiving, Mother and I traveled to Dad's apartment with a family friend, Patti, a former student. Dad had gone to Pittsburgh to pick up Becky and we were to meet up at The Gorgonage, Dad's name for his home-away-from-home, coined in honor of his landlady who lived below.

The Gorgonage was filled with boxes of Dad's work stacked along the walls waist-high. Everything was placed with precision, as if the apartment was to be inspected by the world's toughest drill sergeant. Dad showed Becky and me our pallet on the kitchen floor. Patti's cot took the corner near the sink. We had little space for our bags and Dad told us not to touch any of his stuff; everything was exactly where he could find it and he didn't want to lose any of his work. Becky flipped around the small space and for some reason, found one of Dad's boxes fascinating, the one perched at the top of the steps leading into the apartment.

She hopped up and down next to the box. Whatever that box had, Becky wanted. Even though she'd been told not to bother anything, Becky started flipping the box in such a way as to crack the lid open just a little.

"Quit that, Becky. Come on in here and play Uno. Don't mess with that box," Dad said. Becky ignored him and continued to dance her way around the box. Again, she gave it a flip. The lid opened a tad more.

"Becky, I said leave that alone," Dad said with his most threatening voice. I couldn't believe Becky continued to ignore him. Yet, that's exactly what happened. Becky acted as if Dad hadn't said a word and continued fooling around with the box.

"I'm warning you, young lady... Leave that alone!" Dad said. Again, Becky ignored him.

Suddenly, the box tumbled down the stairs; all Dad's papers fluttered in the air.

"I told you not to mess with that box!" Dad yelled as he tried to catch it. Too late. The box bumped down every single step, all the way into the Gorgon's lair. The Gorgon said in icy tones, "Mr. Clinard, what was that terrible noise?"

"A box, that's all. Nothing to worry about. Sorry to have bothered you," Dad said.

Dad's face was ruddy as he toted the box with all its messy contents back up the stairs. He tried to grab Becky's arm.

"Becky, I told you not to bother my things and you deliberately disobeyed me. You're going to get a spanking," Dad said while Becky flipped farther and farther away from him.

Before he could land the first blow, Becky squirmed out of his reach and ran behind the kitchen table. For several minutes, they played a kind of tag with Dad reaching across to snag Becky, and Becky dodging with the skill of a boxer. He would dart one way, Becky another. On and on they performed their strange dance. After several minutes, Dad gave up.

"Becky, I've decided not to spank you. Instead, you will not have dessert tonight. Next time I tell you to leave something alone, I want you to listen. Understand?" Dad said.

"Yes," Becky muttered. Dad then told Becky to spend fifteen minutes on the pallet and think about her behavior. I wasn't supposed to, but I sneaked in beside her while Patti and my parents chatted in the other room. I wanted to comfort Becky and make her forget about Dad losing his temper. I wanted to be the "good" sister; Becky was so obviously not good.

It was the last time my father tried to spank Becky.

With my father gone, my life flowed a little easier. I was a senior in high school, got decent grades; I'd never done anything too terrible. I'd earned some trust and so my mother allowed me to spend my time pretty much the way I wanted. I'm not sure I could have seen Jimmy as often if my father had been home that year. But Jimmy and I were happy for my relaxed curfews and the extra time my mother allowed.

We knew that year was special; when I graduated, everything was going to change. But we had our year, when we were in love the way the first man and the first woman must have been. Even now, I can remember our tenderness with each other.

With Becky away in Pittsburgh and my father away in Morgantown, Jimmy and I grew closer. So did my mother and I.

My mother is one of the easiest people in the world to live with. With Becky and my father gone, she had few of her usual stresses. Looking back, I'm glad she had this respite and I hope she remembers the time as fondly as I do. Her relief wouldn't last long.

ॐ

The spring of my senior year came early, with the purple crocus at the end of the sidewalk budding in March. By the end of the month, daffodils were blooming. The sky had gone from gray and cloudy with snow, to blue and clear. The sun melted the last of the ice, even the stubborn patches hiding in the shady spots beneath the hemlocks. That spring, the world warmed and felt its blood move. I could feel my own blood on the move, too.

I was filled with anticipation then, with dreams and hopes, imagining my future and its endless possibilities. I saw my future-self, happy and productive, a success. Once again, I thought of starting a special group home for people like Becky. I could take in five or six residents, teach them myself—after all, I'd had plenty of experience. I wasn't sure what to major in at college for such an endeavor. I knew I didn't want to study education, but that seemed the most likely subject if I pursued my dream of making a safe place for Becky. Other times, I considered how much I loved writing. I'd made As in all my English classes and seemed to have a way with words. I wondered what would happen if I followed another part of my heart and majored in literature. I spent many a night, tossing and turning with such ideas, trying to decide my future course.

Other times, I contemplated becoming a social worker. The summer of my sophomore year, I'd volunteered at the Heart and Hand Camp for disadvantaged children. I was particularly taken with one boy, Lee. Lee was seven years old and one of eight children. He was small for his age with blond hair and blue eyes. Something about him reminded me of Becky; maybe the way he held himself apart from the other children or maybe the fact that he had the same coloring as Becky. Whatever it was, something about Lee made me think of my sister far away at Pressley House.

By the end of the camp week, Lee and I had become great friends. He talked to me a little and he held my hand wherever we went. I discovered his older brother, Michael was at the camp, too. Michael was muscular for a ten-year-old with black hair and very light blue eyes, a beautiful boy. Michael vied for my attention and I ended up befriending them both.

I didn't want my relationship to end with those little boys. I can't explain why, but helping them somehow seemed important. I must have believed if I helped them, that somehow that good deed would transfer to Becky. Maybe someone would think Becky was special and would befriend her in Pittsburgh. There was more to it than that, though. In some way, being with Lee was like being with Becky; I could assuage my ache for her by holding hands with him and telling him stories.

I "worked with" the boys until Christmas. By then, something in me had changed. I began to wonder if I was helping the boys. How could trips to the circus or zoo put food on their table? How could my love and care make up for all they didn't have? What right did I have to think my way of life was better than theirs? If Jesus wanted us to help others less fortunate, as I'd been taught and as I believed, wouldn't He tell us how to do it so our helping hand actually made a difference?

I was trying to change the Robinsons so they'd be like my family, have the things my family had, and enjoy the same privileges. But as I got to know the Robinsons better, I saw they were happy. They weren't worried about the layer of dust that covered them most of the time. They enjoyed each other's company and didn't seem to resent not having furniture or new clothes. In many ways, the Robinsons seemed happier than my own family. Who was I to try to change them?

By December, I'd decided that my time with them was over. I no longer believed I was helping them. I'd come to believe I could be damaging them, giving them a taste for things they might never have. The truth was, I didn't know what I was doing. But I loved those little boys. I continued to see something of Becky in Lee. They shared a certain shyness and they both seemed to be left out of things in a strange way—little aliens. Maybe I thought I was pleasing God in some way, doing for "the least of these" and in reward, God would do something for me—heal my little sister. Or maybe I was just a sensitive girl with a soft spot for loners.

My experience with the Robinsons changed me. I realized life and people were much more complicated than I'd thought. There were no easy answers to anything. Perhaps we couldn't help people. The whole subject confused me, but by my senior year, I was still thinking about how I could help others. After all, I was still the girl who cried over newspaper horrors, who became hysterical in movies, who protested the war in Viet Nam and wrote sad stories about the soldiers. I was also the girl who prayed for her sister to be miraculously healed and made normal. Even though I knew I'd failed with the Robinsons, I thought I could make the world better somehow. I believed it was my duty to do so.

That spring, before I'd learned which colleges had accepted me, I thought of what I might do with my life that would make a difference.

I also thought about Jimmy and Going All the Way.

Though I grew up in the 60s and there was a Sexual Revolution going on somewhere, it wasn't happening in Philippi, West Virginia. The new Women's Movement articulated much of what I had observed about the world, but even that enormous cultural shift hadn't fully blossomed yet. I grew up in the time of the Double Standard, which was so unfair, so unjust, it made my blood surge.

The Double Standard went something like this: If you were a boy and had sex, the escapades enhanced your reputation. You became something of a "bad" boy, more macho, more cool. If you had sex with lots of partners, you were really "bad." And that, too, was cool. On the other hand, if you were female and had sex, even if you'd been dating the guy two or three years, you were a slut. Any girl who went all the way was considered a slut, even though some were doing it. The girls who kept quiet were the smart ones.

Though I'd been cautioned by Gwennie when I was thirteen never to let a boy touch me "down there" (it seems Gwennie didn't want touching of any kind "down there!"), I'd read enough to realize lots of people "did it," and they weren't transported immediately to hell. I saw no logical reason to save myself for marriage. I wanted to live for the moment, get swept away by love, ride passion into the sunset. I blame the term paper I wrote on Lord Byron for my free-spirited attitude, that and the hippy influences of the time.

Whatever made me consider having sex with Jimmy left me curious about every aspect of making love. The more I thought about having sex, the more open I became to the idea.

Two popular songs summed up my dilemma. The first was an old song, "Will You Still Love Me Tomorrow?" The lyrics brought every girl's question out in the open. If a girl decided to make love with her steady, would he still love and respect her after he'd "gotten what he wanted." The words to this song made me think boys were only after "one thing," as my grandmother had told me so long ago. Could this be true? Such thinking didn't make a lot of sense to me. It reduced the entire business to a kind of sport. Maybe some boys were like this, but I didn't think my Jimmy was one of them. Still, the song carried a warning.

The other song was "Just Call Me Angel in the Morning." This song was much more my style. I liked the independence of the singer who sang, basically, consequences be damned, let's go for it. That's the kind of spunky girl I wanted to be, dreamed of being. But deep down, I knew I wasn't that independent. I didn't have the guts to be that brash. Those two songs did battle in my head and I didn't know which was going to win. As my graduation approached, I thought more and more about going all the way, but I remained as confused as ever.

It was March and I'd just turned eighteen.

Becky came home for the week of my graduation so she could watch me walk across the stage at Philip-Barbour. I was happy to have her home, though I wasn't so sure about her attending my graduation. I didn't want to have the added pressure of worrying whether or not she'd behave. Though most of my friends knew about Becky's problems, it's one thing to know something in theory, another to witness it. I hadn't thought much about what my leaving for college might mean to my sister. I'd been accepted at several state schools, including Marshall University, in Huntington. I was seriously considering M.U. because I'd grown up there and had fond memories of the place. I'd also been accepted at Alderson-Broaddus, though I didn't want to stay home; I couldn't wait to leave Philippi and see the larger world.

Earlier that spring, while Becky was visiting for Easter, we nuzzled together in my bed. We spent those precious minutes before sleep, talking about her usual subjects, but also about my future.

"Will you go to college, Jet?" Becky said. "Will you have to leave home? Will you miss your parents?"

"I've been accepted to three places—Marshall University in Huntington..." I started to list them.

"Is that where I was born? Is that where we used to live?" Becky said.

"You know it is. As I was saying, I've also been accepted here, at A-B..."

"Do you want to go where Daddy teaches? Could you live with Mom and Dad?" Becky said. She mulled that over, repeating her questions to herself, her hand extended so that the back of her hand was pressed against her nose, both palms together, prayer-like, her usual contemplative position.

"No, I don't really want to live with Mom and Dad. That's why I'm thinking about Marshall or else Wesleyan. I'm ready to get the heck out of this place," I said.

"Why don't she want to live with Mom and Dad? Don't she like her parents? Won't she miss her home if she goes away?" Becky said.

"I'm sure I'll miss everything, Beck. It's just that I'm old enough to move on, you know, see the world a little. Be on my own," I said. I was surprised at the conviction in my voice.

"I'll miss you, Jet," Becky said. She didn't present this information as a question, nor did her voice sound flat. She said those four words just the way a normal person might say them.

"I'll miss you, too," I replied.

Again, I glimpsed what I thought of as the "real" Becky. If only we could figure Becky out, her mind would unfold like a beautiful rose, full and rich and colorful. She was in there somewhere. If only I could rescue her. If only somebody at Pressley House could solve the puzzle. If only...

The week before graduation, my parents were invited to dinner and I was left behind to baby-sit Becky. I asked if it would be okay for Jimmy to baby-sit with me. They agreed.

Jimmy and I had watched Becky before and also his two nephews. We didn't mind hanging out with kids, and we liked pretending it was what our lives would be like when we got married. At least, I liked to pretend that. I knew I wanted to be with Jimmy forever. I loved him, plain and simple. I believe he felt the same way about me. And yes, sometimes he actually did talk about having a family someday, about our being together always.

Though Jimmy and I were in love, we'd kept our virginity. Truthfully, we'd never even discussed making love. We loved making out, but neither of us seriously considered going beyond extended kissing sessions and a little fondling.

Ah, those long, make-out bouts. Kissing literally for hours, taking small breaks to express how we loved one another. Tentative, gentle, slowly growing more passionate but never culminating in anything more than heavy breathing. With Jimmy, making out was like kissing a cloud. His lips were so full, they acted like cushions and the softness moved over my own mouth tender as butterfly wings. He rarely became overpowering the way Richard had. Instead, he was always considerate of my feelings and he was gentle, the way a teenaged boy can be gentle.

Though we'd never talked about making love and Jimmy had never pushed me to do anything beyond kiss, I remained curious about sex. I wasn't curious from a sexual standpoint. I had no idea the act could be physically pleasurable. I realize such innocence is hard to believe in the twenty-first century; but in 1970, no one talked about orgasm. Even my best friends and I didn't discuss our love lives much. We might joke about French kissing or letting a boy touch our breasts, but that was the extent of our gossiping. We were more concerned about who was dating whom than about becoming sexually active. We worried whether our boyfriends were flirting with other girls. We didn't give a thought to safe sex. Safe sex wasn't even a concept back then. Our safe sex consisted of not going all the way. The only other method I knew about was using a rubber. I'd never actually seen one, but I'd heard about them. So, though I was basically ignorant about sex and sexual responsibility, I still wanted to know what the big deal was all about. I yearned for experience, and making love ranked at the top of my list.

That Friday night, Jimmy came over about a half-hour after my parents had left for their evening out. He smelled of English Leather, my favorite cologne. He'd cleaned up and his Madras shirt was soft and slightly wrinkled.

"So, what's Becky up to?" he said as he flopped on the couch next to me.

"She wants to watch *The Monkees*, then *Hee-Haw*," I said, making a face at the mention of *Hee-Haw*. Becky adored Buck Owens and, because she was a "true hillbilly, a real Mountaineer born in West Virginia, my birth state," as she was quick to tell everyone, Becky related to the country antics of the show.

"God. What a lineup," Jimmy said.

I snuggled beside him and lay my head on his shoulder. Becky cackled and sang along to "Daydream Believer" while the Monkees jumped around, doing their cheap Beatle imitation.

"Man, that show is lame," Jimmy said.

"Want to go in the other room?" I said.

"Sure," Jimmy said.

I led him into my bedroom. My mother and I had redone the room just the year before. I'd refinished my old bedroom suite, changing it from a dark wood to antique white, much the rage then. We painted the walls lavender and I'd selected a purple-flowered bedspread with a white background and green ivy twining throughout. The curtains matched. I was pleased with the outcome and kept the room neater than I had in the past. I shoved a few stuffed animals off my bed and sat down. Jimmy joined me.

"So, have you decided?" Jimmy said. He held my hand tenderly.

"Yeah," I looked down at my feet. I knew my answer would upset him. "I'm going to Marshall. They gave me a grant and work study. It's the best deal," I said. I'd dreaded telling him, but now my decision was out in the open. I could breathe a little easier, though I knew he wouldn't be happy.

"Why can't you just go here?" he said.

"I want to get out of this hole. I want to see the world. Marshall's a much bigger school and it's a university. I dunno—I can't explain it," I said.

"I guess you don't care that I love you," Jimmy said.

"Of course I care. I love you, too," I said as I took his hand. "I love you more than anything." I gazed into his eyes, reached my hand to trace the outline of his mouth. His eyes seemed glassy.

"You know what's going to happen—you're going to find some big college man," he said, jerking his hand away from mine.

"I doubt it. But if I do, then that's what's meant to be. But I don't believe I will. I love you," I said. I was a 60s child all the way. Que sera, sera.

"Maybe we should just go ahead and break up now. Save ourselves the trouble of doing it later," Jimmy said.

"What? That's crazy," I said.

I'd actually thought of breaking up with Jimmy because I figured it might be unfair for us to be tied down. I knew long-distance romance would be hard. But I'd decided against it simply because I loved him and I couldn't imagine falling for anyone else. I hadn't considered that *he* might be the one to break up with *me*.

"Not so crazy. Saves having a broken heart later," he said, smiling.

"We're not going to have broken hearts—we're going to live happily ever after," I said. Then I kissed him. I hadn't intended to kiss him, but a force moved through me and I kissed him with all the passion I felt. Suddenly, I wanted to belong to him. I wanted to be his, completely his. I don't know where this feeling came from—it seemed to be coming from a place I hadn't known I possessed. I wanted to kiss him and kiss him and never stop.

He kissed me back and before I realized what was happening, he'd pushed me onto the pillows and was lying on top of me. We'd done this before but never quite so quickly. I could hear his breath in my ear as he nibbled on my neck. I locked my arms around him and kissed him again.

"Jet? Jet? Where are you, Jet?" Becky's voice seemed to be coming from far away.

I pushed Jimmy off of me and sat up quickly.

"I'm in my bedroom. What do you want?" I yelled. I couldn't believe my sister was interrupting such an important moment for me. Damn her!

"The TV's acting up!" Becky screamed to me. "Why does the TV mess up? Can Jet fix it? Will she hurry? Shit!"

Though Becky didn't often cuss, sometimes she'd say that particular word for special emphasis. For some reason, curse words often made her laugh and now she cackled at the bedroom door.

"I'll be right back," I whispered to Jimmy.

"I'll be here," he said as he rolled to one side and propped his head on his hand. He was too adorable lying on my bed like that.

I hurried down the hall and saw that the vertical hold on our old black and white set had gone nuts. The picture turned over and over quickly. I knew which knob to turn since this flickering picture wasn't anything new. The set was on its last legs.

"There. Okay, Beck, I'm going to be in my bedroom talking to Jimmy, okay? You watch your shows," I said. "Don't bother me again, okay?"

"All right," she said in her flat voice.

When I returned, Jimmy had pulled the sheets down and was lying in the bed. I joined him.

"This could be dangerous," I whispered.

"Naw. You can trust me. I just though it'd be cool to get under the covers," Jimmy said.

The thing is, he was right. I *could* trust him.

"Scoot over," I said.

Again, within minutes, we were kissing passionately. He unhooked my bra and touched my breasts. I could feel him hard against me and I wanted him to make love to me. It wasn't so much desire for the sexual release, since I didn't know that was possible. No, I wanted to belong to him, for him to possess me before I left for college. And, if I'm completely honest, I wanted to experience the act itself for its own sake. I was filled with longing at that moment and making love with Jimmy seemed to be the best way I could still the hungry voice in my head.

"Let's do it," I said as he looked down at me.

"You serious?" he said.

"Absolutely," I said.

"I love you. I'll always love you, Green-eyed Lady," he said. That was his special name for me. The song had just come out and he thought the words described me perfectly. He smiled and then he pulled off my jeans and panties. We'd never gone this far before and my legs trembled.

He trailed his fingers down my legs and smiled at me. At that moment, I heard Becky bobbing around outside my door.

"Jet? What are you doing in there?" Becky yelled. She sounded as if she were standing right in the room with us, she voice was so loud.

"Nothing. What do you want?" I said. Jimmy lay very still on top of me, his clothes still on.

"Is the TV acting up again? Why can't Daddy fix it? Why can't we get a new one?" Becky said.

"Can't you just turn the dial a little bit? It'll settle down," I said.

"Why can't she fix it? Why doesn't her sister fix it for her?" Becky said. I could hear her flipping her hand against the doorknob and bouncing in place.

"Damn," I said.

I jumped out of bed and left my jeans on the floor. The large tee shirt I was wearing would cover me. I flung open the door and stomped down the hall.

"There. Now don't bother me any more!" I said, twisting the dial until the picture steadied.

"Why don't you have your clothes on, Jet? What are you doing in there?" Becky said.

"I've GOT my clothes on, see? It was too hot to wear jeans so I took them off. Now, watch your show," I said.

I couldn't believe how Becky kept interrupting us. She didn't usually do such things. I wondered if she knew I was going to do something I shouldn't. I stopped that thought cold and focused my mind on Jimmy, his kisses, and our first time.

When I returned to the bed, Jimmy held out his arms to me. The sheet covered him but he'd removed his shirt. I slipped in beside him and discovered he'd removed his jeans, too. We kissed again and before I realized what was happening, he was inside me, pushing, pushing. There wasn't anything pleasant about the act, except the sheer forbidden aspect. He wasted no time in doing the deed. Perhaps he feared more interruptions or maybe he was worried my parents might come home at any moment. Or maybe it was just his first time.

Afterward, we held each other.

"I love you, I love you, I love you," I said, holding his head against my chest.

"Ditto, ditto, ditto," he said.

We stayed there without moving or talking for a long time. I could hear the theme song from *Hee-Haw* and I knew we'd better dress before my parents returned.

"You okay?" he said.

"Yeah. You?" I said.

"I'm great!" he said.

When we returned to the den, fully dressed, Becky was flipping and skipping around the room. She seemed agitated, though I knew she couldn't have known what had happened in my room.

"Want some ice cream, Beck?" I said.

"Yes," she said, still flipping.

Jimmy went with me into the kitchen.

"You think she knows?" he said.

"Of course not. She doesn't know about that kind of stuff," I said.

"But she's acting all riled up or something," he said.

"Who knows what got her upset. Maybe because we left her by herself for a few minutes," I said.

"It wasn't just a few minutes," he said, teasing.

"It wasn't all that long, either," I said. "She's probably jealous."

We kissed over the ice cream and then joined Becky for an episode of *Star Trek*, my favorite show.

My parents came home full of smiles and that relieved feeling they seemed to get whenever they went out alone; I sent Jimmy on his way. No one knew what had happened except Jimmy and me. Things were back to normal, or so it seemed. But I had a secret now. I was a woman of the world. I had a lover.

Though I felt much closer to Jimmy after that night, the experience hadn't been as earth-shattering as I'd hoped. I decided Jimmy and I wouldn't do it any more. There didn't seem to be much point, and, after the initial euphoria, I began to feel guilty about having lost my virginity. Perhaps that sense of loss seems puritanical now, but I'd been told my entire life by everyone who mattered to me to wait until marriage before you had sex. And, though I'd begun to have my doubts about God and the way He ran things, I still knew He wouldn't approve of my actions. I'd taken a chance and broken the rules. The more time passed, the worse my decision made me feel.

A few days later, I told Jimmy I didn't ever want to make love again. I explained that we were just too young and I felt too guilty. Oddly, he agreed. He said he'd come to the same decision. He told me he loved me too much to do anything that might hurt me and he wasn't sure making love was good for me. He worried about my reputation, not that we would tell, but such things usually got out one way or another. Even though Jimmy and I decided to wait until we were married before we made love again, our relationship had deepened and had grown even more serious. I believe we both made that vow with every intention of keeping it. Indeed, we did maintain our chastity for several months. But neither of us understood the power of love or the pull of passion.

Recently, I emailed Jimmy to get his permission to tell our story for this book. We fell into reminiscing and he recalled my immediate response after we'd made love. He said I cried, handed him his hat and said, "This is a great way to end a relationship." That sounds very much like the melodramatic girl I was, though I have no recollection of saying it. What I remember is Becky hovering at the door, the sound of her flipping her hands against the doorknob. I can still hear her feet skipping in place while she kept bugging me. What did she know?

That June, I graduated with a solid B average, ready to head toward what I was sure would be a life of adventure, romance, and great success. I would be my parents' only child to graduate from high school, the only one to go to college. It was becoming more and more evident that Becky wasn't going to turn, miraculously, into a normal kid. Instead, I was the normal one, the one on whom the hopes for success rested. I, the one who had gone all the way, the one who was in love with Jimmy. I was the one responsible for my parents' happiness. They'd suffered so much. It was up to me to balance that out by achieving something wonderful. But all I'd achieved so far was the loss of my virginity.

I don't know what Becky might have known about sex at that point in her life. Except for her strange experience with the girl at Pressley House, Becky hadn't had any sexual episodes to my knowledge. She didn't have a boyfriend. I don't know if her cottage parents had told her the facts of life or not. I figured my mother had not, since Mother was hesitant to discuss such things. I didn't know if Becky realized what Jimmy and I were doing while she watched *Hee-Haw* that night. I couldn't imagine how she'd know, but she acted so strangely after we came out of my bedroom. And she kept interrupting us, as if she knew something was going on, something she wanted to stop. I often thought Becky understood more than she could articulate—maybe that night was one of those times.

I realized Becky would probably never have a boyfriend, and I knew she'd never allow a boy to touch her—she could barely stand hugs from her family. I was suddenly sad for her; she would never know what I'd shared with Jimmy. Maybe part of what pushed me into activating my sex life was the realization that Becky would most likely never have such a life. But if that were true, thinking of Becky was a very small part. I can't untangle the motivations of my teenaged heart. I doubt if anyone is ever aware of the complicated decision-making processes that take place in a given circumstance. I can only say that after all my talk about chemistry, I had found it.

Finally, the night of graduation arrived. Earlier, Chris, Mitzi, and I had tried on our gowns together, crying over our soon-to-be-lost youth, growing excited with thoughts of the future. We teased each other's hair until we were true "helmet-heads" and then held hands slippery with tears. Chris was headed for business school, while Mitzi was going to Fairmont State. I was heading south to Huntington, back to the town of my elementary years. The three of us felt the same swirl of emotions—fear, excitement, sadness, anxiety, and, last of all, hope. We held on to hope, the hope that we would be able to make it on our own, the hope that we would be happy and the hope that we wouldn't disappoint those who had helped us reach this moment.

That graduation day, my father snapped a picture of me in my blue cap and gown. I was standing in our front yard, my high heels sinking fast into the soft grass. I grinned with confidence and pride. My smile said, Look out world, Here I come! I couldn't wait to walk across the stage, grab that diploma and toss my cap into the air when the ceremony was over.

I didn't know then where life would lead me. I didn't know how close Becky and I would remain, nor did I realize how my responsibility for her would increase over the years. As I walked across the auditorium that graduation night, I was walking toward my future, full of hope and faith that all good things would come my way.

I can't imagine what Becky might have been thinking—all I knew was she was on her best behavior. Though I worried about strange noises coming from the vicinity of my family, that night, none did. Becky knew this was my night and she behaved herself. Perhaps she wondered if I'd ever return from college. Maybe she thought she'd never see me again, once I ventured out into the world. Or maybe she was simply dreaming of the ice cream Dad may have promised her for being good during my graduation.

Becky would be coming home for good soon, though neither of us knew it that night. Her long exile was almost over. Once home, Becky would stay with my parents for the next twenty years—a long, happy interval for Becky between her periods of institutional living. Neither of us had an inkling of that at my graduation.

At that moment, both of us had flown the nest, though Becky was still very much a baby bird and I, a fledgling. I was eighteen with the world awaiting me; Becky was twelve and on the path to something, no one knew what. That night, as I walked across the stage, I knew I'd be going one way, Becky another.

Our adventures were just beginning and who knew where or how they would end. Though it was time to tell my family goodbye, I knew in my heart I'd always be connected to Becky; she was a part of me and I, her. We were, after all, sisters.

Chapter Eighteen

...Why, then, oh why can't I?
—*Dorothy*

When I walked across the graduation stage in 1970, the future was a ribbon of road ahead of me. Now, I look back to see how far Becky and I have traveled.

In her early forties, Becky was still struggling for a self-directed life. After living at home for twenty years, she'd returned to group home living at the age of thirty-two. She had been at Rouse's Group Home for almost nine years and now held a part-time job at Burger King—amazing! But she was ready for a change. I'd seen Becky go through so many changes, so much growth, I believed, once again, anything was possible. Maybe she would achieve her dream of independent living after all. Getting through this interview with the people from UMAR (United Methodist Agency for the Retarded) Group Homes was the first step.

I hurried from the car to join Becky and my parents as they stood at the front door of the brick ranch where the Methodist Group Home staff waited inside. Becky's arm shot out, stiff as a robot's, to push the small doorbell. She was humming very low notes—the lowest organ pipe of all, I imagined. Her nervousness had never been more obvious. She rang the bell a second time before my father could stop her.

Mom, Dad, and I stood behind her. I felt perspiration drip down the inside of my shirt. Becky wasn't the only one nervous about this meeting.

Two women answered the door.

"Hello, I'm Becky Clinard," Becky said, striding into the room as business-like as any executive. She extended her hand to each woman and glanced at each face briefly before looking down at her feet. For her, the awkward effort at friendliness must have seemed as warm as the handshake of a politician pumping for votes. I'm certain she thought she was glad-handing the ladies, working the crowd. I was proud of her for trying to make eye contact, no matter how slight.

"Welcome, Becky," said Mrs. M——, the resident advocate and primary interviewer. The other woman, Mrs. K.——, smiled at us. "And who are the folks with you?"

"These are my parents. And my sister," Becky said.

"Jack Clinard. My wife, Virginia. Our other daughter, Anne," my father said, smiling. We were doing our best to impress the women who had the power to make my sister's life happier.

"Becky, we want to ask you a few questions. Do you understand why you are here?" said Mrs. M——, gesturing for us to be seated.

"Yes," Becky said.

"Would you like to tell me why you think you are here?" said Mrs. M——.

"To get into a DDA group home. Is it because I'm too smart for Rouse's? Do I need to move up to a DDA group home?" said Becky.

"Do you know what a DDA group home is, Becky? Can you explain it to me?" said Mrs. M——.

"Yes. Is it where there's not so much supervision? Do the clients have more freedom? Can they be left alone sometimes?" said Becky.

"Yes, it's all those things. DDA stands for Developmental Disorder Adults and a DDA group home is different from the one you're in now," said Mrs. M——.

"You mean Rouse's?" said Becky.

"Yes. Rouse's Group Home is what they call an ACF group home—Adult Care Facility. The federal government decides on the guidelines for each type of group home. In the ACF group homes, clients must have a caretaker with them at all times—twenty-four hours a day, seven days a week. But here, after a client has taken training to handle emergencies, a client can be left alone for up to four hours," said Mrs. M——.

This was one of the biggest selling points for moving to a DDA group home for Becky. She hated having to be with other people at all times.

"Is it the federal government's fault?" Becky said.

"Is what the federal government's fault?" Mrs. M—— said.

"Is it the federal government's fault I have to ride in the van every time the resident facilitator has to pick up Darryl?" Becky said. She started rocking back and forth in her chair and I sensed she was getting wound up. I glanced at the two interviewers and could tell they had no idea what Becky was talking about.

"Becky has to go with the group every time they pick up Darryl from work, even at night. They have to get her out of bed, drive about twenty minutes, pick Darryl up, then return to the group home. Becky doesn't like that," I explained. I knew if we waited for Becky to explain what she was talking about, we'd be in the interview forever.

"Is the federal government to blame?" Becky said.

"I guess so. They get blamed for everything else," I said, trying to be funny.

"Who blames them?" said Becky.

"All kinds of groups. You're not the only one who doesn't like the federal government," I said. Becky rocked a little faster and I could tell she was enjoying the conversation. "Some groups have even bombed federal buildings to protest stuff," I added, hoping that would make my point.

"Bombed the government?" Becky said loudly. Giggles erupted from deep in her chest and I knew if she weren't careful, she wouldn't be able to stop them. Usually, when something tickled her "funny bone," I encouraged her, saying things to make her laugh even more. Becky was good at finding bizarre comedy and I was guilty of joining in. But now, I tried to calm her down. I didn't want her to blow her chance.

"Remember, Beck, the federal government pays for you to stay at Rouse's. They pay for all the cool stuff you get to do," I said.

"Is the federal government trying to destroy families?" Becky said.

"No, Becky. They're trying to help people who need help," I said. I noticed the two women seemed bored, their eyes glazing over just a little.

"Let's focus on the interview," I said, emphasizing the word interview, hoping Becky would regain control of herself and stop sounding like a saboteur.

"Yes, let's," said Mrs. M——. "According to our preliminary evaluation, you are well-suited for the DDA home and we have a vacancy," said Mrs. M——, again smiling at Becky.

"Yes." Becky grew quiet. She was very interested in this line of talk.

"We already have five ladies selected for the group home we're building in Greensboro. We need to pick one more. We're looking for someone who will fit in with the other women. Someone who has similar interests, personality, and habits. Do you have any hobbies?" said Mrs. M——.

"Yes," said Becky.

Becky remained silent and we all waited for her to say something. She rocked back and forth in a steady motion, looking at her hands and making low noises in her throat. The silence grew heavier.

"What are your hobbies, Becky?" my father said, hoping to prod her along.

"Do the Monkees count as a hobby, Father? How about my dental fascination? Ghosts? I have a ghost collection," said Becky, her voice expressing pride in her interests.

"A ghost collection?" said Mrs. M——.

"Halloween ghosts! Decorations! Is Halloween my favorite holiday? Is black my favorite color? Black and orange are the Halloween colors," said Becky, getting revved up again.

"Oh, decorations. How interesting," said Mrs. M——, laughing. Both ladies were laughing. Becky's enthusiasm for the subject bounded from her body; her energy was almost visible. She began flipping the arm of her chair.

"When I go to the beach, I get more ghosts at the store there. They have new ones all the time," Becky said, her words coming faster and faster. "I buy books about ghosts and scary things."

"You like to see spooky movies, too, Becky?" said Mrs. M——.

"Yes. Does the SciFi channel have scary movies?" Becky said.

"I think so. What other hobbies do you have?" said Mrs. M——.

"Do I play piano with my musical ears? Can I bowl? Do I like ballet?" said Becky. She'd switched from declarative sentences to interrogative, a regression that indicated her anxiety.

As the interview progressed, Becky told Mrs. M—— all the things she hated about Rouse's. She didn't like getting up at 6 AM every morning, even on weekends. She didn't like having her coffee limited to one cup each day. She hated sharing a bathroom with three other people. She didn't like not having any time to herself. She also despised not being able to take an aspirin if she got a headache. Instead of being allowed to self-medicate, she had to see a doctor for each problem, no matter how small or simple. While Becky complained about every little detail of her life at Rouse's, I wondered if such negativity was hurting her chances for the UMAR group home. I wished she sounded more positive.

On the other hand, hearing Becky reel off her litany of discontent, I knew she didn't belong at Rouse's any longer. Ten years was a long time to live in a regimented environment when you no longer needed such structure. Becky had been patient and she'd waited a long time to get this far. I remember how hard it was on the whole family when Becky first went to Rouse's.

My parents and Becky moved to Kernersville, North Carolina when my father resigned his position as professor of music at A-B College to pursue a career in insurance. They wanted to be closer to my family. Prior to their move, Becky had attended high school in Philippi until the age of twenty-one, when, by state law, she could no longer participate. After receiving her certificate of attendance, she worked in the Barbour County Sheltered Workshop, where she cut out cardboard for packaging shirts and sanded wood for building projects. At the workshop, Becky made one of her few friends, Paula. Paula and Becky ate their bagged lunches together. During Becky's first couple of years at the workshop, she even had a boyfriend, Terry. They saw each other only at work—no dates, no phone calls, none of the usual courtship events. However, Becky keeps a picture of herself and Terry in the top drawer of her bureau where she stores most of her treasures. In the picture, Becky and Terry are holding hands, while their workshop teacher and some of the other participants are eating lunch in the background. It is one of the sweetest pictures I've ever seen.

After a couple of years, Terry stopped attending the workshop. Becky never did find out what happened to him. Becky attended the workshop for several years after Terry left and she continued to develop her friendship with Paula. When my parents decided to retire in North Carolina, leaving home must have been hard for Becky, especially saying goodbye to the only real friend she'd ever had, Paula. For several years after Becky moved to Kernersville, they exchanged occasional letters. My parents even took Becky to visit Paula once. Eventually, the letters stopped.

Soon after they settled in Kernersville, Becky began to work at the Kernersville Sheltered Workshop where she stuffed pairs of socks into plastic bags for later sale. She worked for half a day, five days a week. My parents drove Becky back and forth to the workshop and participated in workshop social events—picnics, Special Olympics, cookouts. Becky was content with work, but she started to resent some of the rules and regulations set up by my parents.

"Is Mother not trained?" Becky asked me one day while I was visiting.

"Trained for what?" I said.

"Trained to deal with my emotional disturbance? Does she need to go back to school to learn how to cope?" Becky said, her arms stiffening as she spoke.

"I don't think so, Beck. She's your mother, not a psychiatrist," I said. "Are you mad at Mom for some reason?"

"No. Does Mom get frustrated with me? Does she lose her patience?" Becky said.

"Probably. I've seen you badger her with questions. Of course, she loses her temper once in a while. Has she lost it today?" I said.

"Yes. Does she not want me to watch the SciFi channel when her soaps are on? Is she selfish?" Becky said.

"No. She lets you watch what you want to watch most of the time, doesn't she?" I said.

"Yes."

"Well, then, it's only fair for Mom to get one show for herself, isn't it? That's fair, right?" I said. I knew Becky would see the justice of Mom's behavior, even if she didn't like it.

"Yes." She flipped her hands in the air. I could hear her mumbling something to herself in that sing-song voice she used when contemplating.

"Would I have to share the TV if I lived alone? If I had my own apartment?" she said.

"I guess not. But you're not ready to live alone, are you?" I said. I was surprised she would consider having her own place. I thought she was content at home.

"I don't want to leave home," Becky said.

"Well, then, you'll have to learn to share. Can you do that?" I said.

"I can do that," Becky said.

We had a couple of such conversations, enough to let me know Becky was chafing under the usual annoyances of family living. For almost twenty years, since she'd come home from Pressley House, Becky had said nothing negative about her situation. But lately, she'd begun complaining that Mom and Dad didn't know how to deal with her the way a psychiatrist, or "shrink" would. Becky called them "shrinks" because they "will help you shrink up your mind," whatever that meant. She seemed to think Mom and Dad couldn't help her, and their rules for her rubbed her the wrong way. She became convinced they both needed "training" so they would be better caretakers. Their rules weren't stringent:

- Becky could only use a small amount of toilet paper. (Becky's enormous wads of paper had stopped up every commode she'd ever used. Sometimes, my father even asked me to step into the bathroom while Becky was using the facilities to monitor her paper usage.)

- Becky had to go to bed at eleven o'clock.

- Becky was limited as to her consumption of beer and wine—no more than two drinks on the evenings when she imbibed.

- Becky was limited regarding desserts, and her portion size was controlled.

Though Becky couldn't see how such curtailments were for her own good, they were. She was about forty pounds overweight and, while my father might share a beer with her once in a while, he wasn't going to make it a nightly thing. Becky didn't need the added problem of alcohol dependency. But Becky had begun to resent these rules and she wanted more independence, especially since she was working at the sheltered workshop.

Though Becky had a few rules at home, she didn't have many chores. Mother still took care of Becky as if Becky were a child. Such habits, I know from my own experience, are hard to break. Becky attended the Kernersville workshop in the mornings; Mother picked her up and prepared lunch for her. After lunch, Becky usually watched TV and drank several cups of coffee. She didn't have any regular chores, though my father often tried to institute a few, like making her bed. In many ways, Becky had a cushy life.

After Becky had worked at the workshop for a couple of years, the mother of one of Becky's co-workers suggested that Becky might enjoy a group home environment, and she knew a wonderful place that had an opening. The place was located in Mayodan, about a half-hour's drive north of Kernersville. My parents mentioned the idea to me and we decided to check it out.

My father investigated Rouse's Group Homes thoroughly before our family decided to place Becky there. He called organizations for the Developmentally Disabled across the state, at every level, all the way to the main office in Raleigh. He was told by the person in charge of all North Carolina group homes that if Becky were *his* child, he wouldn't hesitate to place her at Rouse's. That is the kind of reputation the institution enjoys.

After discussing the results of my father's research, we proceeded with the idea, keeping our eyes and ears open for any potential problems or negative aspects to the proposal. First, all four of us visited Rouse's.

To drive by the place on NC Highway 139, you'd never guess the five brick houses that lined the road on the left were group homes. Instead, the cluster looked like a small country settlement. Each house, though not large, was well-maintained on the outside and the interior was equally appealing. Bright-colored curtains and matching bedspreads made each of the four bedrooms seem comfortable and warm. The kitchen was well-appointed with all the conveniences a person could want. The residents were friendly. Most of them seemed to suffer from varying degrees of retardation. A few were in wheelchairs. I knew immediately Becky would be one of the most advanced in this group. She'd always been in the high-functioning level at each institution where she'd lived as a child. I felt sure this was an environment where she could shine—where she could be at the top of the heap rather than near the bottom, the way she was in "normal" society.

I was also impressed with the cleanliness of each house. The staff seemed kind and eager to help us feel at home. We walked into the room that would be Becky's and it, too, was decorated nicely in shades of peach and green. *I* could be quite happy here; maybe Becky could, too.

After a long session with Mrs. Rouse, the woman who ran the home, my parents and I were convinced that Becky might fit in well here and she would be given the chance to grow and develop. Becky wasn't quite so sure about the idea and expressed her doubts on the way home.

My mother turned around from the front to face Becky and me.

"Maybe you'd like to spend a weekend, Becky, just to see what the place is like. Mrs. Rouse said that would be okay with her—matter of fact, she brought up the idea. Just a sort of test to see if you liked them and if they liked you," my mother said.

"Do you want me to leave home? Do you not want me around anymore? Is that it?" Becky got straight to the heart of the matter, at least her heart. The truth was, my parents were getting older. In their mid-60s and in very good health, they had begun to feel the hands of time reaching for them. Who could know how long they could continue caring for Becky at home? We all knew the day would come when they would be too ill, too weak, or just too tired to take care of Becky any longer. In our private discussions, I'd expressed my desire for *them* to make the decision about whether or not to place Becky in a home. I didn't want to have to make that decision about my sister's future. It didn't seem my place.

"You know that's not the reason, Becky. We love you very much. We just thought this might be a good opportunity for you. You'd learn things at Rouse's. And what about all the classes you could take—dance lessons, horse-back riding, aerobics—we certainly couldn't afford to pay for all that," my father said softly.

"And we're getting older, Becky. We don't know how much longer we'll be around. This would be a safe place for you to live, a place where you'd learn a lot of things," my mother added.

"Are you dying? Are you going to drop dead?" Becky sort of yelled these questions and giggled. I could hear the tension in her voice, though she was laughing.

"I hope not. Nothing's wrong that we know about. But that's just it, honey. At our age, you never know," Dad said, smiling at her in the rearview mirror. I reached across the back seat and patted her arm.

"It's a real pretty place, don't you think?" I said, trying to point out the positive aspects.

"Yes." She seemed a little enthusiastic, or so I imagined.

"The room that would be yours looked comfy, huh? You could hang some of your Monkee pictures on the wall—did you see the way the other residents had their rooms all fixed up? One lady had dolls on the shelves and scattered on her bed. You could fix up your room just the way you wanted it," I said.

I wanted Becky to give it a try. I hoped living at Rouse's would broaden her outlook and her experiences. And I desperately wanted her to be happily settled before anything happened to our parents. The truth was, I knew I couldn't take care of Becky at my house, full-time. I didn't want to. I had changed since my girlhood. I no longer had any illusions about running a group home on my own and living with Becky forever. I knew I wasn't cut out for it. I had my own dreams to pursue, my own family to care for. Living with Becky would completely disrupt my life. And, if I'm completely honest, dealing with her questions and her habits on a full-time basis would drive me over the edge.

My three sons were still at home, the older boys in college and the youngest in seventh grade. They needed me. I taught writing part-time and I was trying to jump-start my own writing career, a career I'd put on hold for twenty years while I raised my sons and taught high school. I'd just recently carved out a little time for myself—for reading, playing the piano, working out at the local Y. I didn't think I could handle one more thing, and, if I told the truth, I simply didn't want to take care of anyone else, at least not at that moment.

Maybe my feelings were selfish. I felt guilty for not wanting Becky to live with me. I'd been struggling with the age-old question for years—am I my sister's keeper? If so, to what degree? At what point should I give up my own life, desires, goals, dreams, for the sake of my sister? How could I become a living sacrifice without bitterness and a slow eating away of the soul?

I still don't know the answers.

"Wouldn't you like to take ballet again?" I asked, emphasizing Rouse's positive attributes.

"Yes." Becky's "yes" now sounded much more affirmative. There was a slight shift in the pitch, rather than the usual flatness of tone.

"Why don't you try it for one weekend?" I said. I could see she was curious. She got bored at home; she'd told me so herself. Not quite in those terms, but that was what she'd meant. She wanted Mom and Dad to spend hours with her, answering her questions and reading her stories. She knew they couldn't, but she still wanted it. There was nothing else for her to do except go to the workshop and watch TV.

"All right. I will," Becky said. Suddenly, her voice sounded determined and even excited.

"That's my girl," said Dad from the front seat.

"I think you'll feel better if you try it," said Mother, her voice calm.

"Way to go, Beck. I'm proud of you," I said.

And proud of her I truly was. It was a brave thing for her to decide. Her dissatisfaction at home probably influenced her decision, plus all the cajoling on our part. I didn't feel guilty, though. I had a feeling Becky might like the new situation. I knew she should at least give it a chance.

In the weeks before the trial weekend, my parents and I went for several counseling sessions with Lyn Strickland, a therapist. We needed help with this decision, especially Mother. Mother was the most reluctant to place Becky away from home. The irony was that for the past twenty years, Mother had borne the weight of most of Becky's day-to-day care. It was for Mother's sake I suggested the counseling and for Mother, too, that I desired relief. Twenty years is a long time to cater to someone else's whims, even though that someone is your child.

Mother did everything she could to please Becky. She fixed Becky's coffee in the mornings with "extra cream, please." She prepared Becky's meals, toasting the buns for the hotdogs Becky loved, making sure she cooked spaghetti or lasagna a couple of times a month. Mother would bake Becky's favorite birthday cake and make special hot fudge sauce for Becky every Christmas. She did all her laundry. She even took showers with Becky.

Years ago, one of Becky's doctors had recommended Mother give Becky a thirty-minute "question period" daily to limit Becky's relentless questions. But after twenty years, Becky had found ways to extend these sessions. Mother answered Becky's interrogations with patience but these marathons were taking a toll. Mother also read to Becky for hours on end. She never felt she could go shopping for the afternoon or escape for a weekend getaway. Though I kept Becky several times, Mother wasn't totally comfortable with the arrangement. I think she felt that with my own three boys, my job, and my husband, I had enough to do. I didn't mind keeping Becky, though. I enjoyed it for short periods—a weekend or even a week. When Becky visited, she and I would revert back to our childhood ways and I found myself doing exactly the things my mother did—cooking Becky's favorite meals, taking her to movies, making sure she got her coffee—it was exhausting, but satisfying, too.

I wanted my parents to have some freedom and fun in their golden years. They'd worked hard all their lives. They'd had enough heartache from both Becky and me. It was time they reaped the benefits of their lives, time for them to enjoy life before the last, sad moment. But I knew they took their responsibility for Becky very seriously and placing her in a home would be a hard, hard, step. Therapy helped us take that step together.

In therapy, we learned that no human being is always happy. I believe we knew this already, but for some reason, we tried to make Becky's life one of constant pleasure. I did this more than my parents did, probably because I wasn't with her day in and day out. When Becky came to see me, I wanted her to have a really great time and I bent over backwards to make sure she did. But, no matter how hard I tried, or how hard my parents tried, we could never meet Becky's every need, every desire. Before therapy, I'd never given much thought to my behavior toward Becky. I hadn't considered that by expecting her to be happy all the time, I was actually dehumanizing her, stealing her spirit. I was robbing her of the opportunity for new growth and development by trying to make her contented. It is through adversity we change, and I was trying to remove any adversity from Becky's life. To be fully human, a person must experience a varied range of emotions. My sister is fully human, though her behavior isn't in the realm of what others consider "normal." In therapy, I came to believe that Becky deserved to experience life as richly as any person. That included knowing discomfort, unhappiness, even despair. I no longer thought protecting Becky from some of life's lessons was necessarily a good thing. Facing trouble is one way we learn. Though a cliché, that doesn't lessen the truth of it. Becky was capable of learning, growing. She might even gain some self-esteem in the process.

I think my mother learned to let go a little during our weekly sessions. She'd let go earlier when Becky was a child, reluctantly and with wrenching grief. Mother had never recovered from sending Becky to Amos Cottage. Now, she faced sending Becky away again.

Though Becky had been at home for twenty years, Mother hadn't let her grow up very much. I believed Becky was capable of doing so much more than Mother allowed her to do. Mother often felt it was easier to do a chore herself, rather than to wait and watch Becky struggle with the task. I understood that impulse. A mother myself, I often made the same choice—rather than be dissatisfied with my sons' performance of a chore, I'd do it instead. I often lived the old adage, if you want something done right, do it yourself.

But as the weeks of therapy passed, Mother began to see that Becky might actually learn and improve if she lived in the group home. I think she also began to imagine the freedom her own life might gain, too.

As for my father, I'm not sure how the therapy affected him. By nature, he is a logical person who ferrets out the best approach to something, then pursues that idea until concept becomes fact. Yet he's also sensitive and perceptive with feelings that spring to his eyes easily and without shame. He doesn't share his emotions in words very often. He has never discussed how he felt about my sister, except to explain to me why Becky had to leave us when Becky went to Amos Cottage and Pressley House. But now, maybe as a result of the counseling, he confessed to me that he'd cried himself to sleep countless times, worrying about Becky and her future. He fretted about who would be able to protect her when he was no longer around; he struggled to battle his own sadness and frustration about how to help Becky. His anguish was that of the only man in the house, who probably felt he had to be strong for the sake of the women in his family. His pain was the pain of a man whose heart breaks easily, but who tried, with typical masculine stoicism, to keep others from knowing his grief.

Becky also attended counseling sessions with our therapist. Lyn helped Becky to see that she ought to take this chance. She helped Becky to understand that her family wasn't rejecting her, but rather, they were trying to do what was best for everyone concerned. Becky immediately took a liking to Lyn's gentle voice and calm manner. Becky can spot a phony in a heartbeat, and she knew Lyn was the genuine article—someone who loved her and wanted to help ease her way in the world. Becky still sees Lyn once a month.

Finally, the trial weekend came. The three of us reluctantly, but resolutely dropped Becky off at Rouse's, and I had the same feeling of uneasiness I remembered from long ago when we'd left Becky at Pressley House. We drove home without our usual conviviality, each of us quiet and subdued. Once again, I'd left a portion of myself with Becky, and I felt the loss keenly.

For me, the weekend passed quickly. I had the usual chores to do: laundry, house-straightening, chauffeuring my boys to their various activities. I was teaching part-time and had papers to grade, too. Once I was in my homemaking/teacher mode, I had little time to think of Becky. But I did think of her and each time she came to mind, I said a little prayer for her—that she was comfortable at the new home, that she wasn't homesick, and that she'd like Rouse's well enough to give it a longer try.

My parents invited us to Sunday dinner, after they'd picked Becky up from Rouse's that morning. We couldn't wait to find out what Becky's weekend had been like.

As we gathered at the table to eat, no one mentioned the experimental time at the group home. I couldn't stand the suspense any longer.

"So, Beck, how was your weekend?" I said as I heaped green beans onto my plate.

"It was fun. They took me out to dinner and we watched TV. Will I have to live there?" She seemed excited and in a good mood. I felt something release in my chest.

"Do you think you might like to try a longer stay?" Dad asked.

"Yes," Becky answered in her flat voice. But a "yes" was better than I had expected. She must have really enjoyed herself, and now she seemed ready for more of whatever it was they did.

"I'll set it up with Mrs. Rouse then," Dad said. He wanted to get her commitment right away before she had a chance to change her mind. But I don't think he had cause to worry. Becky seemed genuinely interested in a longer visit to Rouse's.

The next step was to try a six-week stay. During this time, Becky'd be tested mentally and physically and provided with a program of study suited to her needs. Also, Rouse's would enroll her in ballet classes, piano lessons, horse-back riding lessons and an aerobics class right away. They would put her on a dietary program designed to help her lose the forty extra pounds she'd put on as a result of my mother's excellent cooking. Becky's attitude was positive about all the preparations.

My parents bought Becky some new clothes, sheets and towels, toiletries, and pocketbook before she moved in. We loaded up their car and I went with them to deliver Becky for this longer trial.

We unpacked her clothes and put things into the dresser.

"When will I see you again, Jet?" Becky asked me.

"Well, Rouse's thinks it's better if you don't come home for this whole six-week period. They want you to get the feel of the place without the distraction of a home visit. They want you to get into the swing of things here," I explained. I knew this time of isolation would be hard on Becky, but I also understood that she needed to make a break from home and she couldn't do that if she were always visiting. I remembered my freshman year at college, how homesick I was and how I tried to hitch rides home at every possible opportunity. But eventually, I'd adjusted and had loved living on my own. I hoped Becky would make that same adjustment.

"I'll come and take you to lunch, though. How's that?" I said.

"That's all right. I'll miss you, Jet," Becky said as she gave me a stiff hug.

"I'll miss you, too."

When the six-week training period ended, no one mentioned it to Becky. She didn't ask about coming home, either. She seemed relatively content. My parents and I visited her often, taking her to lunch or supper. She had a total of sixty nights per year she could spend away from Rouse's. That meant she could spend holidays at home, plus take a long vacation with the family to the beach. Slowly, the time passed. Becky complained at times about her diet at Rouse's, but she was very proud of her new figure—she'd gone from a size 18 to a size 10 petite and she'd become quite a clotheshorse. Shopping became one of her favorite activities. She might gripe about the new nurse, but she learned to get a shot, something she hadn't done since her bout with poison ivy at Amos Cottage. She was pleased that finally she could get a flu shot each year. She also got a pelvic exam for the first time.

Slowly, the months turned into years and before anyone realized it, Becky had been at Rouse's for a decade.

At Rouse's, Becky learned to make her bed, do laundry, cook simple meals, plan a well-balanced menu, vacuum, and wash dishes. Her reading skills improved and she could read her favorite series, *Goosebumps*, for herself. She worked in the greenhouse where she discovered the joys of digging in the dirt, preparing the soil to nourish new life. She created ceramic mugs and vases with whimsical moons and stars painted in her inimitable style. She made decorative silk flower arrangements for the group home to sell during the Christmas holidays. And, surprising all of us, Becky got a job at the nearby Burger King, where she worked fifteen hours a week.

It was while Becky was at Rouse's that we learned exactly what her problems were. Jason Connor, Becky's social worker, contacted a group in nearby Greensboro called TEACCH (Treatment and Education of Autistic and related Communication Handicapped Children) on Becky's behalf. Then, at their recommendation, Mr. Connor arranged for Becky to be tested yet again at the University of North Carolina at Chapel Hill. In the resulting diagnosis, our family finally discovered that Becky was, indeed, autistic, with possible very mild retardation, though her actual IQ was still difficult to assess given the nature of autism.

At the age of thirty-seven, my sister finally was given the right label. No longer considered emotionally disturbed (and fixable), she now had a place where she fitted in. I believe my parents and I were equally relieved. I was glad to have a jumping off place so I could read about her condition in order to learn how to rise to its challenges.

I believe my parents were relieved to know that they were not to blame in any way for Becky's condition. Finally, they could allay the secret fear that they had somehow mis-parented Becky. They could give up the illusion that Becky might have been cured, had they been able to find the appropriate place for her. And they could learn to deal with the reality of her condition. After all, calling Becky's disability an "emotional disturbance" implied a cause and a cure. A diagnosis of autism simply was.

Our family owes Rouse's Group Home a debt that can never be repaid. They helped us discover an accurate diagnosis for Becky. Their fine staff gave

Becky the kind of instruction she needed to become more independent, though training left Becky desiring more independence than Rouse's could, by law, allow. It was the direct result of their excellent program that caused Becky to apply to the UMAR group home. She was now ready to move up to a DDA group home, thanks to the diligent work of the staff at Rouse's.

❧

But now, Becky was ready to enter the next stage. She'd worked hard for ten years to be allowed things most of us take for granted—sleeping in on Saturdays, choosing when to clean and when to relax, having our toilet to ourselves. She'd forced herself to lose forty pounds and keep it off, even though she loved ice cream and cake, potatoes and pasta, candy and cookies. She'd conquered many of her fears, though loud noises still sent her scurrying for the nearest exit. She deserved to be invited to the UMAR group home. I could only pray the interview tilted in her favor.

As we left the brick building, I couldn't have been more proud of Becky. She had conducted herself with grace in what was a nerve-wracking situation in anyone's life—the dreaded interview. We had no idea how it would come out, but I knew my sister was a charmer and she'd made the interview fun and funny. Everyone was in good spirits as we left the building.

"You did a great job, Beck!" I put my arm around her as we walked to the car.

"You sure did. I was proud of you," my father said.

"Me, too. Very proud," my mother said.

"Do you think they'll take me? Will they let me in?" Becky said, flipping her Monkee book which she'd removed from her purse.

"Who knows? It's in God's hands," my mother said.

"Will it be God's fault if I don't get in?" Becky said.

"No. But we'll pray that you do get in," my father said.

"I'll pray every night," said Becky.

We crawled into the car and headed for the K&W Cafeteria. After that afternoon, we all needed some comfort food. The next few weeks would be difficult—none of us were any good at waiting.

Afterword

About three months after Becky's interview with the UMAR Group Homes, my parents received this letter:

March 31, 1999

Dear Dr. and Mrs. Clinard,

The Admission Committee of the UMAR Greensboro Group Home has completed its review of applicants from which the initial six residents have been selected. Rebecca's application was reviewed, but she was not accepted as one of the initial six. However, Rebecca was selected as the third alternate resident for the Greensboro group home should there be a vacancy.

Please be assured that Rebecca's application will remain active on the waiting list.

When Mom and Dad told me Becky hadn't been selected, I was worried about her reaction. But we had to tell her. Every time I saw her, she asked about the results of the interview. We had to let her know so she wouldn't continue hoping.

The night we told Becky about the results of the interview, Dad took us out to eat at Becky's favorite restaurant in Mayodan, an Italian place called Tiano's.

"The Group Home people sent us a letter, Becky. I'm sorry but they didn't pick you. But you're still on the waiting list," my father said to Becky as she scooped a bite of tiramisu into her mouth. She kept eating as if she hadn't heard.

"Did you hear me, Becky? I'm really sorry about it," my father continued.

Becky took another bite.

"Are you okay, Beck? I know you're disappointed," I said.

"Didn't they like me? Is there something wrong with me?" Becky finally said.

"That's not it, honey. You remember, we talked about how they had to find a good match for the other ladies. It's nothing personal," my mother said, her face pinched with worry.

"Why didn't they pick her? What was the reason? Was she not good enough? Didn't they like her?" Becky started her litany of questions, mumbling under her breath while she stared at her folded hands. My father, whose hearing had become poor in recent years, didn't catch what she was talking about. She wasn't really talking to any of us, so my parents finished their dessert. I listened while Becky mulled things over. She was devastated, though she didn't show it.

Later, we took Becky back to Rouse's. She gave us her perfunctory hug and seemed subdued. Mother and Dad talked about how well Becky had taken the news, but I didn't think she had absorbed what her rejection would mean. I knew she would grasp its meaning soon. I wondered how she might respond once the information had sunk in.

When my parents and I broke the news to Becky, I'd expected a show of disappointment, maybe tears or some kind of tantrum. I knew how badly she wanted to leave Rouse's. She was ready to grow up, finally. And her desire for independence was palpable.

Over the next few months, Becky became more and more vocal about her hatred of Rouse's. No matter what we did to appease her or what the staff at Rouse's did to make her happy, Becky was miserable. When she came to spend the night at my house, she stalled for hours when it was time to return to Rouse's. She'd drink several cups of coffee, something she wasn't allowed to do at the group home. Becky drinks coffee with a spoon and can stretch drinking one cup over an hour, sometimes longer if she puts her mind to it. Of course, after two or three cups of coffee, a trip to the bathroom becomes necessary. Becky has been known to stay in the bathroom a whole morning. She takes her Monkee pictures with her and leisurely peruses them.

Each time she spent the night with me or my parents, Becky incorporated these tactics. And her complaints about Rouse's were incessant. She hated the food, the activities, the other clients, the caretakers, the drivers, Mr. and Mrs. Rouse, their daughter, Deborah, who ran the group home. Becky despised the nurse, the social worker, the psychiatrist, her job—just everything. And she didn't keep her disgruntlement to herself. She let the people at Rouse's know just what she thought. Feelings were hurt; and soon, Becky began acting out her frustration.

She started telling lies. First, she told us that someone at Rouse's had stolen her clothes. Then, she claimed the house parents were picking on her. Finally, she told us that she wasn't receiving the usual five dollars she got each week for incidentals. Since she was earning her own money at Burger King, we were concerned about what was happening to her paycheck.

When my father asked the folks at Rouse's about this, they explained that Becky still received the same amount as always. She had lied. They also reported she made disparaging remarks about some of the other residents, making fun of them if they couldn't do a task correctly and asking, "Am I smarter than they are? Is it because they're stupid?"

By August, Becky's behavior had become a concern. At her quarterly meeting, where the family and the people who worked with her gathered in her presence to evaluate her progress and set goals, her psychological report read:

- Goal: Becky increases appropriate social behavior.

- Objective Statement: Becky decreases inappropriate behavior to 5 or less per month for 6 consecutive months.

- Target Behaviors:

  Non-compliance—Refusing to follow staff instruction in regard to programming or activities of daily living after two prompts.

  Telling untrue stories—Telling staff or other residents or family stories that are untrue.

- Rationale: Becky is a 41-year-old white female who resides at Rouse's Group Homes. She is ambulatory and verbal although she is often difficult to understand in that she talks very quickly. She can make her wants and needs known. Frequently, she is friendly and cooperative. When she is upset, she becomes agitated, nervous, non-compliant and has a tendency to exaggerate or make up stories. This program is being written to give staff a consistent means of dealing with these behaviors.

None of this sounded like the Becky we knew and loved. Something was wrong and I thought I knew what it was—Becky had never processed her disappointment regarding her rejection from the UMAR group home.

After her meeting in August, we went to eat again at Tiano's.

"So, Beck, what's up with all this bad behavior? You've been at Rouse's almost ten years and you've never lied about stuff or said mean things to other people. What's going on?" I asked. My parents knew I could often elicit information from Becky better than they could. I understood her.

"Is it because you weren't selected for that other group home? Is that the problem?" I said.

Becky stared at her hands and made a low, growling sound in her throat. I waited while she continued to make the noise.

"You can tell us, Becky. We're not happy with your behavior but we want to find out what's causing it. We want to help you," said my father.

"Do you need to talk about something with us? Did something happen at Rouse's to upset you?" my mother said.

"No." Becky continued staring at her hands. I could hear her grit her teeth.

"Well, what's the deal?" I said.

"Is it my mind? Is it my autism's fault?" Becky said.

"Is what your mind?" I said.

"Is it my emotional disturbance? Is that why I acted ugly?" Becky said.

"I don't know. Is it? What's bothering you? It's not like you to be mean to other people. Call them stupid and stuff like that," I said.

She laughed, the bubbling-up kind, the kind she didn't have control over. She held her hands close to her face and pressed them against her nose, laughing the whole time.

"What's so funny?" I said.

"I don't know," she said, still giggling.

Finally, the fit stopped and she started talking to me, seriously and without the questions.

"I was disappointed, Jet. I think there's something wrong with me and that's why they didn't take me in the group home. Is that because of my emotional disturbance?" she said.

"Of course, you were disappointed. I would have been, too. I don't think it's because of your brain. Such disappointment is normal. I bet Lyn could help you," I said, hinting to my parents that maybe Becky needed to see Lyn more often than every two months.

"Because Lyn's trained? She knows how to help people get over disappointment?" Becky said.

"I think she'll help, yes," I said.

My father agreed and immediately set up an appointment. After about three months of therapy, Becky seemed better and her negative behavior improved.

In 2001, about two years after Becky's rejection from the UMAR group home, Becky was accepted into Group Homes of Forsyth (GHF), a collection of five DDA homes. Group Homes of Forsyth was interested in Becky because they believed Becky would one day be able to go to supportive living, where she could have her own place, doing most of her own shopping, appointment-setting and working, with the supervision from special staff at GHF. Amazingly, four GHF clients had been able to purchase a house together, a place of their own. Each of the women held a part-time job, thanks to the vocational rehabilitation services of Winston-Salem. The women enjoyed independence found in a supportive living arrangement. Supportive living means the group home staff continues to help the more independent clients with such things as budgeting money and paying bills, arranging transportation and any emergency situations; but for the most part, the clients function on their own, with close supervision. All of this takes place after months, sometimes years, of training. Donna Jenks, the director of GHF, thought Becky might get to that place if she were given the chance.

In 2002, Becky moved to Stockton Group Home, the highest-functioning group of the GHF houses. The women who purchased their own home passed through Stockton first, so Becky was pleased to move. Currently, Becky has completed her vocational training and is employed once more by Burger King where she works four days a week. Though Becky would have preferred working in a book store or coffee shop, she's happy to have a job and she already has more in her savings account than I do in mine. She brags about getting her paycheck, which she deposits by herself, filling out the deposit ticket and signing her name. She also goes to supported living training two days a week, where she's learning to cook (she makes a mean pan of lasagna) and attempting to budget her money. She's also finished training about safety in the home and knows what to do in case of an emergency.

While she's happier at Stockton than she'd been at Rouse's, Becky continues to chafe at rules and regulations. Because of her overly enthusiastic use of toilet paper, she is given an allotment which she keeps in her top drawer—she's given just enough for each day and she must collect the day's supply every morning. Such a setup is an inconvenience, to say the least, but one which the staff at Stockton must insist on. Though Becky doesn't like the current situation, it motivates her to work on limiting herself—it's one of the goals Becky and the staff set at her monthly meetings.

At Stockton, she gets to sleep in on the weekends, is allowed her morning cup of coffee and best of all, she can stay alone if the supervisor must transport another client. Becky washes and irons her own clothes, cooks, and has certain chores to perform around the house each week. For about a year, she rode the city bus by herself to attend the Forsyth Industrial Services workshop each day. Unfortunately, she had trouble crossing the street one day and had to return to square one regarding public transportation. Ten years ago, none of us would have believed any of these things possible. But, through her own perseverance and bravery, Becky has made them happen.

And though she's not made it to supportive living yet, I know she will. She has more determination and courage than anyone I know; I've learned Becky is full of surprises. I believe she's going to surprise this old world yet.

I'm still fascinated by birds. Even now, as the summer wanes, several hummingbirds vie for possession of my deck, dipping and swerving to buzz in for a sip of nectar at the red plastic feeder that hangs by the double glass doors. Sometimes, the resident male will dive bomb the gray females who dare approach his domain. The females remind me of nuns, their feathers arranged in gray habits with white wimples. And the male, glimpsing him is like finding treasure—rubies at his throat, quick flash of emeralds and deep turquoise across his wings.

While I watch the birds skim the skies of my mountain home—cardinals, red-tailed hawks, blue jays—I still think of Becky, her quick-bobbing head and the jerky movements of her hands. And, while she's flown the nest of our childhood, as I have, we will always be birds of a certain feather.

If anyone had asked me twenty years ago whether having Becky for a sister had affected me, I would have told them no, resoundingly. I was convinced that my childhood was normal, perhaps even better than most. I had so many advantages. My family camped all over the Eastern seaboard; I grew up on a college campus surrounded by natural beauty and intelligent people; my parents were unfailingly kind-hearted with generous and gentle spirits. Having Becky in my life didn't change any of that.

Now, after having written this book, I realize knowing Becky changed everything.

From Becky, I learned to treasure my loved ones because who knew when they might be jerked away. I learned that love is stronger than shame or fear; indeed, love is the most powerful force in the universe. I was lucky enough to have two parents and one sister to teach me this lesson. I learned that God treasures the creation in all its varied forms and shapes, even when the shape is autism.

Finally, I learned that Becky is exactly the right sister for me, the sister God placed in my life, perfect in every way.

Butler Area Public Library
218 North McKean St.
Butler, PA 16001

Anne Barnhill would be happy to speak to
bookclubs, libraries, churches or colleges.
She can be reached at acbarnhill@yahoo.com